Composing Capital

Composing Capital

Classical Music in the Neoliberal Era

MARIANNA RITCHEY

The University of Chicago Press
Chicago and London

The University of Chicago Press, Chicago 60637
The University of Chicago Press, Ltd., London
© 2019 by The University of Chicago
All rights reserved. No part of this book may be used or reproduced in any
manner whatsoever without written permission, except in the case of brief
quotations in critical articles and reviews. For more information, contact the
University of Chicago Press, 1427 E. 60th St., Chicago, IL 60637.
Published 2019
Printed in the United States of America

28 27 26 25 24 23 22 21 20 19   1 2 3 4 5

ISBN-13: 978-0-226-64006-8 (cloth)
ISBN-13: 978-0-226-64023-5 (paper)
ISBN-13: 978-0-226-64037-2 (e-book)
DOI: https://doi.org/10.7208/chicago/9780226640372.001.0001

Publication of this book has been supported by the AMS 75 PAYS Endowment
of the American Musicological Society, funded in part by the National
Endowment for the Humanities and the Andrew W. Mellon Foundation.

Library of Congress Cataloging-in-Publication Data

Names: Ritchey, Marianna, 1977– author.
Title: Composing capital : classical music in the neoliberal era /
    Marianna Ritchey.
Description: Chicago ; London : The University of Chicago Press, 2019. |
    Includes bibliographical references and index.
Identifiers: LCCN 2018051863 | ISBN 9780226640068 (cloth : alk. paper) |
    ISBN 9780226640235 (pbk. : alk. paper) | ISBN 9780226640372 (e-book)
Subjects: LCSH: Music—Economic aspects—United States. | Music
    entrepreneurship—United States. | Music and technology—United States. |
    Music trade—United States. | Neoliberalism—United States.
Classification: LCC ML3790 .R57 2019 | DDC 781.68079/73—dc23
LC record available at https://lccn.loc.gov/2018051863

CONTENTS

Introduction: Music and Neoliberalism

At the corporate partner summit of a multinational tech conglomerate, a young composer conducts his recent symphony, a celebration of the wonders of digital connectivity. Meanwhile, hundreds of musicians from all over the world upload audition videos to YouTube, hoping to be chosen for the YouTube Symphony Orchestra, a Google marketing scheme. In Brooklyn, young composers and musicians celebrate their entrepreneurial individualism; in Los Angeles, a new opera company uses headphones and wireless technology to put on performances in diverse urban neighborhoods. And at a global tech showcase, the CEO of Intel triumphantly launches one hundred unmanned drones into the night sky, accompanied by a live orchestra playing a recomposed version of Beethoven's Fifth Symphony that incorporates Intel's mnemonic tone into the famous opening motive.

This book argues that neoliberal capitalism has profoundly shaped contemporary ideas about classical music in the United States. As artists, critics, and institutions work to attain patronage and revenue for classical music within a culture that increasingly cherishes only financial profitability, some are attaching ideas about this music to the most prized ideals of the free market. However, I am not only interested in how music practitioners are transforming classical music in accordance with neoliberal values as a means of survival; in the pages that follow, I also interrogate how the idea of classical music itself has been useful to contemporary capital. Accordingly, I examine marketing schemes and sponsored performances in which multinational tech corporations seek to attach long-standing beliefs about classical music to the products they sell as well as to the kinds of labor formations that allow them to accumulate capital more quickly and easily. Arguably, such partnerships, as well as the critical discourses that support them, are symptomatic of neoliberalism, the increasingly hegemonic form of contemporary capitalism that privileges free market competition as the best means of ensuring individual rights and solving social problems.

Some of the artists I examine have found major success in the corporate realm, composing and performing music intended to valorize contemporary tech giants like Steve Jobs and the founders of Google and Intel. In return, these corporations have offered patronage of various kinds, including commissions and highly publicized corporate-sponsored performances. Other artists have attained entrepreneurial success by advocating dragging classical music into the so-called real world, by which they mean the competitive entertainment marketplace. Deploying keywords from neoliberal theory—including "innovation," "entrepreneurship," "disruption," and "flexibility"—these artists have attracted critical acclaim and relatively large audiences as well as (ironically) more traditional forms of institutional security, such as university teaching positions, high-profile commissions, and residencies with established symphony orchestras and opera companies. Whether through patronage or entrepreneurship, young artists, music educators, and institutions are finding that aligning classical music's long-standing cultural prestige with the prerogatives of corporate power can open new avenues of financial support.

At the same time, corporations often use historical ideas and stereotypes of classical music in attempts to smooth over the discrepancies between what they promise and what they deliver. Corporate globalization has generated inequality and exploitation on a massive scale. Nonetheless, as tech firms like Google and Intel work to extend their reach into every corner of the planet, marketing materials and business journals assure us that their innovative products—and the new forms of labor and sociality that they promote—are making the world a better place for all. Attaching their products and processes to classical music helps these corporations appear virtuous to the populations they plunder.

Such co-optation of classical music is, of course, somewhat anachronistic. Tech firms present the past as a nightmare from which their products deliver us via ceaseless innovation; yet this relentlessly progressive vision does not gibe with the very notion of *the classic,* a term that since the late eighteenth century has been used to indicate objects whose value is perceived as eternal and unchanging.[1] I will argue that this ambivalent relation to time and history is a central feature of neoliberal thought. Indeed, such anachronism is perhaps fundamental to capitalism's ideological formulation.

While practices attaching musical values to corporate agendas of various kinds are becoming widespread, there are certainly also artists in the United States whose work is founded on anticapitalist ideas or on the "spirit of critique" that David Metzer identifies as a primary motivator of music in the modernist tradition.[2] In this book, however, I focus on artists who have attained major institutional success and widespread critical acclaim thanks in part to their explicit rejection of this critical spirit. Arts journalists, funding organizations, and major music institutions applaud the artists examined here for jettisoning stodgy modernist ideas about musical difficulty and audience enjoyment. Instead, these artists work unapologetically to please audiences, attract fans, and widen the market appeal of certain kinds of art music. They also embrace the increasingly hegemonic values of entrepreneurialism, which encourage individuals to approach their lives competitively and opportunistically and to view the market itself as a site for personal liberation. The fact that musical practices affirming the essential rightness of market logic, radical individualism, and corporate globalization have been among the most successful and widely publicized in recent US music history indicates the degree to which capitalist ideology has infiltrated our assessments of musical value.

Neoliberalism and the Reinvention of Classical Music

The mainstream discourse surrounding classical music in the United States is characterized by a rhetoric of decline and failure that cites faltering ticket sales, dwindling public support, and an aging audience as evidence of classical music's imperiled state. This rhetoric signals the widespread acceptance, in US culture at large, of the idea that a product's (or a person's) ability to generate profit on a competitive free market is an index of social value. Hence, classical music's long-standing need for state or philanthropic sponsorship is figured as almost automatic evidence of its social irrelevance. Accordingly, some of the activists who propose suggestions for saving or reviving classical music focus on the need to eschew traditional funding avenues and instead pursue new performance and branding tactics calculated to appeal to wider, younger audiences. Furthermore, they insist that this wider appeal will represent a democratization of the art form that will be good not only for musicians and institutions but for society.

The notion that opening a practice to free market competition is a means of ensuring democratic freedom is perhaps the central tenet of neoliberalism, a school of thought established in the 1950s and 1960s by economists at the University of Chicago, notably Milton Friedman. The Chicago school economists asserted that all social problems have their roots in an overregulated market. They believed that the best way to forge an egalitarian society would be to allow markets unrestrained freedom, be-cause—as eighteenth-century liberals like Adam Smith had argued—a truly free market, which individuals entered voluntarily, would be fundamen-tally rational and thus incapable of causing injustice. Building on these intellectual foundations, contemporary neoliberals juxtapose the absolute freedom bestowed by markets to the oppressive restrictions on that free-dom that governmental regulations (for example, restrictions on corporate pollution or rent control) impose.

Many commentators concerned about the crisis they perceive in US classical music manifest a neoliberal orientation toward the market, one in which market competition is automatically figured as personally liber-ating and socially progressive. This discourse also regularly deploys some of the central keywords and values of neoliberalism, using them to exem-plify how classical music can be regenerated by exposure to market forces. Artists, journalists, concert programmers, and music educators discuss the necessity to "innovate" classical music by enlivening it with technology of various kinds; they advocate new modes of musician training that will encourage young artists to become flexible, adaptable, and self-managing individuals skilled at identifying and securing market opportunities; they insist that the performance of classical music must extend beyond the boundaries of its traditional institutional venues; and they celebrate styles of composition and performance perceived to make music easier for un-trained listeners to consume.

This kind of rhetoric demonstrates the extent to which neoliberal theory has become naturalized in US culture as common sense. Throughout the book, I use the term *neoliberalism* to denote both economic practices and economic theories, and a set of general beliefs about life, individualism, and democracy that on their surface do not seem attached to economic is-sues. The political theorists and political economists who study neoliberal-ism routinely deploy this dual usage of the term in their attempts to iden-tify how some of our fundamental assumptions about human nature, life, and democratic citizenship are entangled with neoliberal values. The po-litical theorist Wendy Brown, for example, has argued that contemporary US culture is conditioned by what she calls a "neoliberal rationality" that foregrounds the free market yet is not only focused on economic matters. Neoliberal rationality entails reformulating all individual and institutional action as "rational entrepreneurial action" in which all decisions are made via an assessment of potential profitability, rather than being grounded in moral or ethical concerns.[3] For example, politicians may speak of progressive goals such as staving off climate change or ending homelessness, but these issues are typically framed in terms of how their solutions would benefit the US economy. For Brown, this kind of rhetoric "economizes," and thus renders hollow, moral values like justice, mercy, liberty, environmental stewardship, and fairness, as well as "the knowledge and the cultural orientation relevant to even the most modest practices of democratic citizenship."[4] One of the goals of this book is to reveal how neoliberal common sense has shaped the academic, journalistic, and pedagogical discourses concerning classical music in contemporary practice.

Although it has been the dominant form that capitalism in the United States has taken since the 1970s, neoliberalism has only very recently begun interesting musicologists. Indeed, for decades neoliberalism was barely discussed publicly at all in this country. It was debated primarily by economists and Marxists, and Europeans used the term as a pejorative describing the United States' increasingly meddlesome role in global politics. More widespread engagement with neoliberalism began in this country in 2008 following the subprime mortgage lending crisis. Since then, musicological interest in the topic has been building slowly, directed mainly toward either popular music, as in Timothy Taylor's *Music and Capitalism*, or the discipline of musicology itself, as in work by James Currie and David Blake.[5]

In this book, I address some of the dynamics emerging from the neoliberalization of classical music. In chapter 1 I examine the young Californian composer Mason Bates, arguing that his popularity is due to the way his music and his self-promotional tactics serve two powerful masters: traditional music institutions, which hang their hopes on "saving" classical music via the incorporation of hip new technologies into orchestral composition and performance; and global technology corporations like Google and Cisco Systems, which seek to link their disruptive innovations to a vague idea of "classical music" as the expression of culturally universal and eternal values seemingly incommensurate with the ceaseless social change technological innovation generates.

The Brooklyn "indie classical" artists examined in chapter 2 manifest a plainly contradictory approach to classical music broadly considered. On the one hand, many prominent members of this community routinely condemn "academic" music or music otherwise safeguarded from the free market as elitist and undemocratic. On the other hand, they also often rely on academic positions and traditional institutional residencies for much of their financial support. Their self-promotion hinges on how they rhetorically orient themselves to music's history; their antagonism toward modernism as well as their appropriation of punk and indie rock's do-it-yourself ethos represents drastic reformulations of musical ideas that were historically critical or even revolutionary. Some indie classical artists seem to strive to exemplify and propagandize the ideal neoliberal subject, but since this ideal would be impossible to fully realize, their rhetoric (and, I will argue, their music) is sometimes shot through with melancholy and contradiction.

Chapter 3 examines the multiple contradictions surrounding the Los Angeles opera company The Industry, which has attained substantial corporate and municipal sponsorship even as its director promotes it as "operating under an absolutely do-it-yourself spirit."[6] While The Industry publicized its 2016 opera, *Hopscotch*, as an example of the kind of participatory art that transforms public spaces into sites for political and social awakenings, the actual performance of the opera brought the company into conflict with longtime residents of the gentrifying neighborhood of Boyle Heights, for whom the influx of expensive art galleries and studio spaces is more threat than opportunity. The Industry promotes itself via keywords from traditionally anticapitalist art practices—for example, those of Guy Debord or Bertolt Brecht—but, just as in indie classical marketing rhetoric, these keywords are divorced from the leftist politics that originally gave them purchase.

Chapter 4 turns to tensions within neoliberalism itself, specifically its vexed relationship with history. Much of the book charts the neoliberalization of musical sounds, practices, and value systems in the United States, but an important feature of my argument is that the idea of classical music is itself socially constituted, and represents a pliable ideology that can overlap with neoliberalism but also contest it in various ways. Neoliberals are eager to find justifications for the social disruption their policies cause, and seek to attach their ideas to the great golden ages of the past. This process of justification has led to the transformations capitalism has undergone over the past several centuries as it has responded to its critics by seeming to meet their demands. It is in this sense, I argue, that ideas and stereotypes about classical music are important to the corporations that use it in marketing their products. Thanks to discourses of autonomy that have sought to separate certain kinds of music from the taint of commercial culture, a whiff of eternal grandeur and high-mindedness still clings to music by Beethoven, Mozart, and other canonized masters. Neoliberals, desperate to locate their ideas within a grand historical narrative, marshal this stereotype in their propaganda. At the same time, the very concept of commercial disinterestedness is anathema to neoliberals, who must chain all human endeavors to the workings of the free market. This ideological mismatch generates a productive tension, one that chapter 4 explores via an analysis of the Intel Corporation's recent rebranding strategy, which relied on a re- composed version of Beethoven's Fifth Symphony that incorporated Intel's sonic logo into the symphony's first movement.

Throughout the book, I undertake a critique of the kind of radical indi- vidualism that neoliberalism promotes, and that has become submerged into common sense, affecting not only our beliefs about music and musi- cal practice but also our beliefs about how to be a good person and lead a good life. In my conclusion, I revisit the ideal of autonomy that gener- ates so much ambivalence in both musicology and neoliberalism. I suggest some ways we might rehabilitate this ideal by reorienting it. Historically, the autonomous ideal has represented the yearning for individual, subjec- tive freedom—a compelling and often beautiful version of freedom that, I will argue, has ultimately come to serve capital. In my conclusion, I instead try to think toward a new, collective autonomy. Along these lines, I explore what a collectively oriented anticapitalist musical practice might look and sound like, and suggest how we might reformulate our ideas about music in order to more productively resist capitalist logics.

Classical music and neoliberalism are only just beginning to be sys- tematically studied in our field; Andrea Moore's foundational 2016 article addresses the neoliberalization of labor in contemporary classical music practice, and has proved to be influential to newer and forthcoming work, including the present study.[7] But as a rule, classical music's relation to the capitalist mode of production in general has been undertheorized, perhaps in part because of the long-standing pretense of commercial disinterested- ness that has clung to the canon since the nineteenth century. I look at many examples of neoliberalism's infiltration of classical music practice, marketing, and reception in the United States; however, I also look beyond practice, and approach classical music as a set of ideas comprising a mal- leable ideological framework that has interacted with capitalist logic in complex ways over time. Since I interrogate the shifting set of ideals and assumptions that have constructed the notion of "classical music" itself, I am also concerned with the ideas on which the field of musicology was founded and which continue to exert a profound influence on how we teach, write, and think about music.

Musicology and the Market

One of the field's foundational debates concerns the autonomous ideal—a debate examining the question of whether, and if so how, certain kinds of music might be understood as existing wholly apart from the imperatives of the market. During the nineteenth century, when the rising financial power of the bourgeoisie was opening concert attendance to anyone who could afford to purchase a ticket, some music lovers tried to argue that certain types of music resisted commodification. In 1813, E. T. A. Hoffmann positioned abstract instrumental music as superior to program music, because it neither seeks nor requires external explanation—rather, "its sole subject is the infinite"—and because its complexity and opacity render it incomprehensible to the bourgeois concert audiences he referred to as "the musical rabble."[8] This kind of positioning of abstract music perhaps reached its peak in the mid-twentieth century, when postwar modernists like Milton Babbitt sought to align musical composition with the purity and logic of scientific research, partially in an effort to attain a space for composition within the hallowed halls of academia. Only by seeking out what Babbitt called "the private life" of the university could composers pursue "genuinely original" music: music untainted by the need to appeal to audiences and sell tickets.[9] In the constructions of artistic autonomy that Babbitt and Hoffmann espoused, true, authentic art was by necessity detached from the marketplace, existing instead in a pure, self-contained, and empirical form that required no outside referent and looked for no outside justification in the form of wide popularity.

One of the goals of the New Musicology that arose in the 1980s and 1990s was to break down this insular, elitist formulation of autonomy, which positions "serious" music—implicitly, music made by privileged white men working within the tradition of European art music—as superior to the various musics of popular cultures. The New Musicology self-consciously incorporated "postmodern" ideas into its methodologies for understanding musical production, and argued convincingly that music must be understood as a changing cultural practice conditioned by specific social, political, and economic realities, and experienced by listeners in myriad ways depending on time, place, and subject position. This intervention was usually presented as an assault on power. For too long, it was argued, musical discourse has been controlled by a prevailing power structure that for centuries has instructed us to value composers and musics reflecting the orthodoxies of patriarchy and white supremacy while denigrating or ignoring others. Merely puncturing this edifice of elitist oppression was figured, perhaps rightly, as a critique of power, since the work of the New Musicologists widened immensely the range of possibilities in the field, not only in terms of newly legitimate topics of research but also materially, by opening academic music studies itself to a more diverse array of scholars.

To argue that music was necessarily embedded in a network of social and political relations, the New Musicology drew major inspiration from the work of Theodor W. Adorno. Like Babbitt or Hoffmann, Adorno was concerned with the question of music's autonomy, but he formulated this question in quite different terms. Adorno argued that the structures of musical works point to the structures governing society; hence, even composers' attempts to construct autonomous music—by which he meant not only music with internal coherence but also music that resisted effort-less comprehensibility and thus commodification—manage to reflect the capitalist society in which such works were produced. For Adorno, the au-tonomous ideal allowed music to stand just slightly apart from its culture, opening a potential space for critique. This conception of autonomy had much in common with Hoffmann's and Babbitt's in that all three envi-sioned an ideal music detached from the marketplace. But Hoffmann and Babbitt valued autonomous music for its supposed ability to show us a divine purity outside the messy realities of human life. By contrast, for Adorno autonomous music would paradoxically be music that truthfully depicted our social reality. These three theorists also differed dramatically in their ideas about the realization of such music. Both Babbitt and Hoff-mann believed that autonomy could be achieved: Hoffmann asserted that specific compositional techniques, like organicism, generated autonomous music; Babbitt felt that such music became possible once the necessity to attract audiences was removed from the composer's consideration. For Adorno, the ideal of autonomy was no less powerful and urgently desired; but, crucially, he did not believe it had been achieved, nor that it could be so long as capitalism remained the dominant structuring principle for society. Rather, the pursuit of autonomy would necessarily yield music that reflected capitalist society, even and especially in the attempt to escape it.

While the New Musicology found in Adorno some of the inspiration and justification for arguing that music is a changing cultural practice, such musicologists tended not to engage with Adorno's overarching critique of capitalism. Timothy Taylor addresses this scholarly lack in *Music and Capitalism*, noting that while scholars in many other fields have been critiqu-ing capitalism since the first interventions of Marx and Engels in the nine-teenth century, academic music studies have been slow to catch on. During the Cold War, musicologists in capitalist nations largely ceased writing about economic issues altogether because of these issues' obvious proximity to the Marxist ideas that had led to the establishment of communist states.[10] Once the Cold War ended and music scholars became interested again in Adorno's ideas about music in society, many nonetheless tended to engage such ideas incompletely. They analyzed music as a social product but without considering the powerful structuring force capitalism exerts on all such products, effectively cutting the heart out of Adorno's critique. This lacuna in fact characterizes many interventions in the 1990s across the humanities. Although in 1984 Fredric Jameson theorized postmodernism as the "logic of late capitalism,"[11] Taylor notes that it quickly became more common "to theorize the supposed effects of capitalism without attending to causes." Scholars discussed Jameson's list of postmodern symptoms but "with all of the thinking on late capitalism excised."[12] Consequently, Taylor points out, even where musicologists have made use of Adorno's writings, they have often been critical of his taste, accusing him of mere snobbery or elitist canon defense, without acknowledging the role that autonomous music plays in his overriding critique of capitalism. Taylor productively reassesses Adorno by foregrounding him as a critic of capitalism first and foremost, an approach that allows us to see Adorno as "a major intellect grappling with the capitalism of his time" rather than merely an elitist or someone who made general claims about art being socially constituted.[13]

Taylor demonstrates the implications that musicology's selective reading of Adorno has had on our understanding of Adorno, but he does not examine specific implications it had for musicology itself, except to note that our field has been slow to grapple with capitalism. He also neglects to assess the musicological implications of Jacques Attali's work, although he cites Attali's *Noise* as "the lone book after Adorno's death that systematically tackles the question of music and capitalism."[14] Attali, a political economist by training, was another foundational thinker whose work shaped our field, yet again musicologists largely failed to engage with his thoughts on capitalism itself, focusing instead on his observations about music's social role. Like Adorno, Attali made claims for music as a social product that has something to tell us about social reality. However, while both thinkers positioned their work in the post-Marxist tradition, each had radically different perspectives on capitalism itself and music's relation to it.

In his writings on music, Adorno sees capitalism as a totalizing system of dehumanizing oppression, and holds that the best music can hope for is to tell the truth about this condition by embodying our own alienation and reflecting it back to us. The prevailing tone in Adorno's work is pessimistic—he is oriented toward the past and has no hope for the future. Attali, on the other hand, provides a substantially more optimistic example for musicologists who want to affirm music's socially empowering potential. In *Noise*, Attali argues that music can and does shape society, and he constructs a timeline for human history in which musical sounds and structures guide the development of capitalism, ultimately taking us into a liberated future. In Attali's utopian final stage of human development, which he dubs the era of "Composing," musical creation metaphorizes the liberation of the human subject.

In a recent *Critical Inquiry* article, Eric Drott reassesses Attali's intervention, contextualizing it within the consolidation of the new French Left that Attali's political economy helped bring to power.[15] Drott points out that while Attali identified as a Marxist, his arguments turn Marx on his head—for example, Attali elevated intellectual labor over manual labor, and asserted that it is knowledge workers, rather than the proletariat, who will bring about revolution and utopia. Drott describes Attali's conception of the social world as one in which "all those whose work does not take place within the empyrean realm of ideas and information but within the grubby, terrestrial realm of material production are demoted to a subordinate position."[16] This formulation of society and of the relations of production stands in stark contrast to Marx's. Indeed, Drott situates *Noise* alongside the rise of neoliberalism in France in the 1970s, demonstrating that Attali's book participated in a broader restructuring of leftist ideology. Attali's insistence that music affects culture "took direct aim" at French communism's materialist understanding of historical progress; furthermore, the idea of order emerging from noise that constitutes the through-line of his book about music was also at the heart of Attali's economic theory. Attali asserted that we should embrace the periodic crises that capitalism undergoes, because they are simply indications that the system is perfecting itself. For Drott, "The ideological work performed by Attali's valorization of the cleansing power of calamitous economic upheaval should not be discounted." Attali naturalized economic disturbances "along with the suffering they entail," insisting that such crises will bring about a better world.[17] This salutary vision of the capitalist process is at the heart of neoliberalism.

Luc Boltanski and Eve Chiapello identify two different forms resistance to capitalism has taken since the nineteenth century: the "social critique," which was directed at the collective injustice and inequality wrought by capitalism; and what they call the "artistic critique," which decried the limitations on personal freedom and self-expression that capitalism placed on individuals.[18] They identify an obvious tension between these two critiques, noting that individual freedom of choice often comes into conflict with what is best for the collective. Using this framework, we could say that Attali's influential writings—including *Noise*—subordinate the social critique to the artistic critique. More specifically, in *Noise* we can see the beginnings of the wider social and political transformation of a once-revolutionary socialism into today's establishment neoliberalism, thanks to the excising of collective politics from the leftist worldview, and the replacement of those prerogatives with the fetishization of individual empowerment and of creative labor. Now that the artistic critique has been appropriated as a tool in neoliberalism's arsenal of self-promotional strategies, Boltanski and Chiapello argue, it is effectively "dead" as a viable form of criticism. Capitalism now enables us to exercise more freedom of personal choice and expression than ever before; thus, when we promote these values we also promote capitalism. The authors conclude that we therefore must begin looking for new oppositional values shaped by social, rather than personal, critiques.[19]

The artistic critique in musicology has tended to take the form of celebrating pop culture as an empowering alternative to the constraints on personal expression and freedom of choice that elitist high culture and the canon impose on individuals or marginalized groups. On the one hand, some musicologists have affirmed the market for its potential to spread, publicize, and amplify a wide variety of musics and voices that have traditionally been excluded from academic consideration as well as from the institutions of high art that have served as the main arbiters of musical taste for the past two centuries. This affirmative gesture is certainly justified in some respects, not only because it attacks the many inequalities that the Western canon has helped justify and perpetuate across its history, but also because it upholds the vibrant heterogeneity of a living and lively pop culture as a salutary alternative to the canon's ancient, suffocating sameness. However, in their efforts to deflate the pretentious universalizing of the canon's defenders, who insisted that authentic art constitutes a transcendent sphere, some musicologists have worked to center the market unproblematically as the only meaningful structuring principle for human life. In his 1994 essay, "Mozart as Working Stiff," Neal Zaslaw ruthlessly dismantles the sentimental belief in Mozart's divine genius represented in hagiographies like the film *Amadeus* (Miloš Forman, 1984).[20] Zaslaw scoffs at the notion that Mozart composed "merely to please himself or because he was 'inspired,'" arguing instead that he composed simply out of financial necessity.[21] Richard Taruskin similarly insisted in 2007 that it is futile for composers to resist the imperatives of the market.[22] To stay fresh and change with the times, classical music must accept that its "gravy train" (state and philanthropic patronage) is over, and that it must "go out and earn its living." This entails composers adopting more "accessible" styles, and venues programming the superstars that bring in the crowds. "Love it or hate it, such accommodation is a normal part of the evolutionary history of any art." Taruskin goes on to accuse artists who refuse this imperative—who "hole up" in the academy—of being defenders of the "status quo."[23]

Like Adorno's, these interventions are meant to demonstrate music's inextricability from its economic context; yet they are self-consciously not Marxist, and are not critical of capitalism itself. For Taruskin, the "status quo" is not the free market that increasingly governs every sphere of our lives but rather the isolated zones of old-fashioned resistance to that force. Moreover, such scholarship envisions participation in the market as not only inevitable but also equalizing. Zaslaw, for instance, invokes the meritocratic fallacy when he insists that the main difference between Mozart and the rest of us is simply that Mozart worked harder than we do. Such interventions appear to reiterate, albeit unintentionally, a simplified version of Marx's understanding of society, in which the economy is totalizing and no human idea or act can arise independently of it. Within this strand of musicology, then, the market is democratizing yet strangely antiindividual. Zaslaw wants to cut Mozart down to human size, and he does so by demonstrating that Mozart wasn't special, he was just desperate to make money, and he used music to do so simply because this was the skill set he happened to have developed. These kinds of arguments expose a contradiction in such scholarship, between its intense privileging of unique individual subjectivity and personal expression, and its absolute subsuming of the individual into the logic of the market. Thus, by ignoring the system's structuring role in generating the various injustices and inequalities it was otherwise concerned to rectify, certain strands of the New Musicology could inadvertently reaffirm the universal character of capitalism even while insisting on the fraudulence of universalist thinking in other respects.

Musicology and Difference

In their attacks on the musical canon and the autonomous ideal, musicologists have often productively affirmed difference as an empowering value, focusing on the unique experiences and intrinsic worth of traditionally marginalized subjects. But a lingering aversion to systemic critiques of power makes it difficult to see how difference itself can be commodified and sold back to us as justification for the continuation of capitalism, a dynamic Boltanski and Chiapello cite as one example of how the artistic critique no longer functions as critique. James Currie addresses this melancholy tension in postmodernist scholarship, asking, If difference is supposed to be so revolutionary, why is it that capitalism actually allows for such a wide array of personal expression? Currie points out that capitalism allows the expression of difference so long as that difference is never formulated in terms of opposition to the system itself. This kind of non-oppositional difference can then be scooped up by the system and used to continue propagating the fiction that capitalism generates equality and justice. For example, once corporations, mainstream media, and the government have publicly embraced "diversity initiatives" intended to raise up individual women or minorities into positions of power within the corporate or political structure, these previously disenfranchised voices are then invited to communicate "the message that difference can be acknowledged without the world economy having to be disturbed."[24]

Whatever its strengths and shortcomings, the New Musicology instigated a major transformation of the field, which has affected not only scholarship but also the way composers and musicians are trained. Whether their teachers embraced or decried this new wave of scholarship, the artists examined in this book were undoubtedly exposed to its central claims during their education. In one way or another, difference manifests as a fundamentally sacred value in each of my four case studies. The artists and marketing schemes I examine are also populist in the same way that some of the New Musicology was populist—again and again, in discourses surrounding classical music in the contemporary United States, composers, musicians, programmers, and arts journalists applaud the fact that there is no longer any distinction between "high" and "low" musical forms, and no longer any stuffy, restrictive notions about music needing to be safeguarded from the vagaries of the entertainment marketplace.

The New Musicology made a strong case for abandoning universalist thinking in favor of a rhetoric of difference. And yet I contend that it remains desperately important to recognize that some conditions *are* universal, even if our individual experiences of those conditions may differ. One such condition is that of contemporary global capitalism, and when we insist—as many postmodernist scholars have—that individual subjectivity or injustice can be understood *only* via the logic of the contextual, the local, and the particular, we overlook a crucial key to understanding our shared condition. As activists have been pointing out for decades, the structuring power of capitalism intersects with other forms of oppression and dehumanization. Refusing to engage with this fact sometimes means we focus on symptoms rather than causes, and we mistake the tools of oppression for tools of empowerment. Real collectivity requires some degree of universalist thinking, and it is this collectivity that is endangered by the postmodernist refusal to think critically about capitalism. The Marxist critic Ellen Meiksins Wood observes that "the cult of postmodernism" treats the market as a universal law of nature while "paradoxically" insisting there are no universals. For Meiksins Wood, this paradox is much more insidious than a simple intellectual blind spot, and actually illustrates postmodernists' more or less conscious complicity in upholding the system itself: "What better excuse for submitting to the *force majeur* of capitalism than the conviction that its power, while pervasive, has no systemic origin, no unified logic, no identifiable social roots?"[25] In reality, our individual experiences of universal conditions certainly differ from one another—a middle-class white American experiences capitalism in a way quite different from a poor person in the Global South—and yet we all live under capitalism, are shaped by its logics, and are affected by its processes. Furthermore, while living under capitalism conditions our ways of thinking and being, as history has shown, different groups' resistances to that conditioning have also forced the capitalist mode of production to undergo periodic transformations.[26]

In this book, I try to chart a middle path between these two extremes. On the one hand, I argue that the total rejection of universalism poses a problem for genuinely oppositional thought, because it precludes the kind of radical collective identification that will be required if we are to survive. When we foreclose on the possibility of there being universal experiences, we foreclose on the social critique; we lose the critique of capitalism as a system that affects the whole world, including not only all people but also all mammals, plants, and insects, the creatures in the ocean, the bacteria in our soil. We cannot afford to lose to absolute relativism the recognition of those aspects of our condition that are shared. On the other hand, I try to construct understandings of music within capitalism that also take particularities—like those of race, gender, or sexuality as well as class—into account. Different kinds of people have access to different pathways of survival under capitalism, for example, and this book tries to untangle some of these. Furthermore, as Silvia Federici has argued, racism and misogyny serve to uphold and strengthen capitalism itself, because the system requires that vast swaths of the population be disenfranchised in order to maintain the class hierarchy and continue accumulating profits off exploited labor.[27] In this sense too, acknowledging difference remains important to any critique of capitalism.

The Critical Project

It would be easy to assume that the artists in this book are simply capitulating—in their practices as well as in their ideas about musical value—to the inexorable requirements of the economic system in which they live. In this book, however, I try to think further than this rigid model would allow. Certainly, much of what we do in our lives is shaped and constrained by the increasingly totalizing logic of late capitalism, and as I will demonstrate, there are myriad examples of this dynamic at work in the contemporary practice, reception, and promotion of classical music. At the same time, I try to acknowledge how capitalism itself develops in tandem with—not always simply determining—concurrent ideas. Max Weber, for example, argued that the "Protestant ethic," an ethos of work as salvation that emerged from Puritanism, lent eighteenth-century capitalism a crucial source of strength and justification.[28] Similarly, as I assess the infiltration of neoliberal values into musical culture, I also examine what we have meant by "classical music," as both an idea and a conveyor of certain values that may help shape contemporary capitalism.

In their expansion of Weber's ideas, Luc Boltanski and Eve Chiapello argue that because the current system is totalizing and also because we are aware of our complicity with it, we need "powerful moral reasons for rallying to capitalism."[29] We suspect that capitalism is generating untenable conditions of life for billions of people, and that doubt must be assuaged via continual assurances that participating in capitalist processes can be, nonetheless, morally right. The same paradigms are frequently, as Boltanski and Chiapello put it, "engaged in condemnation and justification of what is condemned."[30] This ambivalence is not necessarily (although it sometimes is) the result of poor education, cynicism, bad faith, or lack of awareness of the contradictions endemic to modern life; rather, it is an unavoidable feature of subjectivity in late capitalism. Because the system actually has no internal justification (Weber called it "absurd"), it must constantly repackage itself in order to minimize the discrepancy people feel between capitalism's rhetorical benevolence and their actual experiences of life within the system. Also, of course, capitalism needs no justification at all for capitalists themselves—the system works astonishingly well at what it was initially intended to accomplish, which is the accumulation of wealth and the consolidation of elite power.

Academics who undertake a critique of capitalism rarely offer reasonable solutions or ideas for changing the system. Theodor Adorno, for example, does not even attempt to suggest how to move toward alternatives, and his unremitting pessimism has often irritated and even baffled his readers. Writers who do offer suggestions, however, can be just as unsatisfying: those who attempt to chart a practical course toward a possible future often advocate for an incrementalism that seems demoralizing given the enormity of capitalism's challenge to life on earth; meanwhile, those who offer transformative alternatives to capitalism find it impossible to explain how such alternatives might be brought into being.

Two recent musicological studies exemplify these two extremes. Timothy Taylor concludes *Music and Capitalism* by accepting the inevitability of some form of the capitalist system, at least for the near future, and he asks us to let "other regimes of value" besides the purely economic inform the construction of a "kinder, gentler" capitalism. At the other end of the spectrum is Phil Ford's *Dig*, in which he envisions artistic creation in a post-capitalist society and conjures a world in which art becomes an individual practice rather than a productive activity. The concrete incrementalism of Taylor's conclusion is somewhat deflating yet useful in a real-world sense; Ford's conclusion may be more inspiring in some ways, but its utopian vision of a world free from capitalist logic feels devastatingly unreachable. Both authors admirably undertake to envision alternatives to the system, even as the difficulties their two very different conclusions present illustrate Frederic Jameson's famous observation that it is easier to envision the end of the world than the end of capitalism.

I take the tack that criticism need not present a checklist for attaining utopia, nor must it accept the world as it is. Criticism is valuable because it can puncture holes in the justifications for capitalism that convince us to accept it. By deflating capitalist ideology and revealing its many contradictions and flaws, criticism encourages consciousness-raising, which in turn may lead to widespread demands for something different. Criticism is also a means of opening a space to envision alternatives to capitalism; without these we are doomed to accept the system, and thus our participation in it, as inevitable and eternal. For Wendy Brown, critique rescues us from our "entrapment in an unbearable present," because it "aims to render crisis into knowledge, and to orient us in the darkness."[31] For Brown, critiques must affirm life and possibilities in order to be political in this way; and it is in this sense that I find Taylor's focus on "other regimes of value" and Ford's utopian thought exercise most meaningful, because they signal a refusal to submit to pessimism or to simply accept things as they are. I will return to some final thoughts on critique in my conclusion.

The transmutation of economic principles into a common sense governing average citizens' everyday lives and moral codes helps explain how values that originally emanated from right-wing schools of economics can now be seen manifesting all over the political spectrum. Progressives and conservatives alike often agree that innovation is obviously good, and that industries, schools, and individuals must become technologically proficient in order to keep up with the destabilizing social transformations generated by constant technological change; that personal liberty and freedom of choice are self-evidently superior to the values of other social formations, such as communism or socialism; that personal liberties are best protected by the free market; and that teaching and enabling entrepreneurship—for example, giving "micro loans" to poor women in the Global South so that they can start businesses—are admirable practices that will facilitate social justice.[32] Capitalist logic has become an unseen spirit motivating and shaping our lives and the way we see the world. Some of the system's central premises—such as human beings are by nature competitive and profit seeking—have now become commonsense truths, no longer recognizable as the culturally and historically contingent theories they are.

This indicates a fact that can be difficult to grasp in today's polarized political climate, which is that neoliberalism is nonpartisan. Republicans, Democrats, and many people in between espouse its central tenets and contribute to expanding its conditioning logic. Most of the subjects studied here identify as socially progressive, perhaps even leftist, yet they often passionately espouse brutal right-wing ideas without realizing that they are doing so. Neoliberalism's ruthless mercantilism has become naturalized as common sense, which makes it very difficult to criticize or even to notice, not only in political discourse but also in our own perceptions and opinions. By distorting revolutionary rhetoric about freedom and justice into a tool that serves capital, the musical discourses I examine obscure our ability to talk meaningfully about musical aesthetics or the role that music can or should play in society; they contribute to the increasing dearth of politically engaged music and music criticism; and finally, they contribute to the US culture's uncritical adoption of corporate values as common sense, and thus to our growing inability to envision alternatives to capitalism.

My choice to focus on the United States is a conscious one. While neoliberalism has for decades been remaking much of the world, it originated in the United States, and its global spread is widely perceived as an outsourcing of American prerogatives. While all the corporations I examine in this book have become multinational conglomerates, each of them began as an American company, and the values they promote in their foreign markets and workplaces reflect these origins. Additionally, classical music itself occupies different cultural positions depending on the country in which it is practiced. In some countries, for example, classical music is figured as a Western import, the practice of which can signal acceptance of Western values, while in many Western European nations, state funding for musical production is much more widely supported than it is in the contemporary United States, and European composers thus often have more freedom to compose in styles that would be anathema to artists—such as the Americans examined here—who feel they must appeal to broader audiences. For these reasons, I situate neoliberalism as a phenomenon of US culture, and seek to understand how its central tenets are shaping the composition and appreciation of classical music in the contemporary United States.

Furthermore, this book diagnoses discourses and practices of classical music during a historical crisis moment in US capitalism. Neoliberal principles have governed the US economy and conditioned citizens' lives for decades, yet some saw the 2016 US presidential election as indicative of a crisis in this value system, as voters from many political orientations rejected all the neoliberal candidates—including Hillary Clinton as well as the mainstream GOP challengers—and instead elected Donald Trump, an "outsider" who ran against free trade and globalization, and who pledged to dismantle NAFTA and bring back American manufacturing jobs. Trump's election, as well as the return of Democratic socialism to the mainstream via the Bernie Sanders campaign, represents a crisis for neoliberalism, because it indicates the degree to which large swaths of the US citizenry have become disillusioned by its promises. Such crises in capitalism have historically strengthened and reconsolidated the system, because they show it how it must reform so that people will continue participating in it.

While the artists, institutions, and journalists I examine continue to make neoliberal assumptions about music and musical practice, the positioning of that rhetoric in the wider society has changed since the 2016 election. Until recently, valorizing statements about innovation, diversity, and flexibility in musical practice fit neatly into both governmental and corporate promotional rhetoric. Now such statements are increasingly out of step with those emanating from the US power structure, as both the government and corporations attempt to assuage the population's resentment about precarity and pivot toward a more protectionist, closed-off stance (or at least the appearance of one) regarding the rest of the world. In the book's conclusion, I will examine this issue at greater length; here I will simply say that this crisis presents both a challenge and an opportunity to music practitioners in the United States, who will have to decide whether to continue promoting essentially corporate versions of values like freedom and diversity, or else critically interrogate those values in order to turn them into tools for attacking power.

The current mainstream discourse on classical music presents many dangers. Allowing ideas about music to be wholly conditioned by a neoliberal ideology deepens precarity and labor instability in the musical workforce and enables people to accept those conditions as natural—as simply the results of some musicians' lazy refusal to capitalize on their potential. Such conditioning helps entrench the increasingly widespread belief that value can and should be measured only monetarily, and it encourages us to think of human relationships in transactional terms. The historical perception that classical music somehow stands above market considerations also allows corporations to use it to disguise innovations (data accumulation, data analysis, surveillance, drones) that aid US military imperialism and the surveillance state by cloaking these innovations in the inspirational associations that still adhere to music by Beethoven, Bach, and other past masters. Such a disguise naturalizes military and surveillance technologies as normal elements of the human experience. Finally, some of the projects I explore here make neoliberal social transformations like gentrification and corporate globalization seem not only inevitable but glorious by associating them with the timeless cultural value still accorded to classical music and artistic practice generally.

By criticizing some of the most high-profile ways classical music is continuing to find relevance in contemporary US society, I do not mean to diminish or sully the importance, beauty, or worth of music or the people who make it and love it. Nor is it my intention to criticize people for finding ways of surviving within contemporary life; indeed, we are all simply trying to survive, and we are all as complicit in allowing capitalism to continue as we are individually helpless to stop it. Rather, I am interested in interrogating the discursive strategies that insistently celebrate these survival tactics as empowering and good for society. I want to issue a challenge and ask that we work harder to find ways of explaining, presenting, and advocating for music that do not simply celebrate the hegemony of market rationality. The first step in this process of reaffirmation is to recognize how our values are entangled with market logic in the first place, so that we may thoughtfully explore alternatives.

ONE

Innovating Classical Music

Cisco Systems deployed marketing materials, speeches, and videos to advance the slogan for its 2014 summit: Amazing Together. Then, as the corporate partners of the multinational technology corporation met in Las Vegas to network, the event's branding extended to a special performance of the Las Vegas Youth Orchestra (LVYO), which played briefly for the assembled tech executives. The ensemble performed "The Rise of Exotic Computing," a work for small orchestra and laptop by Mason Bates, a Juilliard- and Berkeley-trained composer and a rising star in the world of contemporary classical music (in the 2014–15 season, he was the second-most performed living composer in America, after John Adams).[1] At the Cisco summit, the then thirty-seven-year-old Bates briefly introduced his piece, then took his usual spot behind a laptop and digital sampler, which he used to accompany the orchestra with an array of electronic beats and sampled sounds.[2]

For the duration of its performance of "Exotic Computing," the LVYO was surrounded by large screens displaying images and text. Animated grids were superimposed on footage of leaping dolphins, naval ships, farmland, assembly lines, spiderwebs, and outer space, linking the images and imposing a teleology on the visuals. In one sequence, the interlocking circles representing a dolphin's use of sonar transformed into a naval ship's radar bleeps: an image linking nature and technology. These images were overlaid by segments of text associating the sounds and visuals with Cisco's corporate slogan: "We are all connected . . . one universe . . . one planet . . . one ecosystem . . . thriving as one network . . . working with one purpose . . . we are amazing together." The whole performance naturalized technological innovation and universal connectivity, linked those processes to the timeless grandeur of high art, and presented them as the reason we can be "amazing together."

Cisco had donated money to the LVYO, so the group's performance at the corporate summit demonstrated the company's socially minded endeavors to support not only young people but also the kind of "high culture" that classical music still represents in the popular consciousness.[3] But the music the LVYO played revealed much more than simply a display of philanthropy. Bates is especially applauded for his incorporation of new technologies into orchestral music; most of his work makes use of drum machines and sampled sounds. Furthermore, as I will discuss below, many of his compositions programmatically valorize tech entrepreneurs like Steve Jobs, and he has also been involved in projects like the YouTube Symphony Orchestra (YTSO) that serve to mythologize the valiant role tech corporations like Google are playing in remaking our world. "The Rise of Exotic Computing" also valorizes technology at a musical level. The piece comprises tiny motives that flit from instrument to instrument; it's meant to aurally depict synthetic computing, a process that links computers by instantaneously replicating lines of code without human intervention. Thus, the piece essentially presents Cisco's product, networking technology, as art.[4] The video that accompanied the performance accomplished a similar presentation, by linking man-made technologies with naturally evolving processes like dolphin sonar. In this way, it fit in nicely with the corporate branding strategy of Cisco and its partners, which involves packaging the products required by the surveillance state under inspirational rhetoric about connectivity.

In this chapter, I seek to explain Bates's phenomenal career success, arguing that he serves two related—but not wholly overlapping—functions within the power structures represented by traditional classical music institutions on the one hand, and tech corporations on the other. In his institutional function, Bates represents a heroic figure, someone who is saving classical music by fusing it with contemporary values like innovation, diversity, and connectivity. Popular perceptions of classical music often figure it as a musty relic of the distant past, and as elitist, sexist, and racist; by contrast, Bates presents it as a thriving participant in a tech-savvy, multicultural global community. In the first part of the chapter I lay out the institutional function Bates serves, examining his creative work with the YTSO, a project that positioned classical music as a leader in technological innovation but also as a facilitator of multicultural communication and connectivity.

Bates also serves a corporate function, one similarly grounded in a valorization of connectivity. In the second half of the chapter, I examine his characteristic glorification of digital connectivity via an analysis of "The Rise of Exotic Computing" and its correlations with Cisco's marketing strategy. By sponsoring and promoting Bates and his projects, tech corporations like Cisco and Google can borrow the aura of commercial disinterestedness that still adheres to the idea of classical music, and use it to legitimize capitalist globalization and the surveillance state.

There is a long precedent for the kind of technology-oriented musical-corporate connection such as the one between Mason Bates and contemporary tech giants like Google and Cisco Systems. In the previous generation, institutions like IRCAM, the BBC Radiophonic Workshops, and Stanford and Princeton Universities constructed a similar rhetoric privileging scientific research and technological innovation, one that appealed to power and secured funding and prestige for new music in a changing world.[5] Even from its earliest moments, "computer music" has had strong ties to powerful industry; the first computer-generated music was made via a technology invented by a Bell Telephone Laboratories researcher who was trying to convert audio signals to digital information in order to automate the tasks performed by human telephone operators.[6]

That tech corporations would patronize a symphony orchestra or a young composer should come as no surprise; art music composers and performers have a long history of appealing to those with money and power. Since much of the great music of the past was created with at least one eye toward pleasing the financially solvent of a given era, changing musical aesthetics have often accompanied changes in the ideals of those with the most power and money in a society. To this extent, the YTSO or the Cisco-funded performance of "Exotic Computing" is certainly nothing new; however, the structure in which wealthy people and corporations can become patrons of the arts—as well as what they choose to patronize—has changed, and along with that change has come a shift in cultural beliefs, tastes, and, inevitably, the practice of music. IRCAM, for example, is state funded, and its founding was part of the French government's nationalistic plan for rebuilding its image in the wake of the social turmoil of 1968.[7] By contrast, in the contemporary United States, the power that some of the most successful and widely acclaimed musical innovations are aligned with is corporate power, the power of private enterprise, which is a power that neoliberalism deliberately counterposes to that of the oppressive state and its obsolete nationalisms.

Contemporary discourses of innovation often credit new technologies with both liberating individuals and promoting social connectivity. As the Cisco presentation put it, "We are all connected . . . thriving as one network." Technology's unique ability to "bring us together" was also ceaselessly promoted during the performance of the YTSO, a Google marketing scheme in which musicians from all over the world uploaded audition videos to YouTube, hoping to be chosen for performing in a live concert of classical music broadcast to millions online. Here, too, we can see a difference between the state-sponsored centers for musical-scientific research and Bates's various projects. Composers at Princeton, for example, tended to value computer-generated music for how it allowed the individual artist to maintain total control over the work, and for how such musical research represented a means of safeguarding musical creation from the necessity of appealing to the entertainment industry; these institutions or departments were erected in an effort to construct spaces for autonomous creation, and they did so by emphasizing the idea that music should not have to connect with audiences. By contrast, Bates and his supporters present his use of computers and electronics as entrepreneurial and market oriented, saying it will draw in young audiences and appeal to those who don't like traditional classical music. These qualities, in turn, are praised for being "democratic."

Throughout this book, I document the way products and practices that find wide market success are often dubbed "democratic" and celebrated for promoting "community." Corporations like Cisco and Google present the connectivity their products enable as uplifting—such products allow us to be "amazing together"—and composers like Bates similarly talk about widening music's commercial appeal as a means of bringing people together. This rhetoric is meant to oppose the kind of hermetic, closed-off, individual autonomy that academic music research centers allow, and so on its surface it seems to promote the superiority of democratic collectivity to elitist isolation. However, the version of collectivity offered by Cisco and advocated by audience-pleasing composers is one wholly mediated by the market, and thus I will argue that it is a hollow one.

Bates and the Innovation Fetish

Mason Bates has a prestigious pedigree. He received his BA from the Columbia-Juilliard Exchange Program, where he studied with John Corigliano and David Del Tredici and majored in both composition and English literature. He then went to UC Berkeley, where he studied with Edmund Campion and earned a PhD in composition in 2008. Bates has been highly honored by august arts institutions; shortly after finishing his undergraduate education he received a Rome Prize, and the year he finished his PhD he was awarded a Guggenheim Fellowship. In 2010 he became one of the Chicago Symphony Orchestra's composers in residence, and in 2012 he received a Heinz Award in the Arts and Humanities category. In 2015 he was named the first composer in residence at the John F. Kennedy Center for the Performing Arts. At the Kennedy Center, Bates programs evening concerts that blend the performance of traditional classical music with DJ sets (he calls these evenings "post-classical raves").

Bates himself is also an electronica DJ. In addition to performing regularly (as DJ Masonic), he incorporates DJing into his works for orchestra; not only does most of his music deploy drum machines and sampled sounds, but Bates routinely performs these sounds live with the orchestra, standing behind his array of technology, wearing headphones and bobbing his head to the beat. The impression that he is saving or rejuvenating classical music by infusing it with hip new technologies and the driving rhythms of techno is widely felt in the arts press as well as in the traditional institutions that have rewarded him so highly. His supporters in the classical music world include luminaries like Riccardo Muti, Marin Alsop, and Leonard Slatkin, all of whom maintain that because of Bates's use of digital technologies, programming his music will bring in newer, younger audiences than classical music usually garners in the United States. "Often he's in the orchestra with his laptop," Alsop notes, "and his music resonates with audiences of today, with younger audiences."[8] Reviews, press releases, and bios of the composer regularly describe him as "innovative," and his Heinz Award website profile credits him with having "moved the orchestra into the digital age."[9] In a glowing profile of the composer, Anne Midgette wrote that the secret of Bates's success is multifaceted and includes "his love of electronic music, his active second life as a DJ and his burgeoning activities as a curator of interesting new-music concerts" that "represent a link to the younger audience the orchestra world is so hungry to reach."[10]

One of Bates's most prestigious supporters is the San Francisco Symphony director Michael Tilson Thomas, who has been championing and collaborating with Bates for a decade.[11] Tilson Thomas has consistently recorded, programmed, and promoted Bates's music, and often associates him with the greatest composers in the Western canon (in 2014 the symphony programmed a festival titled "Beethoven and Bates," with performances that alternated works by the two composers). In 2009 Tilson Thomas invited Bates to be a guest soloist at the inaugural concert of the YouTube Symphony Orchestra (YTSO), a marketing project Google undertook shortly after acquiring the video-sharing site in 2006, and for which Tilson Thomas served as conductor and creative director.

The YTSO project was, in part, meant to showcase the radical new possibilities enabled by the internet; hundreds of musicians worldwide uploaded audition videos to YouTube, and the winners performed an evening of canonical classical music that served to celebrate both the West's timeless traditions and the transformative innovations of Google and YouTube. The project has been executed twice: first in 2009, with a culminating performance at Carnegie Hall; and again in 2011, with a concert at the Sydney Opera House. Bates served as one of the creative advisers for the Sydney iteration of the YTSO, and he also wrote a short symphonic piece, "Mothership," that premiered at the performance.

The video that introduced the Sydney concert featured a montage of Turkish minarets, Venetian gondolas, Chinese pagodas, and the Statue of Liberty, interspersed with shots of musicians playing their instruments in iconic global locations and overlaid with the following text:

> From the sands to the seas, from the forbidden city to the city that never sleeps, from their own world to the whole world: 33 countries, 5 continents, 101 musicians, 1 stage.

The concert program contained three new commissions and included one excerpt from a work by the Argentinian composer Alberto Ginastera; the rest of the evening was devoted to well-known pieces and excerpts by European composers of the eighteenth and nineteenth centuries: Berlioz, Mozart, Robert Schumann, Schubert, Stravinsky, Mendelssohn, Percy Grainger, Richard Strauss, and J. S. Bach.[12]

This program of canonical art music was accompanied by "live digital painting" projected onto every surface of the venue, including the building's exterior.[13] During the concert, camera operators moved silently among the musicians, filming close-ups of fingers on keys and rapt expressions that were also projected all over the venue. These were interspersed with short, inspirational video interviews with selected musicians, and with speeches made by Tilson Thomas. The whole performance, including the digital painting, the close-up shots, the speeches, and the musician interviews, was live streamed on YouTube to millions of viewers worldwide.

During the YTSO performance, Tilson Thomas routinely credited the project with using technological innovation to show the world that classical music is an "ongoing" tradition, one fully commensurate with participation in a digitally connected global community. Such attempts to associate classical music with innovation are common in US classical music discourse; commentators associate "innovative" artists, programmers, and venues with saving classical music from market extinction. For Tilson

Thomas, the YTSO project clearly served as a means of associating classical music with the innovative products that corporations like Google have bestowed on us, as well as with the wholesome process of constant change that such innovations generate. He opened the Sydney concert by proclaiming that the performance represented "the culminating of a weeklong celebration and collaboration between the worlds of classical music and technology"; later in the concert, he deepened this connection:

> Well, classical music really does connect the past and the present, and even predicts the future. Over the centuries, as new thoughts, new instruments, new technologies have come along, classical music has initiated many of them, made use of them, and absorbed them. And it's still going on.[14]

Innovation, especially technological innovation, is a key value in neoliberal thought. Milton Friedman described our "dynamic world" as one in which "new products emerge and old ones disappear, demand shifts from one product to another, innovation alters methods of production, and so on without end."[15] Because we cannot alter this constant change, our only option is to accept it and learn to flexibly adapt to an ever-shifting environment in which we experience an accelerating turnover in jobs, fashions, neighborhoods, industries, and ways of life. Friedman argued that "experimentation" as a broadly adhered-to social value is what will bring "tomorrow's laggard above today's mean."[16] He also upheld the great potential of innovation to contribute to individual freedom by demonstrating that most technological innovations in history have benefited "the ordinary person" rather than the wealthy.[17] Since the 1970s, innovation has been increasingly enshrined as a desirable goal not only in economic theory but in everyday life. It has become so commonly accepted as an obvious truth and an unmitigated good by corporate and political leaders as well as by average citizens that the political economist David Harvey goes so far as to call it a "fetish belief" of contemporary culture.[18]

Ironically, the neoliberal prioritizing of innovation has its roots in Marxist thought; the notion that modern capitalism demands constant innovation at the level of production formed the basis of the "evolutionary" economic theory Marx outlined. To successfully compete against one another for profits, capitalists must constantly pursue new methods that lower the costs of producing commodities.[19] These new methods generate new consumer practices, transform the workplace, and destabilize the labor market. In the famous formulation of Marx and Engels,

Constant revolutionising of production, uninterrupted disturbance of all social conditions, everlasting uncertainty and agitation distinguish the bourgeois epoch from all earlier ones. All fixed, fast-frozen relations, with their
train of ancient and venerable prejudices and opinions, are swept away, all
new-formed ones become antiquated before they can ossify. All that is solid
melts into air.[20]

The Marxist identification of capitalism with an ever-evolving process
of periodic crisis and transformation became the core of the German
economist Joseph Schumpeter's work. Writing during the first half of the
1930s, Schumpeter insisted that capitalism is "by nature a form or method
of economic change and not only never is but never can be stationary."[21]
He argued that while there are other historical factors that lead to changes
in capitalism (such as "wars, revolutions and so on"), these are not the
system's "prime movers." Rather, he associated capitalism's condition of
constant change with Marx's notion of "creative destruction," meant to
describe the crises that constant innovation generates within the capitalist
system, as well as the notion—which Schumpeter shared with Marx—that
such constant crises would one day lead to the replacement of capitalism
with some form of socialism. For Schumpeter, as for the later neoliberals
who found inspiration in his work, creative destruction is generated by entrepreneurs. Schumpeter characterizes entrepreneurs as heroic individuals;
he repeatedly describes entrepreneurship in terms of the battlefield, calling
entrepreneurs "generals" and "warlords" and noting how they often have
to fight against a society which resists their innovations in various ways,
"from simple refusal either to finance or to buy a new thing, to physical
attack on the man who tries to produce it."[22] The entrepreneur's valiant
introduction of innovations causes businesses to crumble, industries to
founder, and society to experience periods of economic stagnation, which
can be resolved only by more heroic innovations. This is the "disruption"
that is the goal of contemporary entrepreneurship.[23]

However, while technological change has always been a feature of capitalist modernity, in recent years the term *innovation* has become an extraordinarily prevalent positive keyword in contemporary US discourse. Economists and business leaders have published study after study on the positive
benefits of innovation not only to capital but also to the entire population
of the earth.[24] Business journals are replete with glowing articles about the
necessity of encouraging innovation. The *Harvard Business Review* spon-
sors an annual "Innovating Innovation Challenge" and recently published
an article titled "Who's the Best at Innovating Innovation?" in which the

author demands that businesses work harder to "build innovation into the values, processes, and practices that rule everyday activity and behavior."[25]

The glorification of innovation has also expanded far beyond the walls of business schools, and now manifests in a wide variety of industries and undertakings. An article on the website of the Jerusalem Center for Public Affairs proclaims the need for "innovative solutions" to the Israel-Palestine conflict; articles and blogs promote guided meditations to "boost innovation"; an essay on funeral directing asks, "Is there any place for innovation in the funeral industry today?"; Reuters publishes a top–one hundred list of "The World's Most Innovative Universities," and universities across the United States are opening new "Innovation Institutes" and "Innovation Hubs"; meanwhile the education expert Tony Wagner's best-selling parenting book asserts that "young Americans learn how to innovate most often despite their schooling—not because of it."[26]

These examples reveal how innovation has been submerged into conventional wisdom. Schumpeter and Marx saw the creative destruction that incessant technological change wrought as a means to a grand end—some form of socialism. Friedman and other early neoliberals eschewed this conclusion, but nonetheless saw innovation as the primary engine of capitalist development, for the way it propels the creation of new consumer products and new means of production that lower labor costs. However, for many contemporary commentators, innovation has become prized for its own sake, as a value that should "rule everyday activity," rather than a means to any specified economic, social, or political end.

Because of the way his music seems to innovate old styles and performance models, specifically via the use of new technologies, Mason Bates serves an important institutional function for classical music. In the United States, classical music has been perceived to be in a perpetual death spiral, due to its inability to compete successfully in the contemporary entertainment marketplace.[27] Within this rhetoric, not only is new music (or the new performance of old music) praised when it can be perceived as manifesting innovation broadly considered, but composers and institutions themselves are also urged to be innovative in embracing change and finding new sources of funding. For some critics, in fact, the crisis in classical music is welcomed, for it represents merely the turnover in industries, jobs, and labor practices that constant innovation makes inevitable within capitalism; for them, the failure of old economic models is actually seen as positive evidence that classical music is still relevant. The musicologist Andrea Moore analyzes this perspective, noting that such commentators believe that classical music is thriving "precisely *because* its existing institutions are being dismantled, with new structures rising in their place."[28] This is the seemingly contradictory belief that fetishizing innovation makes possible.

American arts journalists, performers, and composers routinely discuss the necessity of "dragging classical music into the real world," by which they mean the competitive entertainment marketplace.[29] Diversifying classical music's market share, specifically by attracting younger audiences, is explicitly associated with technological innovation. The music activist Greg Sandow, who teaches arts entrepreneurship classes at Juilliard, often amplifies this connection in his many essays on contemporary musical practice. Sandow routinely argues that classical concerts must innovate in order to attract younger ticket-buyers by incorporating new technology (such as video screens showing tweets from audience members during performances), and that orchestras and opera houses must begin catering to the newly omnivorous music-consuming public.[30] In this sense, the YTSO project, with its foregrounding of technological innovation, represented a salutary alternative to the way music by Schumann or Berlioz has been performed in the United States since the nineteenth century. A post on the Eastman School of Music's Music Leadership blog proclaimed that "just the effort to do something like [the YTSO project] helps take the orchestra out of the stuffy, old foggie [sic], we're sophisticated and you're not, white tie and tails image."[31] In fact, as the YouTube marketing director Ed Sanders put it, the YTSO project "helped fundamentally challenge the norms of an entire industry."[32]

The symphonic work Bates composed for the Sydney performance of the YTSO exemplified some of the ways classical music might innovate. "Mothership" combines traditional orchestral sounds and techniques with a constant stream of pulsing beats and electronic noises that Bates loosely refers to as coming from "the world of techno." The music is highly dramatic, and pushes relentlessly forward, driven by the motoric drum machine, which Bates played live with the YTSO in Sydney. The piece, like so much of Bates's music, weaves tiny melodic and rhythmic motives into a thrumming ostinato that grows dramatically as it repeats, with multiple buildups of tension and climactic release.[33] In keeping with almost all his work, "Mothership" is also programmatic; we are instructed to hear the orchestra as a futuristic spaceship that visits alien lands and showcases the marvelous diversity it finds. Bates emphasizes this narrative in many of his score markings. The opening section is marked "Lifting off . . . ," and the first laptop trigger is labeled "spaceship booting up." Bates gives various

Example 1. Mason Bates, "Mothership," mm. 1–10.

triggers programmatic titles throughout the piece: "radio static," "hydraulic doors," "spaceship accelerating," "over and out signal." (See example 1.)

The piece opens with a three-measure brass fanfare made up of swelling fourths and fifths, which heralds the heroic takeoff of the spaceship. In measure five, the drum machine enters; from that point onward, the piece is rarely without the drum machine's regular "four on the floor" beat pattern. In approving reviews of Bates, as well as in his own self-presentation, his dual experience as a classical composer and DJ is often highlighted. Maintaining his image as a DJ is clearly important to his brand as a genre-hopping technological adept, yet his evocation of electronica DJing—hunching intently over his computer while bobbing his head to a regular beat that is never loud enough to drown out the acoustic orchestral instruments surrounding it—represents a fairly tepid, stripped-down version of the art form. When serious electronic music producers like Skrillex, DJ Snake, or Major Lazer perform live, they generate overwhelming, noisy spectacles: at a recent Major Lazer show in Las Vegas, the music was epically loud, enhanced by pounding beats and a wild and frenetic cascade of lights and pyrotechnics that never stopped; Major Lazer flung himself back and forth across the stage, yelling at the crowd; the thousands of crowd members themselves, many of whom were shirtless and covered in fluorescent paint, screamed and ceaselessly bounced up and down (egged on by frequent blasts of air horn); and periodically, huge plastic balls containing flailing human beings went bouncing across the hands of the spectators.[34] Examine a show like this alongside Bates's performance at the Sydney Opera House or even his performances at his "post-classical raves," and it becomes clear that his gentle beats and periodic whooshes of electronic noise are not meant to appeal to hard-core techno fans.

Nor is "Mothership" meant to appeal to hard-core classical music fans, however. As it does with certain obvious markers of techno music, the piece similarly evokes many time-honored clichés of a certain type of orchestral music without really being classical in the sense of the term most aficionados would use. The opening horn fanfare heroically describes the spaceship taking off; sudden transitions into modal collections let us know we are entering an exotic, foreign planet; there is no real motivic, thematic, harmonic, or structural complexity of any kind, and yet it is also worlds away from the kind of hypnotic simplicity manifested by early minimalism; the piece's governing characteristic is a driving forward motion punctuated by climactic blasts of timpani and cymbals. Bates often compares himself to the great nineteenth-century symphonists, and says his compositional approach is modeled on the "dramatic" and "narrative" styles of Berlioz, Liszt, and Beethoven.[35] Yet he also explicitly rejects the Hanslickian ideal of "pure music" often associated with the nineteenth-century symphony. I would argue that the orchestral tradition Bates is most aligned with is not that of Beethoven but rather that of Howard Shore. This is film music, and as such is replete with clichés and musical stereotypes that cue the listener to have certain reactions to the symphonic drama.[36] By using simplified tropes from both techno and orchestral music, Bates can appear cool and edgy to classical music institutions while also seeming to further the practice of old-fashioned concert music. This combination has made him a sought-after composer for traditional music institutions like the Chicago Symphony Orchestra.

Innovation and Labor

Marx argued that technological innovation, in addition to pushing capitalism toward periodic crises, was also a crucial weapon that capitalists deploy in class warfare. Constant innovating at the level of production means that past skill sets and business investments are continuously devalued and destroyed, and workers in a given field are always being "deskilled" and forced to learn new skills in order to continue earning a wage. Such deskilling prevents many workers from gaining promotions and raises, since they must routinely start over in new positions or even new industries rather than working their way up through the ranks and gaining security along the way, as was once considered the norm. It is crucial to note, however, that far from being merely regrettable accidents or exceptions that can be corrected via small tweaks to the system, these negative social outcomes are actually among the stated goals of many of those who advocate for the mutual benefits of constant innovation. For example, Milton Friedman always uncritically accepts the inevitability of innovation-driven creative destruction, and uses it to advocate for a wide array of policies and practices that he claims will lead to economic growth and the betterment of society. But curtailing labor power is chief among his stated goals. Because the process of deskilling lowers wages and limits workers' ability to assemble into skill-based guilds and unions, neoliberals correctly consider it salutary for the accumulation of capital. In *Free to Choose*, Friedman asserts that full employment may seem like an admirable goal toward which a government should strive, but that really it is "a much more complex and ambiguous concept than it appears to be on the surface," because in a world characterized by constant innovation "it is desirable to have a good deal of labor mobility."[37] Friedman's avoidance of a clear subject in this sentence is deceptive; to *whom* is labor mobility desirable? What he means is that it is desirable to capitalists for the working classes to be mobile, so that they can be constantly moved from job to job; this kind of enforced mobility among workers also limits their ability to unite to demand higher wages, retirement benefits, and long-term contracts.

Ever-speedier innovation also conditions workers to accept unpaid labor as the cost of gaining experience in a new field. The culture industry has relied on free labor for at least a century, but its ability to demand free labor has been dramatically aided and expanded by information technologies like wireless internet and mobile phones.[38] The condition of constant connectivity is also erasing the traditional boundary between work and leisure time.[39] Now that work increasingly permeates our lives, the belief that individuals ought to "do what they love" without thought of payment has become widespread. In 2015 Microsoft sponsored a series of tweets proclaiming that "passion and purpose beat pay" and presenting graphed data showing that America's top CEOs care more about "creating something significant" than they do about salaries. Similarly, people—especially but no longer exclusively young people—are increasingly forced to compete for unpaid internships in order to get a foot in an industry's door. The proliferation of "do what you love" rhetoric and the cultural acceptance of unpaid work as a necessary rite of passage both mask the enormous amounts of free labor that such pursuits provide to capitalists.[40]

Another labor formation attractive to neoliberals is subcontracting, which is also enabled by the innovations of the internet and smart devices. Corporations that use subcontractors instead of regular employees rely on information technologies to conduct long-distance coordination, to cease investing in infrastructure or maintaining a consistent workforce, and to unload traditional business expenses like health insurance, paid sick days, workspace rental, and work-related purchases and travel onto individual workers. Subcontracting increasingly characterizes labor under the contemporary phase of corporate globalization; although it is celebrated for bringing freedom and flexibility to individual workers all over the world, the sociologist Richard Applebaum also notes that subcontracting has promoted the "ethnicization" of global capitalism, as the owners and CEOs at the top of a subcontracting chain tend to be white and male, while those at the bottom tend to be from the Global South and female.[41]

The YouTube Symphony Orchestra project was made possible by unpaid internships and by subcontracting. With the exception of a few star performers like Mason Bates, the orchestra consisted solely of nonunionized volunteer musicians, and instead of establishing a stable orchestral workforce and paying them a salary and benefits, Google identified individual workers in disparate global locations and paid them nothing for a single night of labor.[42] This is, in part, what Ed Sanders of YouTube referred to when he said the YTSO project "helped fundamentally challenge the norms of an entire industry."

Diversity Management

Just as the YTSO linked classical music to innovation and the process of creative destruction, it also associated technology and classical music with breaking down cultural barriers and facilitating powerful connections between diverse peoples. Despite the Anglo-European heritage of almost every composer on the program (a program that was also all male), Michael Tilson Thomas presented classical music as a timeless and universal tradition capable of speaking to anyone, anywhere:

> This week has been a real summit conference of classical music, our wonderful 1,200 year old tradition that witnesses everything that it has meant and what it means *right now* to be human. It also shows us the diversity of people coming from all over the world who love this music and make a special place for it in their lives.[43]

The premiere of "Mothership" was the centerpiece of the YTSO Sydney performance, and it was clearly intended to metaphorize the crossing of cultural and national borders that the internet makes possible. In keeping with the rhetorical trends of the evening, Bates's video introduction evoked the wonder of music's status as a universal language, in combination with the righteousness of technological innovation; he insisted that music and technology are what bring us together.

The most celebrated feature of "Mothership" is Bates's inclusion of four breaks in which designated musicians—representing entities from different alien planets—"dock" with the mothership, and take solos.[44] There are four Docking Episodes in total; two are marked "Rhythmic" and two "Lyrical." Each episode is preceded by the "docking signal," a reverberating beep heralding a pause in the mothership's churning movement forward. Like the orchestra members, the soloists at the Sydney performance had competed for their slots via uploaded audition videos, and the ones chosen represented the project organizers' commitment to diversity of both the cultural and the musical-generic varieties. The soloists—Paulo Calligopoulos, Ali Bello, Su Chang, and John Burgess—were from four different countries, and played respectively a distorted electric guitar, a violin, a Chinese *guzheng*, and an electric bass.

"Mothership," and indeed the entire YTSO project, celebrated a particular type of Westernized multiculturalism, one regulated under neoliberalism as "diversity." Initially, multiculturalism was a pedagogical value,

inspired by the civil rights movement and developed by educational re-
formers who tried to remake public education in the United States during
the 1970s so that it would empower minority children and promote inter-
racial friendship and understanding. But while multiculturalism began as
a grassroots movement to work toward a world with no more racism, in
the 1980s government officials and US businesses co-opted it and turned it
toward different ends. In this new form of official multicultural discourse,
attacking systemic racism was replaced with emphasizing cultural diversity;
in fact, commentators from all over the political spectrum insisted that racism no longer existed, and thus that policies and laws intended to protect
nonwhite citizens were unnecessary.[45] By separating culture and class from
racialized injustice, and by opening up participation in corporate life to
previously excluded people and people from other nations, official multicultural discourse also defused the challenge that social movements like
the Black Panthers posed to capitalism when they identified it with race-
and gender-based inequality. Thus, embracing and promoting 1980s-style
multiculturalism makes businesses and the US government seem progressive to a population that increasingly values tolerance of certain kinds of
difference.

Because neoliberal economists maintain that widening the scope of the
free market is the best way to ensure democracy and social justice, neoliberal ideology easily incorporates the value of multiculturalism and mas-
sages it to convey free market principles. As early as 1962, Milton Friedman wrote lengthily about how the free market could bring about an
end to racism. "The great advantage of the market . . . is that it permits
wide diversity," he argues, contrasting the free market with the stultifying
"political channels" through which actions must be taken in an overregulated democracy.[46] Friedman identifies race as an "irrelevant characteristic"
that should not affect "economic efficiency," and he goes on to detail in
a chapter-length explanation how unrestricted competitive capitalism will
automatically create a racially just society.[47] Taking as his starting point the
liberation that the ownership of private property brought the "Southern
negro" after the Civil War, Friedman insists time and again that "discrimi-
nation against groups of particular color or religion is least in those areas
where there is the greatest freedom of competition."[48]

As is often the case in Friedman's writing, his examples conflate political freedom with consumer freedom. He approvingly notes that African
American people can save up enough money to purchase the same kinds
of cars that white people own or send their children to private schools,
and he means these examples to illustrate that in those scenarios African

Americans would be as politically free as their white neighbors, thanks to the color-blindness of the market. In this case, his conflation of consumer and political freedom reveals an especially painful contradiction: although he presents many examples of the way free market competition does a better job than any other system in the world of guaranteeing the rights of African Americans, he never mentions the African slave trade—perhaps the most virulent example in world history of market capitalism impinging on the freedoms of a racialized population. Even today, such brutally racialized oppression is far from merely a regrettable aspect of capitalism's distant past but is rather a necessary ongoing condition for the system's continuing success.[49] Friedman's blindness to the contradiction between his utopian free market rhetoric and the material role the competitive market has played in subjugating racialized others seems almost willful; he devotes several paragraphs to his bewilderment at the fact that disadvantaged groups so often "mistakenly" attribute their oppression to capitalism, when in reality they are freer than ever before, thanks to the competitive marketplace within which they are benevolently permitted to act, so long as they have the money to do so.

The US government's public endorsements of multicultural tolerance may seem comforting to progressives, but they have also functioned as effective propaganda justifying the United States' increasingly meddlesome role in foreign nations as well as its dominance in global finance.[50] Friedman's theories along these lines display his belief that ending racism is not a desirable goal for its own sake, but rather because it is good for the economy and is thus one way of securing US interests. By promoting the idea that the United States is a bastion of cultural and racial freedom, official antiracist statements help establish the benevolence and wholesomeness of the free market principles on which the US economy is founded, and thus of the US government itself. Jodi Melamed details many jarring examples of how these discourses function in political life, including the George W. Bush administration's proud announcement that the prisoners being illegally and indefinitely held at Guantanamo Bay were given copies of the Koran and allowed time to pray in accordance with their own cultural customs. For Melamed, official antiracisms like this one emphasize that the United States is the guarantor of cultural diversity and tolerance, an image that then justifies its military interventions abroad as simply "spreading freedom" to marginalized populations.[51]

In explaining his choice not to be racist, Friedman wrote, "Those of us who regard color of skin or religion as irrelevant can buy some things more cheaply as a result."[52] Since the 1980s, US corporations have increasingly espoused the values of multicultural tolerance and racial diversity in order to appeal to consumers and potential employees, and to establish toeholds in non-Western countries. Accordingly, a new corporate field, called diversity management, has gained visibility and importance in the business landscape. Today's corporations are scrambling to publicize their plans for increasing workplace diversity in the face of growing public concern about the monocultural (and largely male) makeup of most large firms, especially tech firms.[53] Business journals and corporate policies link diversity to "innovation," although specifics are rarely given. One representative study found that "inclusive" companies had 2.3 times higher cash flow per employee and were 1.7 times more likely to be "innovation leaders."[54] In a 2011 *Forbes* article, an IBM official says that "diversity has allowed IBM to be innovative and successful for 100 years and to work across lines of difference in 172 countries, amongst 427,000 employees."[55] And Apple has an extensive "diversity" page on its website, where it informs viewers that "inclusion inspires innovation" and, somewhat alarmingly, that "the future of tech isn't a product. It's people."[56]

Like Milton Friedman, directors of diversity management believe that racism and cultural homogeneity are bad for business, and that this is reason enough to try to eradicate them. Now known as the "business case for diversity," this rationale is based on theories about the best ways to recruit talent, solve complex tasks, and connect with a diverse customer base.[57] Some progressives may argue that this scramble for diversity is simply a case of the ends justifying the means—acknowledging the perspectives of a wider array of people than the US corporate mainstream has traditionally been willing to do seems a self-evident good, even if we also acknowledge the destructive work corporate capitalism seems inevitably to do in the world. But antiracisms crafted to serve the interests of corporate globalization seem unlikely to liberate disenfranchised populations or diminish inequality, since the drastically cheap and exploitative labor corporate globalization requires is contingent on the very uneven social structures multiculturalism was initially created to combat. In reality, official discourses of multiculturalism often serve to promote and naturalize the very racialized divides they seem superficially to bridge.

Official statements valuing diversity disguise the fact that to succeed in a given corporate environment, workers must follow practices and ascribe to values dictated from above. The activist and scholar Angela Davis brutally dissects a *Harvard Business Review* article by the executive director of the American Institute for Managing Diversity, Inc., who wrote, "Given the diverse work force I've got, am I getting the productivity, does it work as smoothly, is morale as high as if every person in the company was the same sex and race and nationality?"[58] For Davis, questions like these reveal corporations' real intent, which is that

> workers may look different and talk (even signify), eat, dance, and act differently from one another, but they will be expected to be as productive "as if" they were all the same . . . we simultaneously can be different and perform "as if" we really were middle-class, straight white males.[59]

Thus, official multicultural discourse subsumes difference into the dominant culture, preserving it only as piquant local color for use in brochures and recruiting.

Within neoliberalism, the free movement of capital worldwide is the only real goal of deregulation; what happens to individual human beings within a deregulated world is of less interest, except insofar as destabilized people provide a source of cheap labor. The YTSO project and "Mothership," however, emphasized cultural exchange and friendly communication between nations. These qualities represent the more positive, human side of globalization, and thus in some respects the YTSO and Mason Bates's piece depicted a humanistic borderlessness very different from the one espoused by neoliberals. Nonetheless, despite their revolutionary claims that they are "opening up" classical music to global participation, the YTSO project and "Mothership" also maintained Western values and Western art products at their center.

The project was designed to be an inspiring celebration of how the performance of music with universal appeal, when combined with the world-changing technology of the internet, can peacefully connect people from diverse cultural backgrounds as they work toward a common cause. The videos encouraging musicians to audition for the YTSO emphasized that the directors wanted submissions from as diverse a pool of cultures and musical traditions as possible. Bates proclaimed that "even if you aren't a classical musician, we still need to hear from you"; musicians who played non-Western or nonclassical instruments were told to simply play along with the audition piece in whatever way they wanted.[60] After the Carnegie Hall performance, the project's coordinators uploaded a video titled "The 'Internet Symphony' Global Mash Up," which featured clips of some of the diverse auditions they'd received, including performances on singing saw, metal bowls, melodica, and balalaika.[61]

But these nontraditional instruments were never meant to be included in the actual orchestra, which after all was a completely conventional one;

rather, the YTSO's diversity manifested primarily in the performance of "Mothership." Within the context of the rest of the Sydney performance, the piece's incorporation of its diverse soloists seemed to metaphorize official multicultural discourse and the kind of diversity management practiced in today's corporate world. "Mothership" begins with the orchestra playing the piece's main theme, which sets the tone, and establishes the melodic motives and tempo, that will govern the whole composition. Then the orchestra pauses in an extended moment of silence that heralds a solo. The overriding material of the main theme of "Mothership"—played by a conventional Western orchestra—thus contains and shapes the solos, yet also sets them apart, their difference foregrounded as exotic but ultimately commensurable with that main theme.

Additionally, while the celebration of musicocultural boundary traversal in "Mothership" did emphasize the YTSO's marketing rhetoric about the internet's ability to bring diverse peoples together, it perhaps also highlighted the unintentional ambivalence of this message. In the symphony, it is the orchestra—a traditional symbol of Western high culture—that is granted the mobility of a high-tech spaceship, which it uses to cross over into other, stationary cultures, which it observes. This reading of the piece—which perhaps counters some of the YTSO project's grand statements about free global movement—is emphasized by the way its performance was staged. In the Sydney Opera House, the four soloists who represented aliens were seated far apart from the orchestra, isolated in small individual niches high above the main stage. When the time for their solo approached, the lights went down on the orchestra, and went up on a given niche; at the end of the interlude, the soloist fell silent and was once again shrouded in darkness. In the staging, then, people from other cultures actually aren't coming together—in fact they remain separate, both musically and physically.[62] This may bring to mind questions of mobility: Who is allowed to freely traverse the globe, and who must stay in place? Luc Boltanski and Eve Chiapello argue that worldwide, the mobility of the wealthy and powerful requires the immobility of the poor and powerless, and they link this new dynamic of mobility to the contemporary phase of globalization as well as to the new labor formations, like subcontracting, that such globalization enforces.[63]

Official multicultural discourse also establishes which kinds of cultures are good, and thus deserving of protection and reward in the form of loans from central banks and the ability to export goods. By this standard, good cultures are those that themselves practice multicultural tolerance; are amenable to free market principles; and give up outmoded traditions (such as communal decision-making and communally run social programs) that do not gel well with individual upward mobility or the consumption of commodities. Bad cultures are those that attempt to maintain communist or socialist governments; are themselves "monocultural" and resistant to tolerating the cultures of others; or are indigenous populations that have not assimilated into the cosmopolitan mainstreams of their respective countries.[64] Official discourses of multiculturalism present free market principles as the means by which disadvantaged peoples can become emancipated, and they advocate against many traditional and communal ways of life, juxtaposing so-called backward, monocultural peoples to those who have jettisoned old ways of doing things in favor of becoming vibrant, tech-savvy global citizens. The anthropologist Charles Hale goes so far as to argue that proponents' commitment to this very specific type of marketable multiculturalism is what puts the "neo" in *neoliberal*.[65]

The YTSO performance in Sydney clearly demonstrated the appropriate way for a non-Westerner to participate in global life. Presenters not only rhetorically conflated classical music and the internet but also positioned them as being stronger avenues for collaboration than traditional ones based on shared culture, nation, or language. For example, the Turkish violinist Ozgur Baskin insisted on classical music's superior universality in his introductory video: "Nobody knows the real Turkey," he said. "Most of them think we are riding camel . . . we are bad, or, you know, terrorists."[66] Over footage of his family playing nineteenth-century European chamber music together, Baskin pleaded, "Please come and see us. Real Turkey."

The United States legitimizes the many invasions and bombing campaigns it perpetrates in countries like Iraq or Afghanistan by presenting terrorism as a race-based emanation from the Middle East; Baskin's sincere and optimistic plea for cultural understanding makes sense in this context. Yet his statement also indicates the degree to which Western values have become normalized as universal—the "real" Turkey is not the one where people ride camels, but rather the one where people play Schubert.[67] Throughout the YTSO performance, in fact, the universal appeal and accessibility of classical music often rubbed awkwardly against the YTSO's equally frequent praise of its inherent diversity. Presenters uttered words and phrases like "all cultures," "global," "all of us," and "the whole world" again and again in describing both the internet and classical music, and yet the event seemed exclusively oriented toward a contemporary Western audience. All presenters, and almost all the highlighted musicians, spoke English in their informational video (despite the obvious possibility the videos presented of using subtitles). Moreover, of the three new compositions performed, two were by Americans: Mason Bates and Colin Jacobsen, a violinist and cofounder of the Brooklyn ensemble the Knights. The third was a piece for solo didgeridoo by the aboriginal Australian composer William Barton, which Michael Tilson Thomas introduced by saying, "Australia has an ancient indigenous tradition of music-making that also goes way back in time."[68] However, Barton's piece was far from a straightforward celebration of an indigenous aesthetic. Rather, it was composed primarily of signifiers from American pop music: beatboxing; the performer "moon-walking" with his fingers; and his repeated yelling—in English—of "Check this out!" to gales of laughter from the audience.[69]

In many ways the YTSO project manifested the same approach to cultural diversity as the one articulated in diversity management: non-Western others are allowed to look, dress, and signify differently, but they must behave "as if" they are Westerners, sometimes by eschewing their own country's traditions in favor of those of the West (as in Baskin's case), and sometimes by packaging their cultural traditions into a form that a Western audience can comfortably consume (beatboxing on the didgeridoo). Official multicultural discourse encourages cultural difference only "when controlled by a resurgent emphasis on 'Western culture' as a repository of unchanging values," as the sociologists Christopher Newfield and Avery Gordon demonstrate.[70] In the case of the YTSO performance, both European art music and personalized use of Google's products represented unchanging Western values, and it was explicitly these values that were emphasized as what bring us together. While the event highlighted its multicultural diversity, it also seemed to praise these musicians for leaving their cultures behind and using the internet to become global individuals.

The YTSO similarly rewarded members of various cultures—including indigenous ones, as in the didgeridoo performance—for taking part in the corporate goal of producing multicultural music-making as a commodity. The YTSO represented difference as sameness—"all of us," "the whole world," "universal"—and presented that different sameness as an advertisement for tech corporations' benevolent transformation of the world. But this effectively masked not only the aforementioned overwhelming whiteness and maleness of the skilled workforce and higher management at corporations like Google, but also the violence done in non-Western countries by US tech corporations—for example, the African slave labor that produces the minerals required to manufacture Intel's microchips and processors (discussed in chapter 4), or the widely publicized human rights violations routinely committed in Apple's Chinese factories.[71] The kind of Westernized, marketable diversity represented by the YTSO was made possible by long histories of pillaging, extermination, and assimilation that the project obviously did not acknowledge. The anthropologist Anna Tsing observes that we don't rely on such stories to understand our world because they are "complicated, often ugly, and humbling."[72] The YTSO project represented an attempt to smooth over these ugly histories and rhetorical discrepancies, as well as the deepening class distinctions generated by corporate globalization, by using a rhetoric of inspiring multicultural connectedness.

The YTSO exemplified the kind of joyful collaboration made possible by the internet, which is in many respects a genuinely miraculous invention that has undoubtedly transformed our world and made possible drastically new social relations, not all of which are necessarily exploitative.[73] The amateur musicians who took part in the project were understandably excited to be performing at Carnegie Hall or the Sydney Opera House, and thus it was easy to be happy for them and to feel basically good about the corporations that make such projects possible. Also, the fact that people without a shared spoken language can play music together is indeed wondrous; it is not merely naïve to feel that such examples of musical togetherness are beautiful. Our desire to focus on the good things globalization enables—for example, positive encounters between cultures and the spread of knowledge, ideas, and friendships via the internet—makes sense. Luc Boltanski and Eve Chiapello note that justifications for capitalism must "coincide" with people's experience of daily life, and must also "suggest models of action they can grasp."[74] Processes of contemporary globalization generate massive inequality, impose conditions of slave labor and forced migration on enormous numbers of people, and render the planet increasingly uninhabitable. However, these processes also seem unstoppable and even difficult to grasp intellectually in their vastness and power; thus, we focus on aspects of globalization that feel as though they take place on a human scale, such as the way the internet enables musicians from all over the world to perform music together. In Rob Wilkie's words, projects like the YTSO help us "maintain the illusion of the possibility of capitalism without exploitation," an illusion we desperately long to believe in.[75]

Two Motherships

For many people, the term *mothership* conjures up a very different musical image from the one Bates created. *Mothership Connection*, the 1975 album by the legendary funk collective Parliament-Funkadelic, is surely the better known of the two motherships, and it is instructive to compare them (although it is also interesting to note that Bates seems never to have heard of the P-Funk album—as far as I can tell, he has never cited it as an influence or precedent). Like Bates's "Mothership," P-Funk's gives prominence to cultural difference, space exploration, and technology. However, the two motherships manifest very different intents: where Bates's is meant to represent all cultures in the universe being connected by technology and classical music, P-Funk's represents the fantasy of black people using technology to triumphantly separate from racist Eurocentric white culture and forge an entirely new world of their own making in outer space.

Thinking about the differences between these two motherships clarifies how official multicultural discourses can leach race-based, grassroots social movements of their revolutionary potential. P-Funk—like other Afrofuturists working in many different artistic genres—believed that white culture is hegemonic, and recognized how it generated the entangled and age-old systems by which nonwhite peoples have been oppressed, from slavery to corporate globalization. Far from wanting to integrate into that culture by playing by its rules and accepting its values in hopes of succeeding by its terms, many social movements of the 1960s and 1970s were founded on essentially separatist ideas. Malcolm X initially wanted black Americans to move to Liberia and build an entirely new social system from scratch—one based on communal values rather than individual upward mobility; artists like Sun Ra or those involved in the P-Funk community fantasized about flying into outer space and leaving the white world behind entirely.[76]

Members of movements like these were perhaps reactionary, and their projects were not always sustainable or even philosophically coherent. But they understood racism and sexism as systemic, as much grander and more totalizing than simply the ignorant prejudices held by individuals, and thus their responses to this system were themselves totalizing and grand. To get outside racism or sexism, someone would indeed have to dream up an entirely new basis for structuring a society, one not grounded on the extraction of surplus value from labor. Many separatist movements were not interested in incremental reforms or in educating the power structure to be more accepting, because their understanding of oppression was predicated on there being a power structure in the first place. Even Martin Luther King Jr., who was not a separatist, explicitly tied capitalism and racism together as mutually reinforcing social ills, saying, for example, "We must recognize that we can't solve our problem now until there is a radical redistribution of economic and political power. . . . We must see now that the evils of racism, economic exploitation and militarism are all tied to-gether . . . you can't really get rid of one without getting rid of the others."[77]

The US government and corporations have responded to such revo-lutionary movements in various ways. For example, FBI director J. Edgar Hoover placed King under surveillance, harassed him ceaselessly, and at-tempted to drive him to suicide.[78] While Hoover surely held personally racist beliefs, these actions were much more powerfully motivated by the threat that movements like King's present to capitalism and class hierarchy in the United States. We can see that this is the case by examining the of-ficial antiracisms the nation has propagated since the 1980s, all of which are focused on maintaining justifications for capitalism. In the wake of widespread demands for change—like those articulated during the civil rights movement—the US power structure has seemed to accept its histori-cal culpability in generating injustice, and thus its responsibility to create a better world via promoting diversity. Such rhetorical acceptance of culpa-bility and responsibility makes the power structure seem more benevolent to socially progressive populations. This also makes it seem like that struc-ture has accepted and incorporated the demands of its critics, such that we can rest easy in our continued acceptance of its basic benevolence and willingness to change. However, in responding to revolutionary critiques like King's that explicitly identified capitalism itself as a cause of injustice, the corporate and political powers have reformulated those critiques in order to establish racism, sexism, and homophobia as merely individual failings that can be fixed by diversity management strategies, rather than as a system of inequality that is implemented from the top down in order to aid accumulation. Today, US governmental officials (including, infuri-atingly, the FBI) and corporate CEOs praise King for his vision of racial togetherness—and of course they sternly emphasize his supposed insis-tence that all protest must be nonviolent—while conveniently ignoring the link he identified between capitalism and systemic racism. This transfor-mation in the definition of *racism* allows corporate power to maintain its dominance in global life, because it can seem to respond to demands for racial equality by simply hiring a more diverse workforce or undertaking various other diversity initiatives.[79]

In projects like the YouTube Symphony Orchestra, classical music lends corporate hegemony an aura of cultural legitimacy and universal virtue, which also obliterates any potential for critique that this music or its per-formance might possess. We can see ambivalence regarding such projects in the way the YTSO was received by arts journalists. Several commentators—even some who also complained of the poor musical quality of the hastily assembled and barely rehearsed orchestra—held the project up as an example of how classical music might innovate in order to survive. On his blog, the widely read classical music activist Greg Sandow wrote that although the YTSO's musicianship was bad and the actual concert "disappointing," he nonetheless loved how it gave classical music "the kind of multimedia treatment pop concerts get," and says he believes that "this event helps classical music" by making it seem "far more accessible and interesting than it did 10 years ago."[80] In Anthony Tommasini's review of the Carnegie Hall concert, he describes the performance as musically unsubtle, and wishes that the concert "had been less gimmicky and more substantive." In pointing out the inevitability of videos and projections given the project's sponsor, he says that "there were so many spotlights and projectors in the hall that pianissimo passages in the music had to compete with the whirring sounds of ventilating fans." He also states that he had been "exasperated" by the organizers' decision to overwhelm the audience with flashy excerpts and "difficult but empty-headed" virtuosic showpieces like "Flight of the Bumblebee" instead of allowing the musicians to properly explore full works. However, Tommasini concludes his review by saying that "after all the spoken and video tributes to YouTube and Google, you can only hope that this project becomes permanent"—a surprising conclusion given his lukewarm assessment of the actual musicianship, staging, and programming the project displayed.[81]

Music and culture are mutually producing—obviously, musical styles and changes in how we think about them are always conditioned by the cultural values of a given time and place, and the reverse is often true. It is obvious that some classical music supporters have, consciously or unconsciously, adopted these ideas in an effort to lend a beloved art form continued validity within the prevailing ideologies of contemporary US society. It is also easy to see how breaking down cultural boundaries can be figured as a progressive value, when contrasted with the racist nationalism currently sweeping the United States and Europe and leading to the tightening of physical borders that prohibit the free movement of human beings. Yet I would argue that the way they serve to aid neoliberal globalization means that the breaking down of cultural boundaries and the advocacy of universal connectivity remain ambivalent values. As we demand open borders so that human beings may find pathways to survival in a world made increasingly untenable by processes of globalization, we also acknowledge how those very processes rely on the breaking down of borders, and on the instantaneous linking of all human beings under the auspices of cloud computing.

Naturalizing Connectivity

Mason Bates serves an important function for classical music institutions in the United States. Because he incorporates technology into the orchestra and embodies a dual career as a highly trained composer and a techno DJ, Bates is perceived as making classical music cool and hip. Moreover, via projects like "Mothership" and the YTSO, he enables classical music to be positioned as an enabler of progressive, twenty-first-century values like multiculturalism, which helps traditional institutions promote the continued cultural relevance of the music they perform.

But Bates serves another purpose, one also revealed by his participation in the YTSO. A *New York Times* article about the project notes that it was part of a corporate strategy to "gussy up YouTube content and make the site more attractive to advertisers."[82] Bates's passionate advocacy on behalf of technological innovations serves a powerful function for corporate power as it seeks to legitimize its products. The above analyses have already gestured toward some of the ways he is useful to corporations like Google. Additionally, he loans corporations the cultural legitimacy and sense of disinterestedness that vaguely adhere to the idea of classical music by writing orchestral works highlighting the greatness of connectivity and of the technological innovations that facilitate communication. In promoting himself and his music, Bates has constructed a historical narrative that emphasizes program music and an understanding of the orchestra itself as technological innovations. He regularly declares that his use of electronics in symphonic composition is not avant-garde but simply a logical application of traditional ideas about classical music, which he says has "always" been engaged in technological innovation. Beyond his rhetorical promotion of such innovation, Bates also glorifies it programmatically in a surprisingly large number of his compositions. His "Garages of the Valley," for example, is a symphonic work honoring "the garages that dot the landscape of Silicon Valley [which] housed the visionaries behind Apple, Hewlett-Packard, Intel, and Google."[83] For his 2011 symphony "Alternative Energy," Bates creates drum sounds based on sampled recordings of Chicago's Fermilab particle accelerator and programmatically depicts the history of tech innovation, from Henry Ford's junkyard to a futuristic Iceland turned tropical by climate change. When he discusses why innovation is so valuable, Bates always emphasizes how technology brings us together and enables connectivity and communication. In July 2017 he premiered an even more focused apotheosis of a tech entrepreneur: an opera, *The (R)evolution of Steve Jobs*, that had been commissioned by the Santa Fe Opera. On his blog Bates describes Jobs as "a man who revolutionized human communication." The opera presents Jobs's life as a *Bildungsroman*, moving from his callow beginnings as an idealistic hippie to his late-in-life attainment of a "deeper understanding of true human connection."[84]

Like "Mothership," "Garages of the Valley," and *The (R)evolution of Steve Jobs*, Bates's "The Rise of Exotic Computing" is a programmatic work that aurally represents a specific technological innovation (synthetic computing). Furthermore, the performance of the piece at the 2014 Cisco partners summit worked to establish a specifically neoliberal worldview—and thus, presumably, to endear Bates and his music to the tech billionaires who espouse that worldview. Essentially, it propagated a corporate marketing strategy within a set of inspirational commonsense beliefs about togetherness, connectedness, and the timeless grandeur of classical music.

In an interview about "Exotic Computing" that took place in the Chicago Symphony Orchestra's server room, Bates eerily invokes the central tenet of capitalism when he says that "the idea of the piece is to accumulate."[85] Indeed, the short, single-movement work is meant to sound like "a self-replicating synthetic computer," which accumulates lines of code without requiring human input. The symphony is built on Bates's characteristically springy deployment of tiny, tight motives (usually consisting of only three or four notes in a very limited range), which are nimbly traded from instrument to instrument atop a pulsing foundation of repeated single notes also traded between instruments. As with most of Bates's music, the piece is very upbeat, and emphasizes an extreme rhythmic regularity aided by the drum machine, which, while often heavily syncopated, nonetheless provides a regular driving pulse.[86]

The work opens with a long, slowly building introduction that establishes both the conceptual framework and the main motives for the rest of the piece. Several instruments begin by trading off a quick thirty-second-note pulse on a single note, which is alternated with a single-note triplet. As this fast repetition is passed from instrument to instrument, we slowly get a sense of an overlapping pulse, as we hear the straight thirty-second-note figure in one instrument against the triplet in another. (See example 2.)

We also hear a ghostly echo of one of the main melodic motives that will organize the rest of the piece—a figure that rocks back and forth in eighth notes, against syncopated single notes or chords in other instruments. (See example 3.) The "accumulatory" premise of the work is established very quickly, as these tiny traded figures combine to create great waves of sound that roll across the ensemble, building and subsiding, until new waves take their place. The effect of this introduction is of the

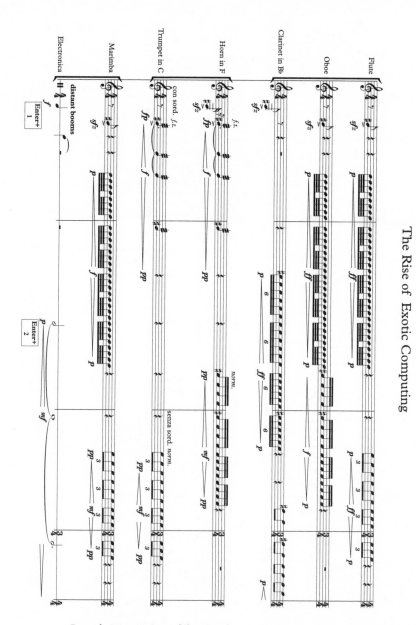

The Rise of Exotic Computing

Example 2. Mason Bates, "The Rise of Exotic Computing," mm. 1–4.

Example 3. Mason Bates, "The Rise of Exotic Computing," mm. 61–65.

orchestra slowly gathering its forces, finding its footing, and establishing lines of communication between the individual instruments as they practice trading short figures back and forth.

As the ensemble enters the main body of the piece, some similarities with early repetitive, pulse-pattern minimalism become evident. Like many young US composers, Bates often relies on ideas drawn from early minimalism. In some ways his "accumulatory" use of small motives sounds like the early "gradual process" works of Steve Reich and Philip Glass. In "The Rise of Exotic Computing" I hear echoes of Reich's *Music for 18 Musicians* (1976), as the piece moves in a modular fashion through soundscapes based on single, simple, repetitive motives. The texture of the two ensembles is also quite similar; both incorporate piano and marimba into a small conventional orchestra, although there are no human voices in Bates's work (and, certainly, no drum machine or laptop triggers in Reich's). But where Reich allows his modules to spin out slowly over great lengths of time, Bates usually spends only a few measures exploring a given figure or key area before crescendoing and climaxing into a new section. This is the kind of "drama" that he says is inspired by symphonists like Beethoven (and that is also obviously in the tradition of postminimalists like John Adams, who combined elements of minimalist repetition with Romantic affect). However, while Bates's motivic style of composing may seem superficially similar to the kind that made Beethoven's Fifth Symphony so compelling to E. T. A. Hoffmann, Bates avoids any semblance of development. His motives do not undergo structural or harmonic transformation; instead, they simply repeat, swept along by great crescendos.

Bates's characteristic version of postminimalist repetition may have something to tell us about how subjectivity has been conditioned by new forms that capitalism has taken since the 1970s.[87] The frantic passing around of motives from instrument to instrument in "The Rise of Exotic Computing" may evoke, for instance, the accelerating cycling of the stock market, in which toxic assets are passed quickly from investor to investor like hot potatoes. The lightning-fast transformations of sonic material may also resonate with Marx's thoughts on innovation, as the force that makes everything solid "melt into air."[88] Bates intended his motivic accumulation to evoke the self-replication of computer code, which evokes notions of the "technological sublime," and the awe-inspiring spectacle of automation that increasingly characterizes the modern condition.[89] The self-replicating motives also bring to mind a central process of capitalism by which capital replicates and accumulates through no labor on the part of its owner.

Additionally, we may hear this piece through the hermeneutic of flexible accumulation, the production model that began replacing the Fordist assembly line model in the 1970s and that is now a primary characteristic of contemporary globalization processes. Flexible accumulation denotes a mode of production—enabled by contemporary technological innovations like cell phones and the internet—in which firms ship unfinished products around the world, where subcontracted workers assemble them piecemeal in various locations depending on fluctuating costs of labor and materials. Those who promote the regime of flexible accumulation rhetorically denigrate stable, consistent employment as stifling, and say that such work places untenable limits on personal freedom as well as on corporations' mandate to do whatever it takes to lower production costs to the barest possible minimum. Bates's jarring motivic transitions echo the ceaseless and increasingly speedy movement of bits of products around the globe. Given the cultural devaluation of long-term stability, perhaps it makes sense that so many contemporary audiences delight in Bates's frenetic transitions between musical modules. There is something exhilarating in his aesthetic of instantaneity, his aural envisioning of constant movement. I examine this hermeneutic of flexibility in more detail in the next chapter.

In all these ways, "The Rise of Exotic Computing" differs significantly from both Beethoven, to whom Bates often compares himself, and from the postminimalist works with which his music bears more obvious resemblance. At any rate, there is no question that in "Exotic Computing," sonic imitation of digitally aided instant connectivity and of flexible accumulation presented the perfect sound to cap the Cisco partner summit in Las Vegas, an event characterized by talk of almost nothing but the innovative approaches the conglomerate was taking toward instantaneous global connectivity. In 2014 Cisco began aggressively capitalizing on the concept of "the Internet of Everything," which it appropriated as an advertising slogan. The term is meant to denote what the world soon will look like: every aspect of personal, social, and professional life across the globe will have been digitized and connected via the internet. As a multinational corporation specializing in networking technologies, Cisco has much to profit from the total global connectivity the Internet of Everything (IoE) will require.

In the 1990s, information technology was heralded as creating a new "information economy" in which facts and knowledge would not only be more widely available than ever before but would also become the drivers of economic growth. However, David Harvey argues that rather than driving new economic growth, the IT revolution instead represented merely an "unfortunate" turn toward the market-driven financialization that is "the hallmark of neoliberalism."[90] Thus—as with technological innovation generally—in the marketing initiatives prioritizing information technologies we can see a tension between neoliberal theory and practice. Theoretically, IT is touted for creating a new economy, and for its promotion of freedom and the spread of knowledge and learning. In practice, however, its main contribution to the economy has been to further concentrate wealth; and in addition to spreading knowledge it has also facilitated the growth of the surveillance state and its encroachment on privacy and civil liberties, which I take up in more detail in chapter 4.[91] We can see this tension manifested in Cisco's corporate advertising strategy.

In promoting the IoE, Cisco officials applaud the universalizing potential of internet connectivity, Big Data, and the surveillance state. Massive databases of information are required to implement the IoE. Accordingly, most of the examples of the IoE that Cisco officials describe rely on the unspoken assumption that one day soon there will be cameras, satellites, sensors, and other tracking devices watching all people at every moment and conveying a constant stream of data about them—their activities, their emotions, their spending habits, their physical bodies—to the Cloud, where Cisco's various corporate holdings and partner firms will sort and analyze it using Cisco technologies. In 2014 Cisco CEO John Chambers gave an interview to *Information Week* at the international Consumer Electronics Show in which he described the IoE's revolutionary potential to change the lives of citizen-consumers all over the world. He suggested, for example, that embedded sensors in a home's garbage receptacles could "allow officials to see how full a can is" as well as whether hazardous materials are inside, and noted that this data could be analyzed to determine when garbage companies should pick up waste, thus solving traffic problems caused by regular pickup routes (intermittent garbage collection would also solve the problem of paying benefits to full-time garbage collectors, although Chambers did not mention this). He discussed smart clothing that could tell its wearers when they were getting sick as well as alert their doctors and pharmacies, and smart cars that could communicate with their passengers' smart homes and smart workplaces. He added that ideas like these will generate billions in savings and allow consumers to live to one hundred years of age.[92] These sorts of marketing speeches applaud and welcome what Andreas Huyssen disapprovingly called "the invasion of capitalism's technological instrumentality into the fabric of everyday life, even into the human body."[93]

Cisco's marketing materials work to present the multiple invasions of the IoE as utopian rather than frightening. One of the most widely circulated advertisements Cisco has produced shows a soothing series of actions that smoothly lead to other actions, instigated or aided by an overriding connected network that benevolently observes every person in every moment: a fully automated house brews coffee; which wakes up a man; who gets into his self-driving car; which communicates with his workplace when it's time for the building's door to open for him, and so on. On top of this visual pattern of technologically mediated actions and reactions, an amused male voice intones a reassuring stream-of-consciousness text reminiscent of a children's book:

> This is the cat that drank the milk that let in the dog that jumped on the woman who brewed the coffee that woke the man who was late for work and drove the car that found the parking spot that alerted the door that opened the control room that secured the data that directed the turbines that powered the sprinklers that watered the grass that fed the cow that made the milk that went to the store that reminded the man to buy the milk that was poured by the girl who loved the cat who drank the milk. The internet of everything is changing everything. Cisco. Tomorrow starts here.[94]

Both the advertisement and "Exotic Computing" pursue a combinatory exploration of time, one perhaps reminiscent of how late capitalism ceaselessly presses forward in history while also repeatedly generating exact replicas of products and experiences. The ad depicts a closed and cyclical system: a series of futuristic, technologically mediated events leads inexorably back to the beginning, back to the cat who drank the milk. Giving in to this repetitive experience of technology, the ad suggests, will carry us into the gleaming future.

Conclusion: Classical Music and Corporate Collectivity

The performance of "Exotic Computing," with its dramatic musical depiction of digital connectivity and data accumulation, and its inspirational example of how technology and musical performance allow people to be "amazing together," was the perfect choice for Cisco's sponsored content at its partner summit, and the accompanying video aptly reiterated the same kind of benevolent total connectivity advocated by the company, its partners, and its advertising materials. At the same time, Mason Bates's suitability for artistically representing Cisco's ideals goes far beyond any particular compositional technique he may use. There are potentially many different ways that musical construction could evoke features of neoliberal reality, some of which I will suggest in future chapters; what makes Bates an even more potent figure for corporations like Cisco has much to do with his positioning as a champion of new technologies, and his passionate statements about how music—his own as well as the great music of the past—is fundamentally interwoven with the concept of innovation, itself interwoven with the logic of capitalist development.

The connection Bates tries to draw between nineteenth-century instrumental music and technological innovation does not merely allow him to appeal to tech corporations; it also represents a rebranding of the traditional repertoire that enables traditional music institutions to change how they promote themselves. For several generations, repertoire-based city orchestras and opera houses have been promoted essentially as museums: hallowed repositories of the great (past) works of Western culture.[95] But in light of faltering ticket sales, bankruptcies, and the dreaded "aging audience" that has supposedly plagued classical music in the United States for decades, critics, trustees, and boards of directors increasingly feel that marketing these institutions as the safeguards for historical high art is no longer a brand that appeals widely enough. From a marketing perspective, championing a composer like Mason Bates thus kills two birds with one stone: it allows city symphony orchestras to prove that they embrace new music and living composers; but Bates's insistent linking of nineteenth-century symphonic music to the ideals of technological innovation and global diversity also helps rebrand the canon itself as hip and relevant. Thus, institutions initially founded to protect high art from the marketplace are now insisting that that art has been a dynamic market innovator all along.

In one sense, associating high art and technological innovations in the manner that Bates and his supporters do represents a newly unproblematic orientation toward the marketplace, one generally not shared by the artists and critics in the nineteenth century who felt that art needed to be sheltered from the more brutal realities of market logic. Such commentators also perform a weird historical slippage when they insist that classical music has always been a part of technological innovation: Michael Tilson Thomas noted that "the enduring message of classical music" is "about that going forward into the realm of technology and the many ways in which that is happening and is going to happen."[96] However, in one sense, when Bates or Tilson Thomas claims that classical music has always been a part of technological innovation, they may be more correct than they know. Richard Leppert argues that part of the nineteenth-century fascination with Liszt had to do with industrialization; for example, many caricatures depicted the piano as a machine, and showed Liszt hard at work at his "steam engine." For Leppert, the appeal of watching virtuosos perform on musical machines was stoked by and in turn stoked "contemporaneous fascinations with and anxieties over the brave new industrial world." These musicians "out-machine[d] the machinery, while at the same time aestheticizing—hence, helping to market—the capitalist-bourgeois work ethic."[97] I would argue that a similar tension between fascination and anxiety undergirds the popularity of contemporary composers like Bates; by penetrating the historical genre of the symphony with cutting-edge technology, Bates shows us the way toward becoming ideal neoliberal selves, individuals who entrepreneurially use technology to disrupt old industries or traditional practices by opening them more fully to the market.

Similarly, we can see that the kind of radical connectivity promoted by Cisco and Google and propagandized in Bates's music differs from the collectivity that revolutionaries of many stripes have worked toward in opposing capitalism. The YouTube Symphony Orchestra centralized and normalized Western corporate values underneath an inspirational rhetoric of multicultural togetherness. The video that played at the Cisco partner summit articulated a vision of a fully connected humanity, which superficially may seem to assuage the growing atomization and alienation we experience because of our participation in capitalism. Yet Cisco's version of connectivity is one wholly mediated by its corporate products; we can connect with one another, but only via our submission to Cisco's IoE, which accumulates wealth from every one of our connections.

As many have observed, the relationship between art and capitalism is a dialectical one—the capitalist system certainly impacts modes of artistic production, but at the same time, artistic critiques of those frameworks have led to reforms in the system.[98] It makes sense that tech corporations so insistently promote their products' enabling of connectivity, given that for decades a primary criticism of capitalism has been that it isolates us from one another and alienates us from the products of our labor. In the book's conclusion I spend some time exploring what a renewed musical critique of capitalism in its neoliberal form might look and sound like. Here, I have sought to demonstrate some of the ways that classical music in contemporary practice is conditioned by neoliberalism, in particular by a value system that privileges—and even demands—constant technological innovation and the chaining of all human endeavors to the logic of the market. In this way, some high-profile practitioners and advocates for classical music are working hard to associate it with corporate power as one potential means of ensuring its continuing survival. However, I have also argued that corporations like Cisco and Google have just as much to gain from such an association. But in many ways they must work just as hard to contort their disruptive products and practices into a form that can be seen as commensurate with the notion of timeless, universal value that adheres to the idea of classical music.

TWO

"Indie" Individualism

This year, 2015, is a fantastic time to be a composer and performer of contemporary classical music. We've moved past the years of an inward-looking avant-garde that made music mainly for themselves, past the self-conscious reactions to that movement and into an era that might be called post-historical in its openness to all styles, forms and approaches to music making.[1]

So declares the young composer, performer, and record label owner Judd Greenstein, in a passionate essay meant to teach musicians how to become "extraordinary" in today's competitive musical landscape. Praising the small, flexible new music organizations that increasingly have been finding a toehold in the music market "even as traditional institutions struggle," Greenstein notes that such organizations are successfully building audiences, "taking nothing for granted and bearing more resemblance to their grassroots peers outside the classical music world than to the philharmonics and operas that used to dominate the musical landscape." The rest of the essay provides a roadmap for becoming extraordinary, and enjoins musicians to master their craft, which might mean the repertoires and techniques of Western classical music, but also every other musical tradition they may choose to incorporate as an influence. "To be extraordinary is to create work of exceptional quality that only you can make," Greenstein observes.

Greenstein is a prominent member of a Brooklyn-based music scene that critics have loosely grouped under the rubric "indie classical." The term was introduced by composers in 2007 and immediately became a flashpoint for criticism and debate.[2] Artists typically associated with the term include Greenstein; the composer and keyboardist Missy Mazzoli; the flutist Claire Chase, who in 2012 was awarded a fellowship (popularly

known as a "genius grant") by the MacArthur Foundation for her arts entrepreneurship activism; and Nico Muhly, currently the youngest composer
ever commissioned by the Metropolitan Opera. While each of these artists
has since disavowed the *indie classical* label, I continue to find the term
useful, in part because it did such powerful early work in establishing the
public profile of this group, but also because it clearly indicates some contradictory tensions that, I would argue, continue to preoccupy the scene.

Though critics have often used the term to point to the ways in which
these composers sometimes draw on styles and sounds from popular
music—namely, those of "indie rock"—composers and performers themselves have tended to use it to denote their entrepreneurial, flexible career
practices. Members of this group are notable for how they have applied certain practices from the indie music scene of the 1990s to successful careers
in classical music (indie rock musicians are the "grassroots peers outside
the classical music world" to whom Greenstein refers above). At the same
time, each of these artists was trained at a prestigious traditional music program: Mazzoli and Greenstein received MMs from Yale; Muhly has an MM
from Juilliard and apprenticed with Philip Glass; and Chase has a BM from
Oberlin.

Indie classical artists, and the critics and institutions that support them,
tend to bemoan the hidebound traditions and impenetrable elitism of
older music institutions like the "struggling" opera houses and city symphony orchestras Greenstein laments in his essay, and applaud the plucky
entrepreneurial spirit of the new do-it-yourself activists of this scene.
Chase's International Contemporary Ensemble (ICE) has made headlines
for its combination of rigorous musical performance with a self-managing,
entrepreneurial mentality. Playing in ICE is said to liberate musicians from
the constraints of contracted or unionized labor, and they can perform
with other ensembles whenever they like.[3] Both Greenstein and Muhly
have cofounded independent record labels to release their own music and
the music of like-minded friends and colleagues, thus sidestepping the
need to appeal to major labels and distributors. Mazzoli not only writes
operas and chamber music for established classical music ensembles but
also plays in her own quintet, Victoire, which functions much like an indie
rock band in that it is a group of friends who play shows together, rather
than an officially hierarchized ensemble like those associated with earlier
models for labor within classical music. Some of these artists grew up playing in rock bands, lending credence to the notion that their engagement
with indie rock culture is deeper than the mere stylistic incorporation of
sounds and rhythms from certain kinds of pop music in their works.

There are many artists working in many communities all over the United States, and their opinions and experiences are diverse.[4] Not every young classical musician or composer in the nation espouses the kind of flexible, market-friendly, casual beliefs about music as those I examine here, nor do all young composers write music using the friendly, tuneful techniques I discuss in this chapter. Furthermore, even the artists I discuss sometimes manifest awareness of and ambivalence about how corporate thinking is influencing musical production, or how their own privileged backgrounds have contributed to their success, or how their promotion of their business practices can sound like union-busting rhetoric. But the fact that these artists have been so richly rewarded by widely respected, powerful institutions signals larger changes in classical music culture as well as in US culture generally. Indie classical composers and musicians have reaped rewards, rather ironically, from very traditional entities: residencies with established symphonies and opera companies, professorships, MacArthur grants, and high praise in the arts press. Tellingly, when they are rewarded, it is often less for their musicianship or artistry than for their perceived disruption of these very traditions. To take only one example, Claire Chase is a brilliant flutist who has achieved a rare mastery of her instrument, but she was not awarded a MacArthur Fellowship for her musicianship; rather, she received it specifically for her entrepreneurship, and for the ways this entrepreneurship is "disrupting" conventional classical music practice. Such recognition by an august arts-funding organization indicates changing ideas about what art is, and what it is for.

The musicologist William Robin has historicized the indie classical phenomenon in his 2016 dissertation, detailing where and when the scene began coalescing and dissecting the complex historical factors and musical traditions that produced it. Basing his reflections on extensive fieldwork, including many interviews with the composers and performers themselves, Robin observes that indie classical artists promote what they do as being first and foremost a "music without walls." As Greenstein's essay indicates, these artists celebrate the end of musical genre and the dissolution of all the old supposed restrictions on how composers ought to create, and to varying degrees they credit themselves with bringing about this end to music's history. Robin, however, demonstrates how this positioning is contingent on excluding "the wealth of historical precedents of composers who similarly ignored genre," for example artists like Laurie Anderson and John Zorn, not to mention the composers in the Bang on a Can Collective. Robin thus sets his detailed historical research against the more "narrow genealogy" indie classical artists themselves have constructed to explain the scene's origins and position what they do as new and exciting.[5]

In this chapter, I also examine indie classical's relationship to music history, focusing on the way these artists jettison the spirit of critique from the historical styles and movements with which they are in dialogue. Specifically, I argue that they have failed to appreciate the very concrete political concerns undergirding both the modernist tradition and the historical indie rock movement. In keeping with the postmodern turn that cultural criticism took in the 1980s, indie classical artists engage with ideas that emerged in opposition to capitalism, but they largely do so without taking capitalism itself into account. Indeed, the indie classical community's self-presentation, its critical reception, and its music reproduce a new formulation of the individual conditioned by neoliberalism. I argue that indie classical artists work to model this new ideal for their fans and supporters, which helps further naturalize neoliberal ideology in US culture at large. At the same time, an ideal, neoliberal subjecthood cannot be fully realized and is thus impossible to attain. Hence despite these artists' great career successes and their embrace of market imperatives, there remains a tension between the ideal for which they strive and their material situation—a tension we might also hear emanating from the music they create.

Neoliberal Individualism

The concept of the autonomous individual is the foundational starting point of classical liberalism. For Adam Smith, the right to enter into market transactions inheres in all individuals, and those transactions are expressions of individualism that should not be coercively regulated by any larger body. Thus, one critique that has been directed at liberalism in all the forms it has taken since the eighteenth century is that it is a doctrine of selfishness, which instructs people to follow their own self-interest even at the expense of the well-being of others. By centering the individual rather than the community in their formulations of liberty and rights, liberals like Smith, Hume, and Locke introduced ideas that would ultimately culminate in the radical conception of individual autonomy that undergirds contemporary economic, political, and social discourse in the United States.[6]

In seeking to understand liberal individualism, Jeremy Gilbert compares Hobbes's metaphor for society with the much earlier one Plato relies on in *The Republic*. Plato figures society as a body—the body politic—in which types of people (leaders, soldiers, slaves) are allegorized as the different parts that allow a unified body to function (brain, heart, hands). Hobbes, by contrast, imagines society as one enormous individual—the Leviathan—made up of countless smaller individuals, tied together by laws. Where Plato's society is interconnected, sharing a nervous system, a circulatory system, lungs, skin, and so on, which implies that the health of each part is contingent on the health of every other part, Hobbes's is radically discrete.[7]

The United States was founded on liberal ideals, and it is easy to see how contemporary discursive formulations of individualism in this country tend to derive from Hobbes's metaphor rather than Plato's. Within liberal thought, every individual is isolated in its own quest to fulfill its self-interest, and is tied to others, not through bonds of solidarity or shared goals or even the brutal physical reality of shared blood vessels, but rather by a larger, immutable force—for Hobbes, absolutist monarchy; for neoliberals, the market. In this conception, every individual is an isolated node, linked firmly to the larger governing force but only transiently with other individuals.

With this conception of society as their starting point, it is perhaps no surprise that twentieth-century liberals like Milton Friedman tended to see social bonds as restrictive, and to valorize individuals who found ways of heroically transcending them in order to work directly with the higher force of the market unencumbered. In 1962 Friedman wrote glowingly of the great geniuses that have advanced (Western) civilization:

> Newton and Leibniz; Einstein and Bohr; Shakespeare, Milton, and Pasternak; Whitney, McCormick, Edison, and Ford; Jane Addams, Florence Nightingale, and Albert Schweitzer; no one of these opened new frontiers . . . in response to governmental directives. Their achievements were the product of individual genius, of strongly held minority views, of a social climate permitting variety and diversity.[8]

For Friedman, not only the individual but the singular individual—one with "strongly held minority views"—represents the fullest expression of human potential. Friedman was suspicious of social bonds and how the necessity to compromise and cooperate with others limited individual innovation and forced us dangerously close to "communalism." In fact, he goes so far as to describe his ideal society as "a collection of Robinson Crusoes": lone, wholly autonomous individuals whose freedom would be guaranteed neither by the state nor by shared goals, morals, or emotional bonds but rather by competitive capitalism, which he declares "a necessary condition for political freedom."[9] In Friedman's ideal society, we would each be marooned on our own little island, scheming single-handedly for our own individual advancement, without recourse to friendship or communal support.[10]

Friedman served as an economic adviser to Ronald Reagan as well as to Margaret Thatcher, who famously declared in 1987 that "there is no such thing as society, there are only individual men and women, and there are families."[11] Throughout the 1980s, Thatcher and Reagan deregulated trade, privatized public resources, and brutally broke labor power and other forms of collectivism in an attempt to implement Friedman's vision of society: a vision more extreme even than Hobbes's in its radical atomization of individuals and its denial of the social.

Whatever rhetorical nods to the betterment of society neoliberals may make, a major feature of the policies they have enacted is the destruction of collective identity. Collectivity—in the form of unions, primarily, but also in the communal administration of natural resources and social services—presents various boundaries to, and restrictions on, the accumulation of capital.[12] In fact, neoliberalism initially emerged as an attack on the New Deal policies and rhetoric that were reigniting class consciousness in the United States and around the world. The New Deal recognized the working class as a political entity; for neoliberals this kind of recognition is unacceptable, because it makes individuals aware of their collective disenfranchisement and encourages them to think of themselves as a large group with shared challenges, rights, and—most dangerously—power.

Political theorists and scholars in the social sciences have carved out understandings of neoliberal individualism from a variety of perspectives. The sociologist Arlie Russell Hochschild focuses on the transformations neoliberal ideology has wrought in our definitions of care and social reproduction, for example.[13] Hochschild argues that older notions of care were grounded in commitment, loyalty, mutual dependence, and a sense of responsibility for the feelings of others; today, by contrast, self-help literature and advice columns figure human relationships as temporary "investments" from which self-contained individuals should expect "returns." For Hochschild, this transformation is symptomatic of neoliberalism's requirement that everything be subjected to the laws of the market; we effectively curtail what we "need" in order to make it fit in with what we can purchase.[14] The anthropologist Ilana Gershon's understanding of the ideal neoliberal self begins with the related belief, ceaselessly propagated, that individuals must be self-managing if they are to be free.[15] Gershon charts a subtle yet powerful transition in liberal thought between the eighteenth century and today. Within classical liberalism, individuals own themselves as though they are property; individuals own their bodies, and can sell their bodies' capacity for labor. Within neoliberal thought, however, individuals own themselves as though they are a *business*; we own a set of skills and traits that we must constantly invest in, cultivate, market, and manage. For Gershon, the self conceived as a "bundle of skills" represents a "fragmented" understanding of personhood.[16]

The result of such fragmentation and monetization of care and of the self is that under neoliberalism, all individuals become wholly responsible for their own well-being and for their success or failure in attaining economic (or social, or romantic) self-sufficiency. For Hochschild, what is heroic and morally virtuous now is to not need others, and to proudly proclaim this lack of dependence: "the ideal self doesn't need much, and what it does need it can get for itself."[17] Since the free individual is one who does not need others, and since the foundation for freedom within neoliberal thought is the competitive free market, individuals conditioned by this thought train themselves to think in what are essentially competitive terms in every sphere of life. What does a body politic based on the ideal of individual competition look like? Within such a society, in which self-care and self-management have become the markers of virtue, those who are unable to take care of themselves are increasingly denied any notion of inherent rights. For Wendy Brown, this formulation means that the individual "bears full responsibility for the consequence of his or her action," such that poverty, poor health, or incarceration become figured as simply the results of a "mismanaged life."[18] Neoliberalism thus reduces individuals to units of human capital available for wise or foolish investment in various enterprises. Crucially, these human capitals "do not have the standing of Kantian individuals, ends in themselves, intrinsically valuable."[19]

Finally, the ideal neoliberal individual is apolitical, identifying their individualism with respect to other individuals not in terms of social responsibility, democratic action, or communal well-being but rather in transactional, opportunistic terms. This ideal subject is adept at identifying, attaining, marketing, and branding products on the various markets—not only the job market but the romantic market, the social media market, and so on—that increasingly stand in for social life. In short, the ideal neoliberal subject is an entrepreneur, and approaches every sphere of life with a competitive, self-serving, entrepreneurial ethos. As Brown points out, "A fully realized neoliberal citizenry would be the opposite of public-minded; indeed, it would barely exist as a public."[20] Neoliberal individualism makes no space for collective identification; we are each a Robinson

Crusoe, striving to take care of ourselves, and our idea of political action has largely been reduced to commodity activism and the display of our individual identities.[21]

The previous discussion paints a brutal portrait, one that does not map as obviously onto indie classical artist statements as it does onto Friedman's profoundly antisocial essays. Artists in the indie classical community tend to think of themselves as left-leaning, compassionate, and communally oriented, and in some ways they certainly are. By starting a record label with the intention of paying artists fairly, artists like Judd Greenstein sincerely want to (and in many respects, do) strengthen their communities and create new avenues for artists to earn livings. Even the strongly stated desires to "widen" audiences for their music or to "communicate" with audiences rather than alienating them can certainly be figured as communal gestures. Rather than simply tarring indie classical musicians with the "neoliberal" brush, then, what I am interested in here is untangling the web of rhetorical values that some of the strongest voices in this community have woven, in artist statements, interviews, and essays, about the state of classical music and about their own prerogatives as composers and musicians. It is my contention that the contradictions within that rhetoric have much to tell us about the role artists can play in upholding prevailing systems of institutional, economic and political power even while purporting to challenge them.

The Composer as (Anti-)Specialist

One effect of the replacement of collective identification with competitive, individualized identity display can be seen in the indie classical community's complicated relationship with specialization and the academy. Indie classical composers tend to rail against the academy, and when they do, they mean to criticize composers like Milton Babbitt who spent their careers isolated in the ivory tower, devoted single-mindedly to composition rather than to reaching and pleasing audiences. Babbitt's infamous 1958 essay, unfortunately titled "Who Cares if You Listen," sometimes takes on the character of a straw man in indie classical artists' attempts to position themselves in the "real world." Greenstein has called modernist ideas like Babbitt's "toxic," and calls Babbitt himself "one of the people responsible for the contemporary music scene being so riddled with bullshit."[22] In a 2011 interview, he said that while he appreciates a lot of the music made through academic or state funding and is "sympathetic to this notion of protecting things that wouldn't otherwise happen," he simply thinks that such protections are no longer necessary: "I don't think that there's work that's being sheltered from the marketplace that really has to fear the marketplace."[23] In an interview with the *Washington Post*, Missy Mazzoli takes this stance even further, contrasting herself with "grumpy and dogmatic" composers that make "academic" music. Mazzoli resents the hold that such composers apparently have over the critical and educational establishments, saying that younger composers like herself who try to reach wider audiences "are looked down on as stupid and uneducated." She concludes by saying that her goal as an artist is simply "to communicate with an audience," and that this goal "sounds obvious to 99 percent of the world, but it really is blasphemy to say that within academia!"[24]

In his essay, Babbitt compares composition to scientific research. Since we do not expect a "layman" to be able to instantly understand or appreciate an advanced lecture in mathematics, he suggests, we should also not expect "serious music" to be accessible to untrained audiences.[25] Babbitt certainly insults the "layman" here, and he essentially outlines the same elitist understanding of "serious music" as the one E. T. A. Hoffmann laid out in 1813 when he counterposed Beethoven's symphonies to the music enjoyed by "the rabble." More specifically, Babbitt advocates "granting to music the position accorded other arts and sciences," meaning creating a space where composers can pursue their own unique goals and articulate their own visions without worrying about being pleasing to those with money.[26] Thus, Mazzoli and Greenstein are correct when they say that postwar modernists like Babbitt sought "shelter" within the university; indeed, for Babbitt this was the only way "serious music" could survive, protected from the brutal realities of market competition. I would add that Babbitt further neglects to grapple with the reality that even academic sinecures can be attained only by composers who articulate certain ideas or pursue certain types of musical research. Even composers ensconced in ivory towers must appeal to money and power; these just come in a different form than ticket sales and wide popularity.

Babbitt's confrontational title has often worked to obscure the more nuanced exploration of artistic creation under capitalism that he undertakes in that essay. But his editor chose the title without his consent, and he himself consistently disavowed it; in fact, regarding the argument I am building about indie classical artists and neoliberal individualism, it is interesting to note that Babbitt wanted to title his article "The Composer as Specialist." The indie classical scene manifests a strange ambivalence when it comes to specialization and expertise. On the one hand, its musicians and composers have been phenomenally well trained by long-established educational institutions, they have highly specialized skill sets, and they evince a rigorous and devoted approach to their craft; on the other hand, they rhetorically embrace career flexibility and stylistic eclecticism, which represent the diffusion of specialization that survival within neoliberalism requires.

For much of the nineteenth and early twentieth centuries, classical music in the United States was produced primarily by unionized orchestras and opera companies, but in recent decades those stable jobs have become contested as traditional institutions struggle against bankruptcy and perceptions of cultural irrelevance. The do-it-yourself ethos and the career flexibility for which the artists examined here are so celebrated is symptomatic of a larger shift in ideas concerning employment in the United States since the 1970s, a shift from thinking of jobs as stable and long term to embracing a "gig economy" in which workers must be flexible in leaping from job to job and in adapting new skill sets so as to compete in a variety of labor markets.[27]

These new labor formations began emerging in opposition to the Fordist assembly line model that characterized production in the early twentieth century. Where Fordism enabled mass production of identical products for sale on a mass market, increasingly the market has fragmented, giving rise to the need for what economists call "flexible specialization," or the ability to create a wide variety of products for sale in a large number of markets.[28] Labor flexibility has also become crucial to the success of businesses, which must be able to quickly change the size of their workforce and move workers from job to job in response to changes in demand. They must also be able to exercise what is euphemistically called "pay flexibility"—in other words, to quickly change how much they pay workers for given tasks—in response to shifting market forces. Contracts outlining wage expectations and establishing basic worker protections limit firms' ability to be flexible in these ways, and thus since the 1970s we have seen the dismantling of a century's worth of organized labor's hard-won gains, and the rise of new precarious labor formations: subcontracting, working from home, part-time and temporary work, and job sharing.[29] The rhetoric of flexibility makes it seem liberating for individual workers, but it also liberates capital, which firms can more quickly accumulate once they are no longer required to make expenditures in the realms of employee benefits, pension plans, sick pay, and maternity leave; under the flexible regime, individual workers must seek out and pay for such benefits themselves.

The new flexibility has interesting repercussions for the status of experts and specialists, repercussions that have resonated into the field of musical production. Not only do the flexible requirements of the gig economy tend to reward those workers who have attained the kind of disparate, varied skill set that is the opposite of the specialist's, but neoliberalism itself also has an ideologically vexed relationship with specialization. On the one hand, perhaps the most privileged, lionized, and highly paid worker in today's economy is the tech worker, who has an extremely specialized set of skills. But on the other hand, neoliberals decry specialization because it leads to monopoly and because it encourages unionizing. In *The Road to Serfdom*, for example, Friedrich von Hayek chastised "all the single-minded idealists, all the men and women who have devoted their lives to a single task."[30] For Hayek, such specialists can see only the benefits of their own work, and thus they strive constantly to implement their ideas on a grand scale, leading to central planning. Milton Friedman also decried specialization. Writing that "the overthrow of the medieval guild system was an indispensable early step in the rise of freedom in the Western world," he goes on to construct a chapter-length argument against the licensure of specialized occupations.[31]

Despite the antispecialist stance neoliberals articulate, however, they also distrust the masses, favoring a "rule by elites."[32] In his chapter outlining what the government's role in public education should be, Friedman states that only those who are already talented and intelligent should receive free educations, since they will be the ones who will grow up to run the country. The untalented and unintelligent should certainly have access to education, but they should have to pay for it themselves, since for them education is more of a luxury commodity than it is for the smart and talented who require education in order to be good leaders.[33] Ultimately, while neoliberals are elitists, they must also posture as populists in order to gain widespread approval for their policies. One aspect of this posturing entails discrediting (and even mocking) experts and expert opinions in favor of crowd knowledge and common sense.

In the realm of indie classical musical production, this ambivalence toward specialization and expertise manifests not only in criticisms of the academy but also in the embrace of stylistic eclecticism. The arts press tends to associate "innovative" music with its ability to appeal to wide audiences, an ability usually associated with this music's supposed lack of generic barriers. Judd Greenstein calls the music of his community "post-historical in its openness to all styles," for example, and the arts press routinely describes indie classical composers as "boundary-breaking" and even as "post-genre."[34] A *Pitchfork* review of Nico Muhly is characteristic in its mélange of generic adjectives as well as its anti-intellectual dig at academic specialists: "His minimal, Neo-Romantic style has a balance of graceful form and emotional generosity that resonates with listeners who are more interested in personal statements than musicology. And his free-handed use of electronics, drones, and fluttering pulses blurs his classicism into accessible shades of post-rock."[35] The supposed diffusion of musical styles in indie classical music is felt to appeal to listeners with no special musical training, unlike the rigorously specialized music of the modernist tradition.

The imperative to make classical music nonthreatening to nonspecialist audiences is widely felt in contemporary classical music practice. The praise for newer venues like (Le) Poisson Rouge and National Sawdust in New York City celebrates how they expose audiences to cutting-edge new music as well as canonical classical music in a nonthreatening, accessible way, by allowing audience members to eat, drink, and socialize to a degree that traditional classical music venues prohibit. This kind of imperative is also manifest in the performance and programming decisions made by many contemporary music ensembles. For example, the musicologist John Pippen has examined the way the Chicago ensemble eighth blackbird (they do not capitalize their name) intentionally masks the extraordinarily hard-earned virtuosity of their playing with a crowd-friendly performance style that makes them seem approachable to audiences of nonexperts, who might otherwise find the spectacle of such specialized labor intimidating.[36] The need to appeal to audiences even manifests in the practices of musicians who continue to play music in the modernist tradition. Claire Chase, for example, often performs music that would be thought of as difficult or inaccessible in comparison with Greenstein's or Missy Mazzoli's, such as the work of Jason Eckardt, a Brooklyn-based composer strongly influenced by Webern. But Chase effectively repackages this kind of challenging music—music otherwise said to be inaccessible or even actively hostile to consumers—and instead identifies her performances of it as "entrepreneurial," thus automatically community oriented.

The doctrine of flexibility and its twin, the rejection of specialization, condition many realms of production. The musicologist David Blake investigates a similar trend in higher education, namely the increasing imperative that all work must be "interdisciplinary."[37] Blake uses Bourdieu's "omnivore theory" to dissect the contemporary value of academic interdisciplinarity, arguing that it has been conditioned by neoliberalism. Omnivore theory correlates class and education with broad inclusive tastes, as opposed to the more specialized taste arrays of the historical upper classes.

Blake notes that discourses of interdisciplinarity generate a disciplinary tension: scholars attempting to align their work with this new value must position what they do as a salutary alternative to the specialized monolith of "musicology," and thus interdisciplinary studies of music may have the effect of endangering the discipline itself, by depicting it as "outdated and hegemonic."[38]

In musical practice and production, the doctrine of flexibility reveals similar tensions. The kind of stylistic flexibility this community embraces is becoming an ever more desirable quality in contemporary composition, one rewarded by institutions as well as promoted by musical entrepreneurs. A certain degree of stylistic eclecticism has been a feature of art music composition in the United States for several decades; one of the reasons critics praised the first Downtown scene in 1960s New York was because it integrated idioms and performance styles from art-rock into more or less rigorous art music composition.[39] However, the increasingly widespread critical and institutional *promotion* of this sort of flexible stylistic boundary crossing is new; for the generation of American composers rising now, smoothly, flexibly, and simultaneously crossing many stylistic boundaries (or at least rhetorically espousing this practice) is fast becoming an urgent market imperative.[40] Accordingly, the number of styles that composers and performers feel they must be comfortable working within has proliferated wildly, well beyond the bounds of what a traditional conservatory education could ever provide. Greenstein's essay instructs his fellow artists to pursue excellence in all kinds of idioms, including those of past and present eras of Western classical music as well as rock, experimental pop, and hip-hop; and this kind of listing of disparate styles is routinely repeated in journalism about the scene.

But such an array of skills is one that only a vanishingly small fraction of extremely privileged musicians will ever be able to attain, and even those will be able to do so only with enormous amounts of highly diverse training and assistance. Equally mastering myriad styles from all over the world and throughout history would turn musician training on its ear; it would mean being a specialist with no specialty—the ideal flexible neoliberal subject—and it could be achieved only via a supremely personalized musical education, one in which every individual musician pursued their own interests outside any kind of established institutional framework. Within this personalized value system, not only does the avant-garde idea that art ought to perform social critique and enable collective political awakening become quaint, but the traditional method of training classical musicians comes to seem medieval, like the crafts guilds whose insular specificity Milton Friedman abhorred. Finally, the injunction to master musical idioms from all over the world and from every genre obviously raises questions about cultural appropriation: the ideal indie classical artist may unintentionally embody the figure of the privileged American who scoops up and monetizes bits and pieces of other cultures—cultures within which people may not have access to the same mobility or organs of promotion that this artist does.

Despite the ways the flexible regime is diminishing worker protections and worsening inequality, many individuals do have positive experiences in the gig economy, and flexible labor formations do liberate certain kinds of workers in certain powerful ways. If this were not the case, the doctrine of flexibility would not have been able to spread so widely or so quickly. When they valorize career and stylistic flexibility, Greenstein, Mazzoli, and Muhly are not simply repeating rhetoric they know to be untrue; in their cases, the flexible regime has truly allowed them to build enriching careers in music—careers that might not have been possible in the same way for past generations of composers.

However adamant, indie classical composers' oft-stated desire to break down generic barriers and create a nonspecialized, boundaryless music that moves among many idioms does not necessarily manifest in the actual sounds they create. In fact, William Robin calls Greenstein's insistence that there are no longer any boundaries between musical styles "willfully naïve"; elsewhere, I have also suggested that this boundarylessness is a neoliberal promotional gesture rather than an apt description of the music.[41] Music by Greenstein, Muhly, and Mazzoli, for example, tends to rely on motivic repetition and a regular rhythmic pulse: sounds that have characterized much of the music in the postminimalist tradition for decades. They imbue this repetition with dramatic expression and a few signifiers from other genres. Muhly's music often evokes Anglican choral traditions, for example, and Greenstein and Mazzoli often incorporate distorted electric guitars and rock drum kits into their works—incorporations that are not new with respect to the history of art music but that do invoke the world of rock. Even though I do not hear a wild diversity of styles in their music, however, I would nonetheless suggest that the doctrine of flexibility does condition their sound. In listening to music by Judd Greenstein, Missy Mazzoli, and Nico Muhly, I have been struck by a technique that recurs with some regularity in their work; while they position themselves as musically idiosyncratic, examining a few representative pieces through a hermeneutic of flexibility reveals some shared characteristics.

Musical Ambivalence

Like the work of Mason Bates, whom I discussed in the previous chapter, indie classical compositions often recall earlier pulse-pattern minimalism. Many compositions by Mazzoli and Muhly, for example, engage in cyclical repetition as well as the churning tension of combined triple and duple meters so characteristic of Philip Glass's work; but on top of these conventional markers of musical minimalism is often a sort of truncated, repetitive agitation: an individual voice or small collective of voices that seems to struggle against the monolithic repeating undertow of the bass line. I hear this technique, for example, in Mazzoli's "Tooth and Nail" and "Magic with Everyday Objects," and in Muhly's "Etude 3."

"Tooth and Nail," a 2008 piece for viola and prerecorded electronics, was commissioned by the violist Nadia Sirota for her critically acclaimed 2013 album *Baroque*. The backbone of the piece is a pulsed single note that, because of stereo mixing, seems to flutter from side to side, almost sounding phased. On top of this relentless pulsed repetition, the viola seems to agitate. Again and again, it struggles against the flow, but can't make a solid statement of its own. For me, the emotional effect is one of anxiety—certainly not the Zen-like submission to repetition that I experience in so much early minimalism. As the piece progresses, Mazzoli effects an even more dramatic fragmentation of the viola line via the use of stereo mixing. The viola, which had been separated from the bass line, becomes separated from itself as it ever more feebly pushes against the dominating repetition below. Many of Mazzoli's compositions deploy this technique of juxtaposing alert agitation to relentless repetition, including works for her quintet, Victoire, as well as her opera, *Song from the Uproar*, and her vocal suite *Vespers for a New Dark Age*. Indeed, I would argue that it is a signature Mazzoli sound.

She explores a related technique in "Magic with Everyday Objects," commissioned in 2012 by the NOW Ensemble. Here, individual instruments seem to follow their own paths while remaining only loosely tied together by the repeated two chords of the harmonic material. As the piece progresses, however, the limitations on the individual instruments become increasingly obvious as they repeat their small motives again and again, and the disjunction between instruments ultimately pulls the whole sonic landscape into chaos. The piece ends in an angry snarl of distorted guitar and a melancholy wail of feedback that fades into silence.

Hearing Mazzoli's music as presenting a semblance of free individual movement that seems to clash against its context offers the potential to hear it as expressing an ambivalence about the neoliberal realities the composer publicly espouses. In one respect we certainly could hear this as a musical expression of Mazzoli's stated frustration with traditional ways of doing things—do these individual voices want to break free of the restrictions imposed by the necessity of sounding together as a collective?—but in another way this technique may sonically evoke the melancholy experience of individualism within neoliberalism, in which freedom is rhetorically valorized but ultimately constrained by the increasing difficulty of simply surviving. Similarly, the disjunction between instruments, which generates sonic confusion and which refuses to come to a satisfying, cohesive concluding statement, may poignantly evoke the dearth of collectivity in contemporary life, the looseness of the social bonds holding us together, and the way this looseness restricts us from sounding together in the kinds of collective statements and actions that might bring about social change.

Muhly's "Etude 3," also commissioned by Sirota for *Baroque*, sounds quite like the Mazzoli piece on the same album. It is grounded by a low, circular bass line, and seems to express an angsty, tightly held repetitive agitation on top. The rhythmic and even harmonic disjunction between bass line and viola part is even more pronounced here than in Mazzoli's piece for Sirota; sometimes it feels as though the viola is freely improvising on top of the chord progression. Muhly often makes use of this technique in other compositions, for example in his *Drones* series as well as in his opera, *Two Boys*—in particular during the sequences in which we hear "the sound of the internet," which Muhly accomplished by juxtaposing frenetic, often inarticulate, repeating vocal statements to grand and implacable orchestral cycling.

In both "Tooth and Nail" and "Etude 3," Mazzoli and Muhly created works with repeating bass lines and seemingly improvised solo lines, mirroring the structure of much baroque music, which is appropriate given the title of Sirota's album. In that sense, we can certainly hear this compositional technique as a new interpretation of a very old style. However, the agitation and melancholy both pieces convey, via the sense of extreme disjunction between the solo voice and the juggernaut of the bass line, do not seem inspired by music of the baroque; this affect feels very new indeed.

For the musicologist Robert Fink, early minimalist process music "is the sonic analogue of the repetitive experience of self in mass-media consumer society," and I would argue that these examples of postminimalist music articulate a similar subjective experience.[42] But where 1960s minimalism often evokes a sense of seamless flow, I hear this new music as articulating a conflict with flow, or at least as exploring a potential difference between mindless repetition and a fleet, alert, but ultimately powerless and isolated subjectivity that resists it. This aesthetic of solitary struggle positioned against an indomitable cycling force represents a meaningful difference between such works and the historical minimalism to which they are often compared. Here, there is no real "groove," no sense that polyrhythms are interlocking to create a timeless flow. These works are not hypnotic or patient; to borrow Fink's image, they do not teach us to "surf" atop unending repetition. Indeed, rather than submitting to repetition, some of these works seem to actively struggle against it, as individual voices attempt to construct meaningful statements that are not in sync with the governing structure of the piece.

If we accept the possibility of a musicoeconomic linkage in the sound of early minimalism, then perhaps we can understand this newer musical trope as similarly linked to the new experience of subjectivity following the implementation of neoliberal policies that began in earnest in the 1970s. Even as we espouse the neoliberal doctrine of individual flexibility in an ever-widening sphere of life, many of us experience a simultaneous growth of anxiety and doubt concerning this value. It is within this zone of cognitive dissonance that I choose to hear the compositional technique outlined above, in which free individual movement seems to clash against its context. Such uses of this technique seem to me to be appropriate sonic descriptions of the experience of individualism within neoliberalism, in which freedom is ceaselessly promoted but ultimately constrained, and in which collective identification is strongly discouraged. I would go so far as to suggest that listening to some of the works by Muhly and Mazzoli in this way might reveal an ambivalence about and a discomfort with neoliberal individualism that is not manifested in these composers' public statements.

Greenstein's compositions often make use of a similar technique, but they are rarely so troubled; his "Sing Along" provides an example. This short piece was written in 2006 for the NOW Ensemble, a composer collective and chamber group (flute, clarinet, electric guitar, double bass, piano) of which Greenstein is a member. "Sing Along" opens with an electric guitar tolling on E-flat. Then the clarinet and bass come in, articulating long sustained intervals of fourths and fifths that alternate. The piano enters and soon takes over the tolling backbone of the piece. Slowly, as more instruments are added and the texture becomes more complex, a regular rhythmic pulse—in a combined duple-triple meter—coalesces. The piano part is scored for four hands; while the player in the lower register (on the NOW Ensemble's recording of the work, this part is performed by Greenstein himself) provides the rhythmic pulse grounding the whole piece, the player in the upper register articulates little runs and fillips that almost sound improvised. The flute and upper piano engage in sprightly imitation, tossing these little gestures back and forth. During its last two minutes, the piece accrues a certain dramatic trajectory as the tolling bass line moves through chords more quickly and the soloing instruments seem to continue following their own individual paths. While there are exciting moments of synchronization, when the instruments all seem to suddenly come together almost by accident in the expression of a new chord, the piece mostly sounds like a pleasant, consonant chaos: a collective of individual voices following their own whims (to me, all the individual parts, perhaps aside from the lower piano part, sound like they were written to seem improvisatory) but never coming into any conflict with one another. In the disjunction between its individual parts, "Sing Along" resembles the Mazzoli and Muhly compositions discussed above; yet here the effect is not one of anxiety or melancholy. In his own description of "Sing Along," Greenstein says, "This is an uplifting piece . . . with everyone doing their part (including me) to make a work that allows individual voices to combine, becoming more than the sum of their parts."[43]

Because they so obviously serve capital, it is tempting to view the transformation to flexible, self-managing labor formations as new means of disciplining workers that are cynically imposed from above, as CEOs attempt to squeeze more and more surplus value out of labor. However, we should also appreciate how flexible labor formations emerged in response to workers' resistance to older, more rigid labor models, because this helps explain why so many people embrace and valorize these formations. The ability to move freely between jobs, to take on multiple projects at once, and to be more self-directed in pursuing those projects can indeed be experienced as liberating. As Luc Boltanski and Eve Chiapello demonstrate, demands for changes in the workplace crystallized post-1968 along several related lines: the rejection of hierarchy in favor of greater personal autonomy and choice; the assertion that central planning is too rigid and authoritarian; and a new foregrounding of the salutary benefits of competition and ever more rapid technological innovation. It is easy to see how these demands have been met by capital, for example with the implementation of the gig economy, which requires workers to be freelancers in many diverse fields of employment.[44] However, although they were quickly co-opted by business and turned into a means of accumulating capital more easily and rapidly, these formations are also to some degree the result of decades of workers' demands for greater autonomy and choice.[45] In this way, capitalism continually transforms in order to assuage the anger and anxiety of its critics (while always maintaining accumulation as its central motivation), always taking new forms that require new critiques.

Today's doctrine of flexibility necessarily generates ambivalence. On the one hand, flexible labor formations allow a greater degree of certain kinds of personal freedom and choice (for certain kinds of people), while on the other hand they very obviously diminish stability, safety, social cohesion, and quality of life for workers across the board. But labor and pay flexibility have proved enormously beneficial to capital accumulation; thus, capital demands new means of convincing workers that this type of flexibility is the freedom they've been asking for all along. Where Henry Ford established a Sociology Department to propagate his utopian ideal of the "New Man" (as well as to monitor employees' moral behavior and the cleanliness of their homes), today corporate advertising inundates citizens with messages promoting flexibility and precarity in their many forms: self-help books tell us to "do what you love," even if it means working without pay, and corporations, city planners, and myriad small firms increasingly prioritize attracting workers who are "creative," a vague condition in which the labor workers perform becomes a cultivated aspect of their personalities and of everything they do.[46]

The flexible regime thus naturalizes constant work and self-management as a necessary condition of making great art. In an interview with NPR, Missy Mazzoli notes with approval what she called the new career "eclecticism" that successful composers practice these days. While acknowledging that the "tricky" situation of arts funding has led to a reality in which composers must teach, perform, have their own ensembles, write for films and commercials, start their own record labels, run websites, keep accounting records, master recording technology, run Kickstarter campaigns, and perform a plethora of other activities, she nonetheless affirms this economic reality as *creatively* generative:

> Everything that I do feeds everything else. . . . I don't think I could be an effective composer without being a teacher. And I don't think I would be an effective composer without also being a performer. So I'm juggling 10 things at once on any given day, but it just feels like my life. It's just what I do.[47]

This brings to mind the distinction Andrea Moore draws between entrepreneurship and freelancing in new music discourse and practice. Whereas freelancing requires that a musician attain a particular array of musical skills and be comfortable playing in a variety of styles and venues, entrepreneurship is figured as a wide variety of nonmusical skills "whose mastery can provide the foundation for a *life*, rather than a living, in music." Thus, Moore concludes, "entrepreneurship resembles freelancing reimagined for the neoliberal era."[48]

Max Weber argued that in attaching "restless work in a vocation" to religious salvation, the Puritans ultimately "sanctified" work itself; they made the diligent performance of work into a spiritual practice that had merit on its own terms. Today, as statements like Mazzoli's reveal, we still vaguely believe that there is something virtuous about being dedicated to constant work as a personally fulfilling practice rather than as a financially enriching one.[49] We have simply replaced notions of religious salvation with the growing dogma of "creativity" that is fast becoming a ubiquitous value toward which individuals and businesses must strive.[50] The artist—and, by extension, any citizen who wishes to be "creative"—under neoliberalism voluntarily submits to precarity and constant work, and claims that condition as an invigorating lifestyle choice, one preferable to constancy and permanence. Discourses of flexibility present the destruction of the work-life boundary and the acceptance of labor precarity as the only creditable way to become creative as well as simply to survive.

Reinventing Music History

Because of their desire to generate music without generic boundaries and their resistance to being linked to any past school of compositional thought, indie classical composers often angrily resist critics' and scholars' attempts to locate them within a historical lineage.[51] And yet, it is interesting that Judd Greenstein's essay does exactly this, effectively periodizing indie classical as an inevitable next phase in musical development, a phase we arrive at by moving past other phases. He begins by noting that we have moved past the "inward-looking avant-garde" that made music "mainly for themselves."[52] Here Greenstein demonstrates how emphatically indie classical artists can distance themselves from high modernist schools of thought. While this group finds the isolation, elitism, and hermeticism of postwar academic music research appalling, however—a stance that might actually ally them with the earlier interwar avant-garde—they also reject the notion that music itself ought to be critically engaged. Despite the socially progressive politics these artists tend to espouse, and despite their often referring to themselves as "activists" on behalf of classical music both new and old, they are strangely apolitical and vague when it comes to their beliefs about the concrete work that music could or should do in society.

They speak often of the composer's responsibility to communicate with audiences, but what that act of communication should actually impart in terms of thoughts or ideas is rarely specified; the communication they advocate obviously has little to do with the historical avant-garde's desire to shock or challenge people into a state of political epiphany. Rather, the indie classical composer believes that there is nothing wrong with giving people what they want, and indeed insists that doing so is the only healthy means of ensuring music's survival in the marketplace. What David Metzer calls modernism's "spirit of critique"—critique itself as a principle of artistic creation—falls by the wayside.[53]

In the case of Greenstein, Mazzoli, and Muhly, their idea of music that communicates with audiences seems to mean music that is consonant, primarily tonal or at least diatonic, and organized in very steady, compelling rhythms. The music critic and scholar Kyle Gann describes Greenstein's "happy" music as manifesting "almost a prelapsarian innocence: it doesn't seem to bear scars from the fractures and antagonisms of 20th century music."[54] A review of Greenstein's music says that it mixes genres, manifests "little interest in difficulty," and sounds like the rock band Vampire Weekend, in the sense that it "intelligently and satisfyingly reflects the status quo." The author also notes that these composers' music "aims plainly to please" and is exciting to audiences because it is "rigorous but unintimidating."[55]

As a rule, journalists intend to be complimentary when they characterize work by these composers as lacking difficulty. The perceived easiness of this music not only is its greatest selling point but is also held up as political activism. In a representative review, Daniel Johnson—who is a fan of these artists and writes engaging, insightful essays about the scene—compares Greenstein's music to that of the thornier, more politically oriented ensemble Bang on a Can, but says approvingly that Greenstein is "far more amiable—even tuneful—and seldom so obsessive or intimidating." Johnson ultimately concludes that this tunefulness makes Greenstein "more democratic."[56] This kind of evaluative framework strips away a more political understanding of democracy, leaving only the vague notion of majority appeal.[57]

In contrasting themselves favorably against modernist composers, indie classical artists tend to reformulate the modernist ethos dramatically by simply identifying modernism as a set of stylistic choices that given composers make based on personal preference. A recent episode of Nadia Sirota's podcast, *Meet the Composer*, exemplifies this reconfiguration of critically engaged musical ideas, and reveals what Greenstein means when he says in his essay that we have also moved past "the self-conscious reactions" to modernism that he feels characterized the work of his predecessors. In the May 15, 2017, episode of her podcast, titled "New Music Fight Club," Sirota examines the great battle between composers from the modernist and minimalist traditions that dominated US musical discourse in the 1970s and 1980s. She notes in astonishment that this fight "had the tenor of, like, a Facebook political argument or something," and says:

> If you're not aware of the conflict in the twentieth century between tonal composers and atonal composers, I think it must sound *insane* to hear that creative people were antagonizing each other, belittling each other, calling each other names.[58]

Sirota says that the "crux" of the argument between modernists and postmodernists was "a classic one: left brain versus right brain. Head versus heart. Chromaticism versus melodicism." Composers in the modernist tradition wanted to compose serial music or music based on algorithms, while minimalists wanted to be more expressive; for Sirota, the argument was essentially one about aesthetic choices—what kind of music sounds good or bad. If this were a fully accurate representation of the argument, then the bewilderment she expresses would be justified. How could composers have cared enough about chromaticism to fight bitterly and hatefully with one another, to write impassioned op-eds in the *New York Times*, and even to say "incredibly shitty things" behind one another's backs? After all, chromaticism and melodicism merely represent different stylistic choices composers are free to make depending on their personal aesthetic preferences. When put in these terms, the conflict does indeed sound "insane."

However, characterizing this artistic battle in such a way misunderstands what was actually at stake for many of the composers involved. In fact, in its most sincere iteration, the "crux" of this argument had less to do with chromaticism versus melodicism and more to do with music's political importance and composers' political responsibilities. Modernist composers like Charles Wuorinen and Brian Ferneyhough, for example, genuinely believed that tonal music's expressiveness was dangerous, because it had the capacity to provoke emotional reactions independent of intellectual thought, a power they associated with political demagoguery and fascism. They also maintained a modernist orientation toward time: they believed composers should move composition "forward," and that music should "evolve" along rational lines; they felt it was the composer's responsibility to pursue such rational evolution. In contrast with ideas like these, repetition-based minimalist works (Greenstein's "self-conscious reactions" against modernism) are themselves political; in contrast with modernist progressiveness, the idea of constructing a music that eschews powerful goal orientation—that in effect refuses to strive toward the future for which modernism yearns—articulates a very different orientation toward time and history, one that perhaps can be heard as valuing the present and articulating a Zen-like attempt to "live in the now" (or as insistently drawing our attention to the politics of the present, as is perhaps the case in a work like Steve Reich's "Come Out").[59] Furthermore, the early minimalists had been trained in serialism and had been told that that was the only way to write music; by rejecting that imperative and striving to find a totally different musical language, we could argue that they were performing the kind of dialectical engagement with received wisdom that Theodor Adorno insisted was the hallmark of truly new music, music that "calls this age by its name."[60]

So the fight about musical styles that characterized the 1970s and 1980s "had the tenor" of a political argument because it *was* a political argument; for many of the composers involved, it wasn't merely about pleasant or unpleasant aesthetic choices but rather about the real-world political work those choices performed. Indie classical artists seem to misunderstand this when they characterize modernists as merely "grumpy and dogmatic" and minimalists as merely "reacting against" that dogmatism. Even Sirota, who presents a compassionate and even-handed portrait of the two sides in the musical debate, ultimately comes to a postmodernist conclusion about it, triumphantly asserting that there is no right or wrong way to compose; rather, modernist techniques make one kind of statement while minimalist techniques make another, and both are equally good and meaningful, and equally available to all artists who might wish to make use of them in their efforts to communicate with audiences.

The notion that technique is simply a matter of personal choice generally forecloses on serious, heated discussions and analyses of aesthetics—ostensibly a realm of discourse that ought to be (or at least has been historically) of prime importance to musical producers. Indie classical artists tend (publicly, at least) to uniformly celebrate one another for "breaking down boundaries," "speaking to audiences," "widening the appeal of classical music," and so on; rarely do they engage in the kind of spirited, specific debates about styles and sounds that have characterized so many past schools of composition. William Robin addresses this unusual discursive lack—for example, indie classical concerts and recordings rarely include program notes or extensive liner notes—and points out that for these composers, their much-vaunted incorporation of musical idioms from other times or cultures "does not require any intellectual justification or theoretical exegesis"; instead, such artists praise one another for their "honesty" in expressing their unique musical tastes—tastes that, by virtue of being wholly personal, cannot be criticized or theorized.[61]

This indiscriminate approbation suggests that for the artists examined here, any historical ties between musical sound and a critically oriented politics have been severed cleanly. Compositional techniques and musical sounds themselves appear to have no real political significance; if they did, then the idea of arguing ferociously over them would seem not mystifying or silly but rather urgently necessary. In this light, the passionate musical advocacy that these artists undertake becomes somewhat ironic, since insisting that compositional choices have no serious significance beyond a merely personal aesthetic preference effectively lessens music's social importance, and returns it to the realm to which Kant relegated it in the eighteenth century: that of pretty background noise. Indeed, Judd Greenstein observes in an interview that "outside of making music for other people to listen to, I don't think we really have any function at all, and so that's the end of the story for me."[62] If this is the case, it is hard to understand what these artists are so passionate about when they call themselves advocates for new music.

Do It Yourself

In addition to reformulating modernism in order to strip it of its political implications, indie classical artists repackage another set of historically oppositional ideas in order to instrumentalize them as skill sets for individual success: those contained in the do-it-yourself, or DIY, ethos that characterized the historical punk and indie rock movements. As I mentioned above, workers navigating the gig economy must take on burdens that employers once would have carried. In the absence of stable jobs, freelance, subcontracted, and part-time workers must research and purchase their own health insurance and plan for their own retirements while also constantly learning new skills, marketing themselves in an increasingly competitive job market, and surfing from gig to gig. This cultural context has given rise to a new formulation of DIY as a mainstream value toward which everyone—including, confusingly, businesses—should strive.[63]

Within this new discursive formulation, DIY artists must be able to build a website, read a spreadsheet, manage myriad accounts, found an ensemble, play in other ensembles, network with classical musicians as well as with rock and hip-hop artists, snag opportunities to compose for film and television, attain the equipment and technical skill to record their own albums for sale in the marketplace, and, through it all, make a comfortable living without the burden of an employer or a steady paycheck. In fact, in many respects *DIY* has simply come to mean "entrepreneurial," in the sense that it describes people who take care of themselves and are adept at identifying and exploiting opportunities for individual success. For example, a Boston *Globe* article identifies Claire Chase as the "poster child" for "musical DIYism," implying that this quality is the reason she was awarded a MacArthur Fellowship for her arts entrepreneurship.[64]

But this formulation of DIY differs considerably from its original iteration as an ethos that emerged from the punk and indie rock movements of the 1980s and 1990s, where it defined an anticapitalist stance toward art and life. The first, most hard-core members of DIY-identified scenes worked to establish networks for making, listening to, and distributing music that were deliberately arrayed against what they saw as the corporate homogenization of musical styles and products, as well as the fragmentation of communal life that late capitalism enacted. Thus, DIY was for many practitioners an explicitly political stance and a fairly rigorous way of life, one that influenced the sounds and styles of the music bands made as well as their kinship networks, discursive strategies, and ways of supporting themselves and one another.[65] Many of the people who self-identified with this scene attempted to counterpose their activities, aesthetics, and value systems against the wastefulness and greed of corporate culture: they played free shows and gave away their music for free, or sometimes participated in a barter system in which burned CD-Rs were exchanged for other homemade goods. Some vowed to eat only food they had scavenged from the dumpsters outside corporate grocery store chains: a lifestyle that is far from glamorous and that does nothing to establish practitioners as successful entrepreneurs. Importantly, musicians in these scenes also used musical performance and sounds to contest the standardization and commodification of appropriate expressions of beauty, sexuality, and gender.[66] This network of political ideas—more than any specific musical or fashion aesthetic—was what comprised DIY culture for many people at the end of the twentieth century. Like so many political attempts to revolt against capitalist ideology, these practices and the myriad musical styles they generated were subsumed by the culture industry, both commodified and dismissed as merely hipster lifestyle choices.[67] But for many people at the time, they represented a deeply sincere attempt to rethink collectivity and social responsibility in the face of the financialization and alienation imposed by capitalist modernity.[68]

Where punk rock DIY was profoundly community oriented, however, today's individualistic DIY entrepreneurs pride themselves on not needing others; as traditional support networks weaken, radical self-care has become a highly valued act.[69] Indeed, while they may use the word *community* in advocating for the social importance of what they do, members of what the urban planning consultant Richard Florida has memorably dubbed "the creative class" cannot afford to think in truly collective terms, even if they wanted to. Angela McRobbie argues that the contemporary privileging of DIY undertakes "labour reform by stealth" by creating this class, a group she instead wants to call "the risk class."[70] Corporate advertising has encouraged members of this class to think of themselves as creative, and to value work that enables them to exercise creativity, personal autonomy, and lifestyle flexibility. Members of this class go to art school and get MFAs, they open dance studios, they become composers, they start fashion blogs, they enjoy good wine and nice home furnishings. In short, for McRobbie, members of the new "risk class" think of themselves as middle class and have learned to appreciate the products and lifestyles associated with the middle class, but they have been conditioned to accept a life without any of the benefits once associated with being middle class: health insurance, home ownership, pension plans, and job security, among others. In discussing feminism in particular, McRobbie observes that the precarious socioeconomic environment this new middle class inhabits actually "militates against an ethos of solidarity and collectivity," because it requires members to be self-serving and self-managing, and to engage with other people in a purely competitive way.[71]

Commentators confusingly present such competitive individualism not as self-interested and isolating but rather as good for society as a whole. For example, in a now-infamous address at Northwestern University's Bienen School of Music, Claire Chase enjoined the graduating class to fulfill their "destiny" of becoming musical entrepreneurs, saying that this will build "better organizations and stronger communities." But in the same speech, she declared, "I'd love for every single one of you to put me out of business. Then I will know that I have done my job." In a *New York Times* article about Chase, Anthony Tommasini calls this statement "empowering," and says that Chase makes "the most positive case [he has] ever heard for the new entrepreneurship."[72] It is difficult to see how deliberately attempting to put one another out of our jobs builds stronger communities, but this is the contradictory logic that becomes naturalized under neoliberalism's conception of individual freedom.

Where musical DIYism was initially identified as a sort of workers' resistance movement, for many indie classical artists DIY represents merely the savvy circumvention of traditional classical music institutions as a means of reaping greater personal financial rewards. This neo-DIY philosophy is thus not a rejection but rather an acceptance of the terms of contemporary market capitalism—specifically, of the flexibility neoliberal labor policies impose, and of the kinds of corporate channels that the historical DIY movement arrayed itself against. As Andrea Moore notes, the codification of entrepreneurship training in music schools "belies any claims to resistance" that such musical entrepreneurs may make; furthermore, "concert music, with its roots in the aristocracy and the bourgeoisie, is explicitly not punk."[73]

Aesthetically, too, indie classical DIY is quite different from punk rock DIY. Appealing easily to a broad fan base was definitively not on the agenda of many original punk and indie musicians. Their music was often intentionally grating and destructively loud, and had obscene, violent, explicitly political lyrics. Even the sweeter, "twee" style of the bands that gathered around K Records was irritating in its way: musicians were often untrained or played intentionally poorly or awkwardly (using an overturned yogurt container for a drum kit, for example), and lyrics were often deceptively saccharine and infantile.[74] The annoying qualities of this music were intentional, however, and were meant to oppose emotional and political authenticity (in the form of amateurism) to the glossy, overproduced sound of corporate rock.

Kat Bjelland, lead singer of the punk band Babes in Toyland, discusses the deceptive ugliness of the band's sound, saying that "our music is like Pepto-Bismol: really pink and nice, except it tastes like shit! But it makes you feel better."[75] This punk rock principle does not apply to indie classical music, which the critic Justin Davidson once infamously accused of "badly needing a machine to rage against."[76] But clearly, this music's noted lack of ugliness is related to its economic pragmatism. Describing his vision of new music, Judd Greenstein himself supplies a very different sort of gastronomical metaphor than Bjelland's, saying that "you don't [gain an audience] by shocking people. You do it by adding spice to their food gradually, by introducing new flavors, by broadening their palette [sic] in a way that feels simultaneously comfortable and exciting because it's both new and familiar."[77]

On his blog, Nico Muhly writes sensitively about musical economics and the conditions musicians and composers face in the contemporary

United States. Muhly observes that in today's economic landscape, for example, composing for small ensembles (rather than for the large groups associated with established opera houses or city philharmonics) is "practical and sensible." He goes on to add, "It doesn't mean that in such a making, one is saying that DIY music is the *only* way forward; it's just a different skill set. Writing a chamber opera doesn't mean you don't believe in grand; writing a piece of electronic music doesn't mean you've abandoned the viola."[78] However, in the most idealistic formulations of the indie scenes of the 1980s and 1990s, DIY practices like releasing dubbed tapes and playing in garages instead of aspiring to arenas and major label deals were considered not merely "a different skill set" that could be instrumentalized in moneymaking but rather a whole different way of orienting musical production—and life itself—away from consumer capitalism. Like most revolutionary stances, this philosophy was idealistic, sometimes hypocritical, and often irritatingly pedantic, but it was deeply felt; it is the reason that "selling out" was such a highly emotional topic in these communities. When bands like Nirvana signed major label deals, fans and fellow musicians saw it as a real betrayal of what the community stood for politically. Furthermore, such selling out did imperil the DIY community, as corporate labels tried to replicate Nirvana's huge success by starting subsidiary "independent" labels and commodifying "indie" as an aesthetic rather than a political orientation.[79]

By contrast, no one in his circle, or in the arts press, appears to begrudge Muhly his Nonesuch release or his Met commission; in fact, musicians and critics hold these achievements up as proof that approaching a musical career with a DIY (that is, entrepreneurial) spirit—one that is flexible, adaptable, diversified, pragmatic, and self-promoting—can lead to mainstream success at the hands of corporations and large traditional institutions. These ideas could not be more diametrically opposed to those of the early punk scene, and, to his credit, Muhly (unlike many of his peers) seems very aware of the contradictions that arise when critics refer to what he does as "DIY" or "indie." In a 2013 interview, he noted:

> At heart I'm really quite a traditionalist. . . . I'm not interested in breaking anything down. I have an opera at the Met and when you write an opera for the Met you're not like, "Oh, I'm going to fill it with weird electronic beats and whatever." No, you write something that's appropriate for the space. That's why I'm so bristled at this indie classical designation because it's so dumb, and I can literally think of nothing less independent than a big ol' classical music institution. It doesn't get any less indie than the Met.[80]

Conclusion: The Starving Artist as Ideal Citizen

It is easy to see how US society could come to value the figure of the flexible, self-managing entrepreneur so highly, given the country's traditional self-conception as a nation of pioneers, adventurers, and individualists. But strange phenomena grow out of such an insistently individualized conception of creativity, such as the notion of the "maverick" composer in the United States. Although a maverick is by definition someone who does not do things in the way of an established tradition, two centuries of American composition have nonetheless given us a "maverick tradition."[81] Within this tradition, composers who have won Pulitzer Prizes, who have been commissioned by the Metropolitan Opera, whose works have been performed nationally and internationally to massive acclaim, and who have chapters devoted to their work in standard music history textbooks are described as rebels who challenge the status quo.

Given that the maverick tradition is such a strong one in US culture, and the fact that it has in recent years been combined with the requirement for musicians to approach their careers with an entrepreneurial, monetized DIY ethos, many composers have actively fought critical attempts to align them collectively. On his blog, Muhly complains about the "relentless and sort of obsessive focus on genre that people constantly throw around." By this he means the critical tendency to observe that the music made by him and many of the most successful composers in his community sounds a lot like minimalism. Muhly says that this critical desire to describe and explain music in terms of historical lineage is not only lazy ("How hard is it to just write about how the music sounds without invoking anybody else's name or slapping a name on it?") but also hurtful to composers, who start writing "to one's press-generated biography, rather than from a musical core."[82]

Muhly raises thoughtful points. Certainly, being pigeonholed into a given genre makes it difficult for artists to make different kinds of statements as they age and as their interests develop, and critics (and scholars) do have a disturbing tendency to regurgitate descriptions of artists that may not keep up with how those artists have changed over time. However, it is nonetheless difficult to analyze a piece of music in a culturally engaged way if each piece needs to be seen as completely individual, and as emanating from an isolated, Crusoe-like composer. The sort of musical discussion Muhly calls for ("talking about notes and rhythms" instead of genres or lineages[83]) would produce the kind of dry, socially detached analysis that seems to have so infuriated these composers in their academic music theory classes. If this is the only kind of analysis we are allowed to perform, then we won't be able to assess music as a product of its culture, or as revealing anything substantive about the social and historical situation in which it was produced. Finally, I would argue that insisting that there are no genres, no schools, no lineages, no generational or regional tendencies, can also obscure social relations, labor formations, and inequalities of various kinds. If, to paraphrase Margaret Thatcher, there is no such thing as genre, only individual composers and compositions, then we have no way of knowing that rock 'n' roll was founded on African American musical styles, or that the nineteenth-century symphony emerged part and parcel with German nationalism.

The indie classical scene provides a case study for observing how cultural assumptions about art—and about the figure of the artist—are changing in the contemporary United States, as well as how artists can be used to exemplify the virtues of neoliberal individualism for the rest of us. These artists have been trained to think and act individually rather than collectively, which on its surface seems in keeping with the older nineteenth-century model of artistry, because the stereotypical Romantic artist was also highly individualistic. Yet where Romantic individualism was meant to dramatize the artist's difference from others and isolation from (and critique of) society, commentators confusingly present today's radical individualism as being good for society as a whole. In contemporary US discourse, artistic individualism has been reconfigured as flexible, competitive entrepreneurialism, and repositioned as an ideal toward which every citizen should strive.

In our present moment, members of the indie classical scene are envisioning the market's penetration of artistic life as not only inevitable but empowering, and a new mode of flexible subjectivity more amenable to capital accumulation is being modeled in the figure of the "DIY" composer. Even the more general name for the preferred new labor market— "gig" economy—enshrines the labor formation of the freelancing musician as a potential condition for all workers. Today, business schools, urban planners, corporations, and grant-making organizations position artists' flexible, self-managing approach to their precarious lives as an ideal for all to emulate. Thus the artist, once the outsider—someone who refused to play by society's rules, and who often "starved" because of it—now becomes the icon of the ideal neoliberal citizen; today, all work aspires to the condition of art.

These new ideas about art and artists are doing something more insidious than simply transforming notions of artistry to conform to entrepreneurial necessity. They are helping to further condition the rest of us to accept neoliberal flexibility as a social good and as the best practice for individuals to follow. Because artists are the original "creative class"—their work is their life, and they have long been accustomed to precarious labor conditions—and because of the lofty position art and especially classical music still hold in much of the popular consciousness, artists' activism on the part of neoliberal flexibility makes following such a tenet seem like the best way to become "creative."[84]

Artists, like the rest of us, are in an untenable situation, caught between the desire to pursue their craft and the need to survive in the new world that the free market and its attendant ideologies have wrought. Our paths to survival may also seem to come into conflict with our desire to be good citizens of the world: on the one hand, we know deep down that the freedom promised by the free market will never quite materialize, and we are also aware of the many dramatic examples, both at home and abroad, of the limits on freedom capitalism can and does enforce; but on the other hand, because we have no other option we must continue believing in this freedom and in the market competition that will allow it to fully flower. This conflict generates unresolvable rhetorical contradictions as well as ambivalence and melancholy.

Thus, in some respects it is certainly unfair to criticize artists for the pathways to success they can identify; indeed, despite the highly critical orientation of this chapter, this has not been my goal. Music educators are in a similar bind, after all. How can we train our students in the cultivation of a highly specialized musical skill set, knowing how vanishingly slim are the odds they will be up against once they graduate and try to make a living in music? It makes sense that we have fixed upon entrepreneurship as our savior. With its rhetoric of individual empowerment and its envisioning of a world of endless possibilities—and given the fact that entrepreneurial activities are being so generously rewarded by major funding organizations—entrepreneurship seems like a viable orientation toward work and life, one that offers at least some hope that our students will be able to survive, however meager we suspect the chances of that survival to be.

I have tried to show that despite artists' public statements to the contrary, it is possible to hear some of their music as exploring certain allegorized neoliberal realities without necessarily celebrating them. In some of this music, for example, flexible boundary crossing seems to be a guiding compositional ethos in the same way that it governs these artists' career choices, yet in its very flexibility such music sometimes seems to express ambivalence, anxiety, or even sorrow. This interpretation points to a powerful aspect of music, which is its peculiar unspecific quality. By existing only in time and not in space, music cannot be pointed to or pinned down; its ephemeral nature lends it the ability to mean differently to different people. As James Currie puts it, "Almost anything can attach itself to the same piece of music."[85] I have argued in this chapter that these composers have come to symbolize the ideal neoliberal individual, and yet they also have a unique ability to express ambivalence about that condition. Other members of the creative class—tech workers or management gurus, for example—may not have much of an opportunity to use their work to explore the confusion and melancholy that adhere to the neoliberalized, fragmented, solitary self; composers, simply by constructing music, can and do articulate such contradictions. They consciously inject their music with certain marketable elements, and yet, because it is music, their work opens the possibility to say more than they may intend. Even as we espouse the doctrine of constant flexible movement across boundaries, many of us experience a simultaneous growth of anxiety concerning it, perhaps an anxiety we struggle to articulate in words. Maybe this dissonance—between what is and what ought to be, or between what we are conditioned to think and what we nonetheless feel—is reflected in music that has attained the most market success within this new reality. If this is the case, it offers the possibility that music could be made more consciously oppositional to capitalist logics, an idea I return to in my conclusion.

Ultimately, I want to problematize neither survival tactics themselves nor the artists who use them. Rather, I've been concerned to dispel the emergent myth that these tactics are necessarily wonderful, liberating, and superior to other labor formations and past ways of making a living. Surely we can work pragmatically to survive within the oppressive reality of late capitalism without proclaiming, as Judd Greenstein does, that "this is a fantastic time to be a composer and performer," or insisting along with Claire Chase that ruthlessly competing with one another is good for the community. It is one thing to participate in flexible labor or entrepreneurial activities as a means of paying the rent; it is altogether another thing to actively participate in propagandizing those practices as progressive, exciting, and good for art and society. By loudly extolling the virtues of their flexible, precarious lives, by valorizing the liberation afforded by free market competition and the necessity to work hard for popular appeal, and by relentlessly eliding such popular appeal with vague affirmations of "democracy," these artists effectively reassure the rest of us that neoliberalism's promises are real, and that the glowing possibilities it holds out to us can be achieved with hard work and a creative spirit, despite all evidence to the contrary.

THREE

Opera and/as Gentrification

> Imagine getting in a car without knowing the destination. Sharing the car are singers, actors, and instrumentalists who draw you into a story. The car stops at an incredible site, where another chapter of the story commences—until another car pulls up, with different artists, depicting another chapter of the story. And so on, and so on, in a 90-minute journey throughout the unsuspecting city.[1]

This was the promotional copy advertising *Hopscotch*, a "mobile opera in 24 cars" that took Los Angeles by storm in the fall of 2015. Ticket purchasers were told to wait at a certain time and location; then they were picked up by a limousine and whisked to various historical areas of the city, where they briefly disembarked and encountered actors, singers, musicians, and dancers. The opera also took place inside the limos, as well as in elaborately timed encounters on the road. *Hopscotch*'s diverse musical and lyrical content mirrored the disjointed manner of its presentation: its music was composed by six different Los Angeles–based composers, and its texts were written by six different librettists. It tells a nonlinear story loosely based on the myth of Orpheus.

Hopscotch was the brainchild of the Los Angeles experimental opera company The Industry, which director Yuval Sharon founded in 2012 to "expand the traditional definition of opera."[2] In *Invisible Cities*, The Industry's previous opera (based on a score by the young Brooklyn composer Christopher Cerrone), musicians, singers, dancers, and an eleven-piece orchestra performed scenes throughout LA's Union Station, while headphone-wearing ticket holders as well as other onlookers walked through and around the action. *Invisible Cities* was fantastically complicated to arrange and successfully pull off, and *Hopscotch*, which followed in 2015, was even more so.

Both operas were critical successes. Reviews raved about The Industry's innovative approach to an old art form, and many critics noted that it had taken opera out of the stuffy, inaccessible opera house and "into the streets," where not only audience members but even passersby could be engaged in the creative process and drawn into a new appreciation for opera.[3] The Industry's creative directors along with arts journalists used words like *immersive, accessible,* and *participatory* in describing these operas, thus linking the works to the tradition of participatory art associated with the postmodern turn in the 1990s. They also emphasized these operas' relationship to the city of Los Angeles and the physical locations in which scenes took place.

Many reviews of *Hopscotch* and *Invisible Cities* noted that The Industry is innovating, disrupting, and redefining a historical art form, making it relevant for the twenty-first century. *Wired* magazine's Jeffrey Marlow touted *Invisible Cities* as "the leading edge of operatic innovation," *Los Angeles Magazine* warned readers that there was only "one last chance to see LA's wildly innovative car opera," and The Industry's submission to *Good* Maker (a platform allowing users to vote on awarding grants to projects proposed by artists, companies, and entrepreneurs) asserts that the company has hired some of "LA's most innovative composers" in creating an opera in keeping with "the spirit of innovation" that "has always defined LA."[4]

An important reason these operas were considered innovative was that they foregrounded their use of cutting-edge technology. *Invisible Cities* used wireless microphones and antennae in constructing the soundscape its audience heard on headphones, and *Hopscotch* used an even greater array of high tech, including video feeds, smartphones, and cars themselves. Both operas relied heavily on "technology partners," who donated equipment and, in the case of *Invisible Cities,* actually created new custom-built technology for the production (a managed antennae system, designed by the company Bexel).[5] In interviews, Sharon routinely praises his company's use of innovative technology; in an essay he wrote for KCET's *Artbound* blog, he promotes The Industry's collaboration with the Sennheiser Corporation, which donated headphones to both operas. Noting that "opera is exciting only when the eye listens and the ear sees—that is, when the collision and confusion of your senses ignites your imagination," Sharon points out that headphones offer us this experience every time we use them.[6] He observes elsewhere that while the musicians and singers might be thousands of feet apart, they play "perfectly in time with each other because they're connected across this huge distance with wireless technology."[7]

Sennheiser was the most prominent technology partner in both operas, burnishing its public image by aligning itself with classical music. On its website, Sennheiser declares, "This one-of-a-kind intersection of the classical arts and state-of-the-art technology was not possible even ten years ago, and would remain unrealizable without Sennheiser's pursuit of innovation and perfection." Its director of strategic marketing, Stefanie Reichert, notes that "our world is characterized by fast-paced, interactive communication," and that because of this, "consumers seek experiences that touch them in a much deeper and more meaningful level." *Invisible Cities*, she says, "showcases how innovative technology and cutting-edge artistic vision drives innovation in the arts."[8]

The Industry's operas are considered innovative not just because they rely on new technology but because they are perceived as participatory, as breaking down an out-of-touch historical art form and making it relevant to contemporary life, and because they don't take place within a certain highly marked space—that of the opera house. Alex Ross concludes his review of *Hopscotch* by saying that it "triumphantly escapes the genteel, fenced-off zone where opera is supposed to reside."[9] Unusual performance spaces are a major feature of immersive theater, which often embeds performers and audiences in giant, mazelike warehouses or other constructed environments, as opposed to the single stage and rows of seating that characterize conventional theaters. The Industry is part of a similar and much-lauded trend in contemporary classical music, toward alternative venues and staging.[10] In classical music discourse, the space in which this music has traditionally been performed has seemed to become a problem. Opera houses and concert halls, particularly in the United States, have taken on the perception of being cold bastions of wealth and cultural capital, spaces in which an untutored audience member might feel underdressed and self-conscious.[11] It is this perception of opera that The Industry is trying to combat with its unusual staging practices and its rousing rhetoric about taking opera out of the opera house and into the world.

The fact that *Hopscotch* and *Invisible Cities* took place in ordinary, unmarked spaces made them seem accessible to people who would not normally attend operas. But I question whether simply leaving the designated space of a certain type of building automatically makes opera more accessible to different kinds of people. Then, too, in its aestheticized jaunt throughout the city, *Hopscotch* came into conflict with residents of the gentrifying neighborhood of Boyle Heights, creating an uncomfortable tension between the opera's goal of engaging audiences and bringing art to the people, and the reality of disenfranchisement and displacement faced by locals in some of the opera's locations. Meanwhile, The Industry used common rhetorical devices to market and promote its operas as innovative, accessible, and participatory.

Participatory Art

Participatory art began being theorized in the 1990s as part of a postmodern turn away from fixed meanings and hierarchies of knowledge. Art inhabiting this category can take a number of forms, including installations intended to allow audiences to interact with a constructed environment; delegated art, in which the creation of an artwork is done by people other than the artist; or immersive theater, in which audience members move freely throughout a performance space, interacting with actors and one another, and even playing improvised roles in the narrative.[12] Such artistic practices were initially meant to challenge age-old assumptions and beliefs about art. Does an artwork have to be static and passively contemplated? Who controls the meaning of a given work of art? Do artistic performances have to take place in certain spaces? What is the nature of the relationship between artist and audience, or artwork and exhibition space, and should/could those relationships be transformed in some way?

In its most basic and ideal form, participatory art is meant to challenge what its practitioners feel is the traditionally passive role of audiences or viewers. This goal can manifest in many ways: participatory theater pieces, like those constructed by the London troupe Punchdrunk, may invite audience members to act, sing, walk around, ask questions, or help with equipment; interactive art installations like David Shrigley's *Life Model*, in which audience members create drawings that are then hung on the wall, require the input and activity of viewers in order to be fully realized; the installation *Do We Dream under the Same Sky* is a collaboration by an artist, a chef, and an architect, in which audiences cook, eat, and clean up after a meal and then discuss whether this experience constituted art; the sound collective Lucky Dragons builds musical instruments in the form of long electronic ropes or rocks fitted with electronic sensors, which they pass out into the audience, which then experiments with touching these objects, holding hands, and creating different collective space configurations with their bodies, all while the electronic current flowing through them changes the sounds coming from the speakers. In all these formulations, participatory art engages people socially in some way—it facilitates social interaction and encounter—and asks audience members to think about what art is, as well as what art should or could be.

The Industry uses some of the words and concepts of participatory art and immersive theater in describing what it does. Director Yuval Sharon cites Punchdrunk as an influence, for example, and many proclamations about audience engagement and immersive stagecraft can be found on The Industry's website. Reviews of *Hopscotch* and *Invisible Cities* also promote the idea that these works are participatory. The critic Michelle Lanz observes that these operas are part of a recent boom in experiential art, in which "audiences are frequently becoming participants," and the critic Jim Farber calls *Hopscotch* "an immersive, participatory environment."[13] However, this alignment represents a misunderstanding of participatory art, one that conflates "participatory" with "personalized" in ways that resonate with neoliberal conceptions of subjectivity and agency.[14]

In its most political spirit, participatory art is meant to create powerfully social situations that promote new relations between people and challenge the audience's traditional role as passive observer.[15] But *Hopscotch* and *Invisible Cities* did not actually allow audience members to be engaged with the performance or with one another. In fact, in several interviews Sharon and other producers discussed the difficulty of *preventing* audiences from interacting. In an interview with the journalist Dan Crane, Sharon said one of the problems performers had to address with these works was how to "deal with audience members who tried to sing or dance along with them."[16] Audience members' desire to engage—as well as the unpredictable reactions of passersby—were seen as interesting problems to solve, not as part of the guiding concept of the work. Thus, as in many projects conditioned by neoliberalism, The Industry rhetorically conjured up individual freedom and liberation while actually making sure audience members would restrain themselves from participating.

Furthermore, in both operas, Sharon instructed the performers to scrupulously avoid interacting with or even noticing audience members in any way. Reviews of *Hopscotch* often note how surreal it felt to be sitting, wholly unacknowledged, three feet away from someone singing at the top of their lungs. Farber wrote that the opera "deconstructs" the separation of performer and audience, which is indeed one of the goals of much participatory art. However, he goes on to say that "the performers, the singers, and musicians never acknowledge the presence of the audience . . . the audience is guided but encouraged to view the action from any angle they please." Rather than deconstructing the traditional separation of performer and audience, then, *Hopscotch* simply allowed viewers slightly more flexibility in choosing their observational vantage point than what is allowed in a traditional performance space. Similarly, several reviews say that these operas "break the fourth wall," but it is unclear what the critics mean when they use this phrase; "breaking the fourth wall" was a political technique of early twentieth-century avant-garde theater (associated with Bertolt Brecht's "epic theatre") that entails performers recognizing, speaking to, or otherwise acknowledging the audience (or looking or speaking directly into the camera, in a filmed work) as a means of jarring viewers with the revelation of the form's artifice.[17]

In The Industry's productions, then, the implementation of a few carefully chosen elements of personalization—audience members choosing where to stand while watching a performance, for example—stood in for the kind of mass social interactions that participatory art was initially meant to encourage. In this substitution of personalization for political action, The Industry's projects are in line with contemporary business theory, which holds that consumers are demanding more and more personalized products, spectacles, and services, and that businesses must become innovative and flexible in meeting this demand.

In interviews and reviews about The Industry's works, "participatory" is conflated with "personalized" again and again. The *Invisible Cities* website observes that the use of headphones enables audience members to have "a highly private experience in this public space"; thus, headphones actually sealed individual observers off from one another rather than encouraging "participation," and were approvingly advertised as doing so. In describing both these operas, Sharon noted that the experience of the work will be different for each audience member: with *Invisible Cities*, wherever you chose to stand or walk determined the strand of narrative or the dramatic angle you experienced; with *Hopscotch*, your perception of the opera was determined by whichever route you had chosen to go on when you bought your ticket. Both projects were advertised as "choose your own adventure" operas. But this is the language of personalized consumption, not social engagement. The art theorist Claire Bishop expresses concern with how this kind of rhetoric and these kinds of artworks begin to "dovetail with an 'experience economy,' the marketing strategy that seeks to replace goods and services with scripted and staged personal experiences."[18]

The Industry's innovations in audience experience are in keeping with other high-profile marketing trends that orchestras and opera companies around the country are undertaking, using new technology to personalize the classical music experience for consumers. Many orchestras have been trying to incorporate electronic gadgets like iPads and Google Glass into their presentation of classical music in an effort to make performances more appealing to today's consumers. The Boston Symphony Orchestra handed out iPads to personalize its performances by allowing audience members to surf through themed content while listening. The Philadelphia Orchestra has developed an app that lets audience members browse program notes during performances. The Sacramento Philharmonic offers "tweet seats," where audience members can interact with Philharmonic personnel on Twitter during concerts. "It's about making the experience more intimate," says Jesse Rosen, the president and CEO of the League of American Orchestras, noting that this is "something younger audiences really seem to value."[19]

But classical music institutions' embrace of personalized technologies represents an imperfect and uneasy alliance between very different cultural entities. Tech corporations like Cisco and Intel want to dramatically individualize every aspect of life; they market their innovations as enabling an ever more personalized consumer and work experience. Their products are designed to reduce the individual's need for other individuals, as I will discuss in the next chapter. Meanwhile, the production of classical music—especially of the kinds of large-scale operas and symphonies associated with major music institutions—remains a notably group-oriented and highly regimented affair. Many of the aforementioned marketing schemes seem to be designed to overcome the "problem" caused by this group orientation; while a symphony may need to be performed by hundreds of people (an activity that musicologists have long considered to be a resonant metaphor for social practice), individual audience members ought to be able to encounter that group labor in a highly personalized environment.

One of the reasons *Hopscotch* was called "participatory" had to do with how it was produced. While the actual opera took place on each of the three limousine routes, video of it was also live streamed to a temporary viewing station called "the Hub," which had been built by architecture students at the Southern California Institute of Architecture. At the Hub, people could watch streams from each of the opera's three routes for free, using video screens and headphones donated by Sennheiser. This meant that at each of the opera's locations, a producer handed an audience member a cell phone with instructions to shoot video of the performance, so that it could be live streamed to the audience at the Hub. The Industry's executives cited this aspect of the opera's performance as one reason *Hopscotch* was innovative and participatory, and it was a major feature in the company's fund-raising activities—many grant-making organizations require that a project offer a certain number of free tickets or that its organizers perform a certain amount of community outreach.

Yuval Sharon said he got the idea for the Hub because he was thinking about how people interact with the world using their phones, but it also conveniently enabled video content to be generated by unpaid labor. The art theorist Jen Harvie argues that the contemporary trend toward "delegated" art (like that made by Andy Warhol or Jeff Koons, whose ideas are realized and produced by others) raises many potential problems, among them the devaluation of expertise, lost jobs for trained artists, and the naturalization of labor precarity in the production of art.[20] This facet of *Hopscotch* was participatory in the literal sense of the term, but it is strange that audience members who had paid $125 to see an opera were then asked to produce a document of the event to be consumed for free by others. The phenomenon of audience members doing the unpaid labor of providing live streamed video models the contemporary figure of the "prosumer" that is increasingly encouraged and required under neoliberalism. Prosumers are people who produce what they want to consume.[21] Scholars of neoliberalism, media, and the internet have written extensively about the free labor that prosumers contribute to corporations.[22] The Industry positioned the Hub as a major reason *Hopscotch* was accessible and intended for everyone; like social media, anyone could join, and the content provided was user generated.

The rhetoric of accessibility swirls around The Industry's projects and contributes to their perception as socially engaged, participatory art. Reviews of *Hopscotch* and *Invisible Cities* applaud The Industry for making opera "for the masses" or "for everyone."[23] In a promotional video, Sharon says that his operas have taken opera out of its traditional setting within a building and "into the public sphere." On its Maker web page for *Hopscotch*, The Industry states that the event "will benefit all of LA County," and that the opera company seeks to make its work "accessible to as wide an audience as possible in truly compelling ways."[24] Yet these events were unusually exclusive, even for opera. Furthermore, despite The Industry's claims to accessibility, this exclusivity was obviously a major selling point in its marketing efforts.

The number of people who could experience *Hopscotch* was very limited. Four audience members fit in each limousine, and eight limousines traversed each of the three performance routes on each day of the opera's run. Thus, not counting the nonpaying audience watching amateur cell phone video at the Hub, ninety-six people could see a given performance of *Hopscotch*. By contrast, the LA Opera's Dorothy Chandler Pavilion—the kind of traditional venue The Industry is rejecting in its quest for greater accessibility—has a seating capacity of 3,156. This means that a single performance of the LA Opera can be seen by almost thirty-three times as many people as could view a single performance of *Hopscotch*. The British opera director Netia Jones discussed the exclusivity the *Hopscotch* staging practice necessitated, saying that "inevitably you're limiting the amount of audience that can actually experience the event—which makes it very special for the audience that are in that lucky select few, but it does become a little perverse in terms of what's going into it and who's going to witness it in the end."[25] On the *Hopscotch* donor page, in fact, this exclusivity is highlighted: donors are assured that "tickets for *Hopscotch* will be extremely limited, and priority access will be given to donors."[26] Also, tickets were expensive, at $125 for a full route and $155 for a route plus the finale, which took place at the Hub. By contrast, the LA Opera—like all traditional music institutions—offers tiered pricing, and tickets can cost as little as ten or twenty dollars.

The Industry's rhetoric of inclusion came into conflict with the actual exclusivity of its operas in less obvious ways as well. The headphones that personalized *Invisible Cities* for individual audience members also isolated them and set them apart from the regular citizens occupying the train station. This sense of being set apart was made even more explicit in *Hopscotch*, where audience members were chauffeured around the city in limousines with tinted windows. These two observational strategies—the headphones and the limousines—literally separated audience members from one another and from other members of the public spaces in which these works took place.

Similarly, reviews of these works often hint at a terminology of exclusion in describing the nonpaying passersby who encountered the operatic scenes. Dan Crane wrote about the "confounded commuters" who tried to navigate around the performers in *Invisible Cities*. Alex Ross also described these "unsuspecting commuters," as well as the "tourists" who gazed in confusion at the "cryptic doings" at *Hopscotch*'s Bradbury Building site, and the many people who "wandered" into the background of scenes. Michelle Lanz wrote that *Hopscotch* "will also transform its random passers-by into an unwitting audience," and Jim Farber noted that *Invisible Cities* "combined audience members, singers, musicians and dancers with unsuspecting travelers and the city's itinerant homeless."[27]

It is clear from reviews and from The Industry's fund-raising rhetoric that these events' exclusivity—in the sense that participation in them enabled members of the paying audience to feel special and knowledgeable in comparison with the tourists and homeless people wandering around in the background—was a selling point and part of the reason these works received so much attention. In interviews, Sharon says he believes that engaging a wider community in this accidental way has the potential to expand the audience for all opera. I would argue, however, that trying to engage new audiences by involving them as extras without their knowledge or consent—without even explaining what it is they're participating in—is not in keeping with the revolutionary aims of many artists who make participatory work.

Hopscotch and the Gentrification of Boyle Heights

Examining *Hopscotch*—and The Industry's stated intentions regarding the project—alongside the history of gentrification in Los Angeles brings many of the opera's neoliberal contradictions to light. One of the sites in which *Hopscotch* took place was Hollenbeck Park, located in the Boyle Heights neighborhood of East Los Angeles. During the first half of the twentieth century, Boyle Heights was a thriving manufacturing zone as well as one of the most ethnically and racially diverse neighborhoods in the United States. It had large populations of Jewish, Russian, Portuguese, Japanese, and Latinx people; during World War II it was known as the Ellis Island of the West Coast. The neighborhood's demographics changed slowly, and for a number of reasons. During World War II, most of Boyle Heights's Japanese-American inhabitants were forcibly removed and placed in internment camps, which deeply unsettled the social foundation of the neighborhood.[28] Because of its being a racially diverse, working-class neighborhood, Boyle Heights was also redlined by financial institutions, making it difficult for residents to become homeowners.[29] Redlining policies in the first half of the century targeted Jewish people just as brutally as they did African American and Latinx people, but over time, racist policies against Jews loosened. Once they were allowed to purchase homes in other neighborhoods, most Jewish residents left Boyle Heights, as lending policies at the time made it impossible to buy property there. By contrast, the ongoing redlining of the Latinx population prevented its migration to other parts of the city, and so by the late 1960s Boyle Heights was predominantly poor or working class and Latinx, which it remains to this day (as of the 2011 census, Boyle Heights was 95 percent Latinx, and its median household income was $33,235).[30]

In *Capital*, Marx wrote about the ceaseless "improvements" of towns that "drive the poor away into even worse and more crowded corners."[31] This process, which Marx dubbed "expropriation," allowed for the consolidation of capitalist enterprise; across the sixteenth century, wealthy English farmers brutally ejected thousands of peasants from their homes and burned down their villages in order to turn the land into massive sheep pastures with only a few families living on them. Marx presents these harrowing descriptions of mass expropriation as a rebuke of Adam Smith's utopian vision of the liberty guaranteed by market exchange. He also notes that while at first such expropriation was illegal—Henry VII tried to put a stop to it early on, not only because it was immoral but because it was destabilizing the English economy by pauperizing vast swaths of the population—it soon became legalized and officially carried out by the state.

Contemporary processes of gentrification, dispossession, and homelessness need to be understood within this vast history. While Marx believed that this kind of "primitive accumulation" was a bounded aspect of the prehistory of capitalism, contemporary scholars like Silvia Federici and David Harvey have argued persuasively that it is rather a constant and ongoing feature of capitalism in all the historical forms it has taken.[32] Today, some of the means of expropriation may have changed, but the effect is the same: the expulsion of the poor from their homes and their means of subsistence, which then liberates property to make it useful for capital.

The term *gentrification* was coined in 1964 by the British sociologist Ruth Glass, who used it to describe what was happening in parts of London at that time.[33] Gentrification defines a process of urban transformation in which a long-term population of poor or working-class people, often but not always members of an ethnic or racial minority, is displaced by an incoming population that is middle or upper class and predominantly white. Gentrification is most commonly associated with the influx of wealthier residents and upscale businesses that heralds a neighborhood's "up and coming" status, but it actually begins decades earlier, when businesses and the city government systematically disinvest from the area. Business disinvestment takes the form of deindustrialization, as manufacturers move factories and warehouses away (often overseas), resulting in local job loss as well as devaluation of abandoned industrial property, which is left to deteriorate. City disinvestment takes a number of forms, from redlining to unfixed potholes to the closing of schools and hospitals. Often, cities rezone these areas to allow the construction of hazardous waste facilities,[34] and they sometimes break up and seal off an area with new freeway construction.[35]

Boyle Heights has experienced all the major processes identified with gentrification from the beginning of the twentieth century to the present day. First redlined, then cut off from city life by the construction of the East Los Angeles Freeway Exchange (which I will discuss below), in the 1960s the neighborhood was also deindustrialized, which generated massive unemployment and general urban decay. Since the 1980s, crime waves, drug addiction, and gang violence have plagued the area.

At such a point in a gentrifying neighborhood's history, the presence of artists there becomes important. Artists play a major role in the stage of contemporary gentrification that urban planners euphemistically call "renewal": they move into blighted zones in search of affordable housing and cheap studio space, which they find in the abandoned warehouses and factories of deindustrialized urban areas.[36] Once enough artists have moved in, demonstrating the new "vibrancy" of the area, banks lift redlining policies, and the city redirects municipal funds into that neighborhood—fixing potholes, planting trees, and building bike lanes. It can now be rebranded and sold as "up and coming" to corporate developers as well as "creatives," a relatively new term encompassing a wide variety of practices, from the actual creation of art to management and tech.[37] Following the recommendations of the urban studies scholar Richard Florida, who wrote the 2002 book *The Rise of the Creative Class*,[38] many US cities actively encourage artists to move into economically struggling neighborhoods (by offering discounted rent on studio spaces and various other incentives), hoping that corporate developers and private investment will follow.[39] The influx of predominantly white, highly educated upper-income residents, as well as the city's new encouragement of home ownership and business, causes property values to rise and landlords to raise the rent. In turn, property taxes rise, and the city begins directing more and more municipal resources at the now-profitable neighborhood. The municipal government may also implement new policing strategies or laws regarding public nuisances and loitering, establishing which kinds of people may inhabit these newly vibrant spaces.[40]

New art galleries began popping up in the abandoned warehouses and factory spaces peppering Boyle Heights in the early 2000s, and property values in the area have been inexorably rising ever since. Now that artists have moved in, the City of Los Angeles has identified that neighborhood as an area ripe for renewal, and has begun directing municipal resources toward it. In 2009 the city spent $31 million on a new police station on First Street; Los Angeles Metro is constructing a new light rail connection corridor that would link the neighborhood to more affluent parts of the city; and the Sixth Street Bridge, which connects Boyle Heights to the downtown arts district and had been a crumbling, graffiti-covered hazard for years, was demolished in early 2016 to make way for a gleaming new structure replete with bike and pedestrian access, which will cost the city $428 million.[41] The *Los Angeles Times* declared the new bridge to be "better suited to a gentrifying, forward-looking downtown" than the old one, noting that it "looks tailor-made for the hipster renaissance."[42] The downtown arts district itself was part of LA's infamous Skid Row until very recently. But the artists who moved there in the 1970s and 1980s to take advantage of abandoned warehouses are long gone, and their studios have become high-priced luxury condos.[43]

These changes have made the housing situation in Boyle Heights predictably dire for its original inhabitants, a group that typically disappears in the final stages of gentrification. Home owners may sell their property at a profit and move of their own accord, although historic redlining policies as well as generations of impoverishment mean it is much more likely that the longtime residents are renters, who become unable to pay the higher rent the renewed neighborhood can now demand. These residents may also no longer feel welcome in the changed community.[44]

Additionally, once the renewal stage of gentrification has begun, cities often sell public housing to corporate real estate firms as part of a shift of public resources away from social services and toward marketing and tourism; this typically results in the loss of hundreds of rent-controlled or otherwise affordable housing units. In Boyle Heights, the historic Wyvernwood Housing Projects have become the focus of conflict between locals resisting displacement and the forces of corporate investment. Wyvernwood, built in 1939 as part of a nationwide public housing effort and providing 1,175 rent-controlled housing units to the area, is about to be torn down and replaced by an immense complex of condos, parks, offices, and retail space. The Miami-based real estate investment firm Fifteen Group is responsible for the New Wyvernwood plan, and on its website it seeks to assuage fears of displacement, proclaiming that 15 percent of the new units will qualify as affordable housing. Not only would this development represent a neoliberal process in which city-funded social services are outsourced to private for-profit firms, it would also represent a devastating loss of housing stock to the poor and working-class residents of Boyle Heights; if the firm is successful in building this development, a complex that once offered 1,175 affordable, rent-controlled units of housing would then offer around 600.[45]

Boyle Heights has been resisting these forces of gentrification and displacement with a certain degree of success, due partially to residents' savvy observation of what has happened in other African American and Latinx areas of Los Angeles, but also to the fact that the neighborhood has been a hotbed of leftist activism for decades. In the 1930s, when the Home Owners' Loan Corporation began giving race-based grades to Los

Angeles's neighborhoods in order to determine its redlining strategies, it gave Boyle Heights a D, and declared it to be "a 'melting pot' area, literally honeycombed with diverse and subversive racial elements."[46] Today, Boyle Heights is home to many revolutionary activist groups with many different orientations—Marxist, Maoist, feminist, and so on—as well as coalitions of mothers who have been working since the 1980s to resolve gang violence within the community. In recent years, groups like Union de Vecinos, Ovarian Psychos Brigade, and Serve the People LA along with newer hybrid groups like Defend Boyle Heights and the Boyle Heights Alliance against Artwashing and Displacement have begun organizing, joining together to resist the increasingly powerful gentrifying processes that they feel are transforming their community in harmful ways and without their input or consent. In 2014 an agent with a real estate firm called Adaptive Realty papered Boyle Heights with fliers advertising a bicycle tour of attractive properties in the area followed by "artisanal snacks." The company was protested so furiously and with such sustained intensity by locals that the tour was canceled.[47]

Activists accuse the city of widely disinvesting from the neighborhood during the decades when local residents were fighting desperately for jobs, schools, and getting drugs off the streets, and they say that the city is now investing resources in Boyle Heights only because rich white people are moving in. "The position of the community," wrote Serve the People LA in a July 18, 2016, Tumblr post, is that

> art galleries and other high-end businesses are a key factor in the speculative development of neighborhoods like Boyle Heights. These galleries help to establish the perception among investors than [sic] an area is "up-and-coming" or is being "revitalized" into a place hospitable to the super-wealthy, further driving investment in the area and objectively increasing the property values in an area overwhelmingly populated by renters who will see the material effect of this increase in property value as an increase in their rents and ultimately the total loss of affordable housing options.[48]

This statement does not outline a leftist conspiracy theory; it simply describes the exact process that city planners and consultants like Richard Florida openly and proudly work to encourage. The gallery PSSST, which opened in 2016 thanks to an anonymous donor who purchased and renovated a warehouse at a cost of $2 million and gave the gallery a twenty-year rent-free lease, has particularly concerned activists in Boyle Heights. As Defend Boyle Heights states on its blog, "Behind all new art galleries in the so-called arts district of Boyle Heights are developers, real estate agents and sell-out city officials. . . . Here, art is used as a smokescreen to cover up the horrors of capitalism"[49] In the summer of 2017, after sustained community protests, the PSSST Gallery closed.

For at least a decade, artists and art galleries have been a target for anti-gentrification activism in Boyle Heights, which also means that the activists are often criticized for being "anti-art" or, ironically, resisting diversity.[50] As I mentioned above, the neighborhood was once more diverse than any other in the United States, but racist, classist municipal and corporate policies destroyed that diversity in order to devalue the area for profitable resale to wealthy white people and corporate developers.[51] Furthermore, activists point out that Boyle Heights already has a long and rich artistic tradition—the area is known for its large, historically informed murals, for example, and is home to numerous activist art collectives—and that locals do not require wealthy outsiders to "give" art to them. "Artists don't have to be pawns in the schemes of city developers," Defend Boyle Heights declared on its blog. "Art is a weapon. Let's point it at developers instead of community."[52] Defend Boyle Heights, the Boyle Heights Alliance against Artwashing and Displacement, and other activist groups say they have one simple demand, which is that all nonpolitically active artists leave, and all art galleries immediately close so that the community can use those spaces for emergency housing and job training. This was the political situation into which *Hopscotch*'s fleet of limousines drove in October of 2015.

The complexity of *Hopscotch*'s logistics was epic. The opera's routes wound throughout a city legendary for its traffic, yet countless dramatic moments had to be timed with incredible precision. Actors, singers, and musicians had to perform short scenes repeatedly and in sync with one another despite being separated by distance, and despite not ever being quite sure when a given limousine would arrive at a given location. *Hopscotch*'s composers built "vamping" segments into the music so that performers could play for time if a limo got stuck in traffic or otherwise delayed. Because the opera's scenes took place in sites all around the city, which had not been closed down or blocked off in any way, singers and actors performed amid tangles of everyday activity—people walking dogs or eating lunch, children playing. For some scenes, audiences had to walk from place to place, which created another timing complication. It is not surprising that almost every review of *Hopscotch* devoted significant space to marveling over the technical complexity and enormous scale of the project, with some going so far as to call it "Wagnerian."

To pull off this elaborate undertaking, The Industry required the cooperation of dozens of municipal and neighborhood entities, like the Department of Cultural Affairs, the Department of Transportation, the Mayor's Office, the Department of Recreation and Parks, the Army Corps of Engineers, and the Home Owners' Association of the Toy Factory Lofts, new luxury housing in a restored 1924 factory in LA's warehouse district. Yet although The Industry worked with a wide variety of offices, neighborhood coalitions, businesses, and city departments in planning *Hopscotch*, the company does not appear to have consulted with the Boyle Heights community. Consequently, residents were surprised and bewildered on October 24 when limousines began pulling up to Hollenbeck Park and people began singing, dancing, and shooting cell phone video.[53]

Over several performances, local activist groups mobilized to put increasing pressure on the opera and its audience members. Serve the People LA was the primary group involved in the protests, which began with heckling. Then, activists used bread to lure ducks from the Hollenbeck Park pond into the operatic scene being staged in the nearby gazebo, in hopes that their loud quacking would interrupt the performance (from the group's blog: "A spin on Malcolm X's 'by any means necessary.' By any quacks necessary"[54]). At what proved to be the opera's final Hollenbeck Park performance, local groups rallied and protested loudly, carrying signs that read "Your 'Art' Is Displacing People of Color #AntiGentrification." The *Hopscotch* performers soldiered on for a while, but when the marching band walked over from nearby Roosevelt High School and began playing in an effort to drown the opera out, they conceded defeat and left the park, the limousine surrounded by jeering protesters.[55]

Representing Diversity

Hopscotch was written by six composers and six librettists; musically, it deploys a plethora of styles, and its sections of dialogue are stylistically diverse as well. Some numbers sound like folk songs, employing acoustic guitar or accordion along with straight-tone singing; others are more conventionally operatic and virtuosic. Interspersed among the opera's sung scenes are sequences of pensive spoken narration, in which different actors provide details of characters' backstories and motivations. There are also repetitive "vamping" gestures peppering the sonic landscape; it is easy to imagine these sections being extended indefinitely if a limousine were caught in a snarl of traffic.

The plot of *Hopscotch* transposes the myth of Orpheus into contemporary Los Angeles, and it foregrounds the kind of multicultural diversity LA is known for. One of the opera's main characters is Lucha, a Latinx woman whom we meet at different points in her life; though many different singers and actors of different ages (and ethnicities) portray her, she is always recognizable, thanks to her yellow dress. In "Lucha's Quinceañera Song," composed by David Rosenboom, we hear Lucha reflecting on her life and her family history as she prepares for adulthood. This is a newly composed folk song, with acoustic, vaguely flamenco-style guitar accompaniment, straight-tone singing, and a repetitive verse-refrain structure. The verses are in English, and describe Lucha's maternal ancestry: her grandmother's life in Mexico; her mother's immigration to the United States to forge a new life. In between each verse, Lucha sings a Spanish refrain: "Porque ahora, soy mujer."

Hopscotch insistently emphasizes a type of marketable multiculturalism similar to the one I diagnosed in the YouTube Symphony Orchestra performance (chapter 1). The opera is about a Latinx woman, bits of its libretto are in Spanish, and it takes place in Los Angeles, a city celebrated for its diversity. These aspects contribute to The Industry's ability to market itself as a vibrant, relevant part of the real world, in contrast with the elitist traditional opera houses it has vacated. *Hopscotch* also celebrates contemporary progressive political resistance. Lucha's parents are political activists—"My mother turned fifteen at a protest for migrant rights," she sings in the *quinceañera* song—and their illegal immigration to the United States is depicted sympathetically: "It was the future they'd been dreaming of, so they danced that night beneath a full moon sky." Just as the YTSO's praise of its own diversity was belied by its actual programming and the makeup of its orchestra, however, *Hopscotch*'s rhetorical celebration of Latinx Los Angeles came into conflict with actual Latinx residents of the city.

The Industry's promotional rhetoric presents a vague notion that music is an undifferentiated social good; simply by "bringing" an opera "about Los Angeles" into the various neighborhoods of the city, its marketing materials assert that the company is undertaking positive political action. Boyle Heights activists also discuss this rhetorical ploy; on Defend Boyle Heights's blog, for example, they note that gallerists and developers talk about art's social benefits in vague, even metaphysical terms, when in reality the neighborhood residents require concrete things like shelter and food.

The vagueness of this conception of art's social benefit can also be seen in the awkwardness of the opera's representational politics: rather than taking an interest in what the actual people of Boyle Heights say they want—which is for white artists to leave them alone—The Industry seemed to believe it was being a good political ally simply by operatically representing elements of Latinx culture. Serve the People LA was specifically enraged by this element of *Hopscotch*, writing on its blog that the scene in Hollenbeck Park was an "exclusively white" performance complete with "white *paleteros* banging on the *paletero* cart like a drum, and other sights of bourgeois absurdity." STPLA said that residents "complained that they couldn't understand what the singers were singing about," and also that the vendors at the park—"predominately Mexican immigrant women"—said that no one involved in *Hopscotch* purchased any of their products; instead, audience members were given ice creams from the prop-*paletero* cart.[56] The opera was meant to serve a social good by exposing people to art, yet in its plot and staging it produced Latinx culture as a commodity it could sell to wealthy, outsider audience members.

Gentrification and Car Culture

The Industry strongly associates itself with a very particular space: the city of Los Angeles. As previously mentioned, it claimed that *Hopscotch* would benefit all LA County, and Yuval Sharon noted that he wanted to introduce people to a Los Angeles they might never have known existed. The fact that audience members were driven in cars was also emphasized as being highly site specific: "What could be more LA than an opera that takes place in a car?" asks Dan Crane. The opera's plot also gives prominence to car culture and driving as signal features of Angeleno subjectivity. A narrator describes Lucha's coming of age specifically in terms of her mastery of the Los Angeles freeway system: "Lucha can feel herself moving, her hands on the car's steering wheel. Her life is taking shape. She's twenty-six, and she's from Los Angeles. She knows these roads. She knows what exits to take, what sections of freeway to avoid."[57]

But the fact that The Industry entered Boyle Heights in limousines in order to perform an opera about freeways and cars is the final irony with respect to that neighborhood. In a research report commissioned by the Poverty and Race Research Action Council in 2002, the historian Raymond Mohl presents an array of data proving that "official housing and highway policies, taken together, have helped to produce the much more intensely concentrated and racially segregated landscapes of contemporary urban America."[58] Boyle Heights is the location of the largest freeway interchange in the world; seven different freeways converge there, creating a nearly perfect rectangle enclosing the entire neighborhood. Gilbert Estrada demonstrates the many ways that the city of LA used the construction of the freeway system to deliberately reinforce racial segregation and disenfranchise working-class African American and Latinx areas.[59] In Boyle Heights alone, around two thousand homes were demolished for freeway construction, and the communal space of Hollenbeck Park is now dissected by a ten-lane stretch of the I-5 and I-10 freeways. The interchange, as well as the minimal public transportation service to the area, has made it difficult for locals to move freely throughout the city, thus limiting where they can work. Estrada also presents a disheartening list of "accommodations" that the Los Angeles Highway Commission made to affluent white neighborhoods— rerouting the freeway so that it would not destroy churches, landmarks, or parks, and providing expensive landscaping to dampen the effects of freeway noise on the Hollywood Bowl—and contrasts these with the lack of accommodations given to East LA areas, in which churches, parks, and landmarks were bulldozed freely. Not only did the freeways literally tear up Boyle Heights, displacing families and disrupting communities, but they also contributed to its economic downturn and racial homogeneity: Eric Avila observes that "the age of the freeway" turned Boyle Heights into one of the United States' many "isolated centers of racialized poverty."[60]

In a promotional video for *Hopscotch*, Yuval Sharon is shown driving a car while talking to the camera. "This is really the way that most of us experience Los Angeles," he says, "by driving through it and listening to our own music on the radio, and living in our, kind of, own private world."[61] This was the experience he wanted to recreate and "explode" with *Hopscotch*, using "all of the city as our backdrop." The kind of language Sharon and many critics deployed in describing the opera reveals assumptions about the experience of living in Los Angeles that are highly colored by class: Sharon believes that "most of us" experience that city by driving around it in private cars, while in reality huge numbers of Angelenos are too poor to own cars, or are not legal citizens of the United States, and are not allowed to own registered vehicles. Then there are those who are homeless, perhaps living in cars. Another irony is contained in the opera's plot: on the way to her *quinceañera* celebration, Lucha is orphaned when her parents are struck and killed by a car. The backstory of the opera's main character serves as a metaphor for what car culture has done to many of the working-class and nonwhite people who live in Los Angeles.

Gentrification Discourses

Decades of media narratives have covered up municipal and corporate complicity in the collapse of poor and/or minority neighborhoods and presented socioeconomic downturn as the fault of lazy residents who refuse to work for a living.[62] These narratives are neoliberal constructions, meant to demonstrate that hard work and self-reliance are the sole means not only of attaining success but of being a morally upstanding person, as well as reinforce the corresponding assumption that economic failure is the result of moral failure. One of the most prominent features of neoliberal policy is its erosion of social services and any other city investment in helping the poor. Milton Friedman was vituperative in his criticism of any state initiative meant to alleviate housing difficulties for the poor, for example; included in his long list of governmental activities that "cannot be justified" are rent control, enforcement of a legal minimum wage, "so-called 'public housing,'" and all other housing subsidy programs.[63]

From the neoliberal point of view, poverty is never the fault of structural inequalities or the decisions businesses or cities make (among others, outsourcing manufacturing jobs overseas or redlining individuals because of their race); rather, individual poor people have simply failed to maximize their potential in changing with the times. Adopting an attitude that dehumanizes the poor and castigates them as the makers of their own demise, cities and developers can easily package the displacement gentrification causes with words like *renewal*, *renaissance*, and *rebirth*. As the gentrification scholar Loretta Lees notes, while public policy used to ensure some degree of protection for vulnerable populations, since the 1980s it has been increasingly imbued with the profit motive. Now, urban planners, policy makers, businesses, and even regular citizens see gentrification "as a positive result of a healthy real estate market, and they understand 'the market' as the solution, not a problem."[64]

Likewise, in the pro-gentrification argument that gentrification promotes diversity, progressive politics transmutes into market logic. Richard Florida's city plans treat racial, ethnic, and sexual diversity as assets that add value to an area in the form of potential future corporate investment, but not because they are good on their own merits (he famously developed a "gay index" that cities can use to assess which areas are ready for investment). Additionally, the reason gentrification supposedly promotes diversity is because it entails wealthier white people moving into racially or ethnically homogenous neighborhoods. The argument that this represents healthy "social mixing" is disingenuous for two reasons: first, as the urban studies scholar Nick Blomley observes, if social mixing is so good for society, then surely cities ought to make it possible for poor people of color to move into rich white neighborhoods, instead of only the other way around;[65] and second, since the gentrification process begins with a significant degree of economic and racial segregation more or less intentionally implemented at the municipal level, it is cruelly ahistorical to insist that municipal policies encouraging wealthy white people to move into those previously segregated areas represent a purely progressive impulse toward greater diversity. Finally, as the urban studies scholar Tom Slater points out, the rhetorical promotion of the social mixing that gentrification causes actually "deflects criticism" of its more harmful processes.[66] Because social mixing is so self-evidently good, residents who complain of white people colonizing their neighborhoods come under fire for being obstacles to diversity or even "reverse racists."[67]

The sociologist Malcolm Miles argues that members of Florida's creative class do the free labor of rebranding neighborhoods and cities as prosperous, global zones of creativity and innovation. For Miles, gentrifying artists work—perhaps unintentionally—to generate "a dominant image of a city in which signs of conflict are erased in favour of the glitzy, spectacular and supposedly non-contentious signs of culture and innovation."[68] By misappropriating political and even revolutionary ideas from participatory art traditions, The Industry's marketing materials and the critics who support its operas do just that. The company presented *Hopscotch* as engaging in an open and participatory fashion with the city of Los Angeles, but in practice the event was exclusive, it isolated its audience members from performers and from one another, and it presented just the sort of glitzy branding spectacle Miles accuses gentrifying artists of constructing.

Hopscotch was meant to display the city to audience members, asking them to look at neighborhoods and locations with fresh eyes. The opera's scenes took place in visually or historically striking areas of Los Angeles, from the roof of the Toy Factory Lofts, to the inside of the historic Bradbury Building, to Chinatown, to Boyle Heights. "I'm proud of this celebration of our city," said costume designer Ann Closs-Farley. "These routes show off the depth and history of the place, they show how diverse our communities are and how much art there is on the street."[69]

Yet while *Hopscotch* may have shown audience members areas of Los Angeles they had never visited before, this did not necessarily mean that it engaged in an intentionally political way with space, or with ideas about how space is constructed, bounded, and inhabited. While all space-based art by necessity asks us to think about space, it does not all do so in a productively oppositional manner. Noting that "space is socially contested," Jen Harvie goes so far as to argue that some space-based art actually contributes to "social ghettoization" by privileging the already privileged, and using art to cover up the disenfranchisement of others.[70] *Hopscotch* inadvertently aestheticized and glorified the processes of gentrification that are currently displacing many working-class and minority communities from some of the very areas the opera was meant to celebrate. The role that art and artists play in gentrification is a complicated and ambivalent one, and many artists have engaged with this issue in their work. But *Hopscotch* did not do this, and instead simply foregrounded inequality by aestheticizing the artist's colonization of blighted areas.

The Industry presented *Hopscotch* as an opera for everyone, an opera that would show Los Angeles to itself, an opera that would take art out of the exclusive, moribund zone of the opera house and deliver it out into the real world. Like its rhetoric of participation, though, The Industry's lofty claims about space and community disguised a biased worldview and a consumer-oriented attitude toward space. Boyle Heights residents were, quite evidently, not part of the "everyone" the opera was intended to reach; rather, they served as a backdrop, the kind of local color Richard Florida prizes for its attractiveness to web developers and boutique shop owners. This aesthetic invisibility mirrors the geographical and political invisibility of Boyle Heights.

Conclusion: The Future of Opera

In The Industry's self-descriptions as well as in critical reviews of its productions, once-powerful concepts from participatory art movements and even earlier avant-garde practices are reconfigured as advertisements for the personalized consumption these works encourage. Yuval Sharon cites the Marxist revolutionary avant-garde intellectual Guy Debord as a major influence on works like *Hopscotch*, for example, but detaches Debord's keywords from his anticapitalist politics and practices.

These rhetorical appropriations represent the same sort of historical misunderstanding that allows commentators to paint gentrification as good for the poor. The artists and thinkers who developed revolutionary ideas about art in past eras were concerned with political issues like democracy, racism, the commodification of art, and the degrading effects of capitalism on social life. When keywords from these movements are appropriated and used to make corporations look good, or to make the status quo appear progressive, or to enable corporations to displace poor people from their homes, or to allow an opera company with millions of dollars of private and corporate funding and the backing of one of the biggest cities in the world to claim it operates under "an absolutely do-it-yourself spirit," this reveals how deeply the infiltration of capitalist logic has penetrated our understanding of art and society.[71]

The Industry's success—both critical and economic—is meaningful with respect to the neoliberal reinvention of ideas about classical music that is currently under way in the United States. In the company's self-promotion as well as in its critical reception, we can see the workings of a neoliberal ideology that emphasizes personalized consumption at the expense of civic responsibility or collective identification. One opera company does not represent the totality of operatic practices in the United States today, but The Industry is widely acclaimed as "the future of opera," and has successfully attained funding and praise from some of the most august arts institutions in the world.[72] The LA Philharmonic recently created a new "Artist-Collaborator" position and granted it to Sharon as a three-year appointment, and in 2018 he was awarded a fellowship by the MacArthur Foundation.[73] While The Industry is not representative of all new music collectives working in the United States today, the fact that its practices and self-positioning have been so richly rewarded by wealthy institutions and donors, and applauded by arts journalists, tells us something about the condition of—and expectations for—art in contemporary American society. It is not so much the practices themselves as the discursive formulations of their praise and promotion that I find dangerous, given neoliberal rationality's ever-deeper infiltration of our lives and worldviews.

The Industry and the arts journalists who heralded it very likely did not intend the kind of complicities I have depicted here, but it is this very lack of intention that emphasizes how insidiously neoliberal values have crept into the production and appreciation of art. Defend Boyle Heights activists themselves acknowledge in a blog post that individual artists are "low-intensity" gentrifiers compared with "high-intensity" gentrifiers like Fifteen Group or the city of Los Angeles itself, and they recognize that artists "behave with ignorance" rather than with malice. Nonetheless, as Dont Rhine, a founder of the radical sound-art collective Ultra-Red, noted in an interview about Boyle Heights, "We don't have time for artists to figure out how they feel."[74] Individual artists (like individual white people, or individual rich or middle-class people), regardless of their personal politics, goals, hopes, or community orientations, do play a pivotal role in drawing corporate and municipal resources into poor and minority communities, and—as commentators from Richard Florida to the revolutionaries of Serve the People LA point out—this new investment causes rents to rise and cultures to change, ultimately leading to the displacement of people who increasingly have nowhere to go. The urban studies scholar Neil Smith foresees a future in which working-class residents are priced all the way out of cities and into the deep suburbs originally built as refuges from them.[75]

Artists, like all citizens, must find ways of supporting themselves within the framework of their society, and attaching artistic claims to corporate values is currently one way of achieving success. I would suggest, however, that artists—again, like all citizens—have a responsibility to confront the role they sometimes play in gentrification and other neoliberalization processes. Art can indeed be a weapon—the Boyle Heights protesters certainly experienced *Hopscotch* as an existential as well as a physical threat—and I would submit that part of practicing thoughtful citizenship under neoliberalism entails acknowledging this fact, as well as clearly identifying what such a weapon ought (and ought not) to be aimed toward.

FOUR

Intel Beethoven: The New Spirit of Classical Music

In November 2015 at the Flugplatz Ahrenlohe, an airport in Tornesch, Germany, the Intel Corporation set a world record. As a live audience watched, technicians launched one hundred unmanned drones into the air, where they performed a synchronized light show meant to mimic a fireworks display. Representatives from Guinness World Records were present and officially decreed that the event—which was called Drone 100—had flown the "Most Unmanned Aerial Vehicles airborne simultaneously."[1] To accomplish this epochal happening, Intel marketing directors had worked for months with engineers at Ars Electronica Futurelab, a small group of artists and technology researchers based in Linz, Austria.

Intel produced a short documentary of the occasion, which played at Intel CEO Brian Krzanich's keynote address at the 2016 Consumer Electronics Showcase in Las Vegas. The documentary video begins with short interviews with Intel employees and drone technicians. Soon, we hear the sounds of an orchestra tuning up, and then we begin to see classical musicians, dressed in traditional concert black, carrying their instruments to a site on the airport's runway where music stands have been set up. The video intercuts shots of the musicians unpacking their instruments with shots of hands carefully unpacking drones from padded cases. Night falls, and all is in readiness; suddenly the drones launch into the sky and spread out into a synchronized formation that swirls and changes color in response to orders given by computers—running on Intel processors—on the ground.

Accompanying this dizzying display of unmanned drone technology, we hear the orchestra launch into the first movement of Beethoven's Fifth Symphony—the familiar four-note "ba ba ba BUM" colloquially known as the "Fate motive."[2] In the original symphony, these opening four notes are capped by a fermata, which causes a moment of silence that feels weighted and portentous.[3] However, the version of the symphony the orchestra played during Drone 100 eschewed this moment of silence, immediately answering Beethoven's opening motive with another one: the perhaps equally well-known four notes of Intel's mnemonic tone. That little sonic logo we hear at the end of every Intel commercial is, in the words of Teresa Herd, Intel's VP-global director, what "defines Intel as a brand."[4] While the impulse of a classical music lover might be to laugh at this bizarre juxtaposition, the orchestra performed it with the utmost seriousness; the music was meant to dramatically underscore an exciting and even awe-inspiring event. For the rest of the fireworks show, the orchestra continued playing this transformed version of Beethoven's symphonic movement, in which every main iteration of the "Fate motive" was answered by Intel's mnemonic tone.

Drone 100 and its soundtrack were a major part of a yearlong marketing initiative Intel undertook in an effort to change its brand image. Intel invented the microchip in 1971, and is primarily known for making chips and processors—nuts-and-bolts hardware that other companies purchase and use to run their computers, laptops, robots, and drones. As a result of this position in the industry, it has long struggled to make itself more visible in a marketplace dominated by glamorous consumer electronics like those made by Apple; for over a decade, the company's advertising slogan has been a plea to Look Inside. Krzanich rolled out the new marketing campaign in his 2016 Consumer Electronics Showcase keynote address, a two-hour-long multimedia presentation during which he played the documentary about Drone 100 and ceaselessly reiterated a new, tweaked version of the corporate slogan: Experience What's Inside. Entering the stage on a hoverboard, Krzanich noted that "almost every part of life that we enjoy today is defined by the power of technology, but the technology alone is not our focus. Instead, I want to emphasize the experiences this cutting-edge technology will deliver to you."[5] The emphasis on experiences continued throughout the two-hour presentation, and was reiterated by the pro gamers, fashion designers, composers, and robot technicians who periodically joined Krzanich onstage, and by a video presentation by Lady Gaga. The new slogan and the focus on experiences are deliberate: for years, industry insiders have been charting a marketing transition from products to experiences, as everything increasingly becomes managed by the Cloud and product turnover becomes ever more instantaneous.

The recomposed Fifth Symphony that underscored Drone 100 was also used in the commercial that Intel produced as part of its marketing transition, and that first ran during the 2016 Super Bowl. The ad—titled

"Experience Amazing"—presents a bewildering array of images intercut at lightning speed. In the first seven seconds alone we see a woman jumping off a cliff; a person silhouetted against a galaxy of green lights; a face with a digital web projected onto it; a laptop screen showing a mixing board; a close-up of a microchip; a skateboarder in midair; a close-up of an eye opening and its pupil dilating; a pixelated image of a violinist; a camera's pulling back to reveal a live violinist standing in front of that image; a robot; a grid of glowing ones and zeroes; a person emerging from underwater; a hand holding a microchip; a camera zoom into circuitry; and a sudden wide shot of a space shuttle taking off. There is no voiceover, and very little text. Instead, the images are tied together by the recomposed version of Beethoven's Fifth.

Walter Werzowa, the Austrian composer who created the remix, also created Intel's mnemonic tone, in 1994. That tone—which in the tech world is known as "the bong"—consists of four notes of equal rhythmic value that outline a fourth and then a fifth (D♭–G♭–D♭–A♭), and it is constructed from multiple synthesized instruments, including a lot of xylophone and marimba sounds.[6] Weaving the bong into the opening of Beethoven's symphonic material was, at least from a purely logistical perspective, actually quite easy, given that Beethoven's famous motive is also four notes long and is frequently being played by different instruments throughout the movement. Werzowa simply replaced certain iterations of Beethoven's motive with the Intel bong. He titled his composition "Symphony in Blue" and recorded it in Vienna with a ninety-piece live orchestra conducted by Claudius Traunfellner.

In this chapter, I will discuss how Intel's new marketing campaign uses Beethoven's Fifth to naturalize capitalism's myriad disruptions of human life, a move symptomatic of neoliberalism's vexed relationship with history. I also examine how the campaign and its use of Beethoven work to naturalize and sanctify the US military-industrial complex and the conditions of endless war and total surveillance that increasingly characterize global life under late capitalism.

Neoliberalism and History

Neoliberal writers and economists manifest a fraught orientation toward the past. On the one hand, because of the instability and inequality their proposed practices generate, neoliberals often try to position free market principles as revivals of ideals from lost historical golden ages, in an attempt to make them seem like timeless virtues rather than historically and culturally contingent economic theories that can be criticized. On the other hand, however, neoliberals champion innovation and creative destruction as the foundations of a healthy society, and to do so they must present the past as a nightmare from which entrepreneurial innovations deliver us.

Examples of the rhetorical devaluation of the past abounded in Krzanich's Consumer Electronics Showcase keynote address. Discussing Drone 100 and what such innovations will mean for humanity, he said dismissively that fireworks "have been around for over 2000 years" and have barely changed at all during that time. However, the Drone 100 project has "completely redefine[d] the firework experience." Krzanich said that he sees "a future where fireworks, and all of their risks, and smoke, and dirt, are a thing of the past. And they are replaced with shows that have unlimited creativity and potential, powered by drones."[7] Other people who came onstage to demonstrate various new Intel-powered products also reiterated this rhetorical formula, which takes as a given that a process or activity must be disrupted simply because it is time-honored: someone who created an app to help farmers manage herds of livestock noted that "for centuries, herds have been managed in the same way. Our app is going to change all that"—without explaining what, exactly, is so bad about the way herds have traditionally been managed or in what way the app will represent an improvement.[8] Similarly, Krzanich credited the Bollywood film composer A. R. Rahman with "transform[ing] the experience of music" because of his demonstration of motion-sensing wristbands that electronically generate synthesized musical sounds.[9] Watching the keynote address presentation, it was difficult for me to understand what it was about music's conventional modes of performance that needed innovating: the wristbands were presented as exciting simply because they were new and used technology, not because they solved any existing problem with musical performance.

Although neoliberal rhetoric about innovation presents aspects of the past as dirty, dangerous, or otherwise in desperate need of an update, it must nonetheless also find ways of grounding the disruptions and destructions caused by the ever-faster cycling of markets within some notion of historical precedent or sense of timeless truth. Neoliberalism desperately requires such precedents, because otherwise its disruptive role in human life would be unbearable to the societies it ruptures. If we did not believe that everything is always and has always been changing, and that the only viable approach to this change is to become adaptable, flexible, and self-sufficient, we would be less likely to accept neoliberal facts of life such as outsourcing, downsizing, and the loss of benefits traditionally provided by employers, like health insurance and pension plans. In *The Condition of Postmodernity*, David Harvey examines this issue at length, arguing that the cycling of capitalist markets generates a "maelstrom of ephemerality" that grows increasingly unmanageable as "time-space compression" intensifies.[10] Harvey argues that we have been forced to accept the maelstrom of ephemerality caused by creative destruction, which leads us to value instantaneity and disposability above permanence—in marketing terms, we begin to value experiences and spectacles above solidly built products that last a lifetime. However, he considers that a major social ramification of this disposable culture is the loss of a sense of historical continuity, which generates a rising demand for mementoes and symbols of the continuing presence of a lost past. It is in this sense that the revamped idea of classical music I have been assessing throughout this book becomes most useful to corporations like Intel.

The rhetorical tension between evoking the greatness of the past while also scorning the past's old ways of doing things can be seen in the writings of liberals from Friedrich von Hayek to Milton Friedman and beyond, as well as in a wide variety of contemporary corporate marketing schemes and public statements. Marketing efforts in the classical music world can also display a similarly contradictory attitude toward the past. For example, the Los Angeles Philharmonic recently embarked on VAN Beethoven, a marketing project in which a large van fitted with comfy seats and Samsung Gear VR Oculus–powered headsets drove around Los Angeles to "bring the experience of Walt Disney Concert Hall to the people of Los Angeles!" in the words of the press release. Individuals climbed into the van, donned the headsets, and experienced in virtual reality a four-minute snippet of the LA Phil performing Beethoven's Fifth as swirling animations enhanced the concert footage. On the one hand, brochures and press releases advertising such schemes describe classical music as timeless, universal, and the carrier of humanity's highest values—"Music is a fundamental human right," proclaims a VAN Beethoven press release—while on the other hand, they attempt to align classical music with hip new technological innovations, like Oculus headsets.[11]

Many other orchestras and opera houses have attempted to draw in new audiences via the use of new technology, such as incorporating digital light shows or projecting animations during concerts. In general, US classical music institutions large and small have accepted the idea that incorporating new technology of almost any kind is the best means of attracting new and larger audiences and imbuing old art forms with social relevance: a collaboration between Vice Media and Intel called the Creators Project focuses on rewarding arts institutions for using technology to make art more appealing to consumers; a press release about the new music group NovaTrio emphasizes that classical music and "advanced technology" are wholly compatible, and says that the group's performances are meant to "remind people of these ties and to raise the performance of music into an immersive total-sensory experience to the audience."[12] Such marketing rhetoric—which implies that the latest consumer electronics are not only commensurable with but even inextricable from the authentic performance of centuries-old music—has become commonplace. Thus, classical music hops onto technology's coattails, but at the same time, tech corporations get to be associated with enabling the "fundamental human right" classical music is said to represent.

Neoliberalism was born in an attempt to rescue the free market from the socialist ideals that began encroaching on economic liberalism during the first part of the twentieth century, when the New Deal granted legitimacy and political recognition to the working class and Keynesian economics held sway over much of the Western world. Although neoliberalism is not simply a recreation of eighteenth- and early nineteenth-century liberalism, it does look to this past for its justification, finding in the work of writers like Adam Smith or David Hume the idea of "pure" free market principles, unsullied by misguided communalism.[13] Tellingly, however, neoliberal writers often look even further back than the eighteenth or nineteenth century in establishing the moral justification for an unregulated free market. When contemporary tech corporations appropriate classical music in their marketing schemes, they are seeking a similar sort of precedent for their products and the value system necessary for propagating them.

Friedrich von Hayek, who served as both inspiration and mentor for Milton Friedman, wrote in the 1940s that the value of personal liberty—and, by extension, free market principles—is not only associated with classical thinkers like Smith, Hume, and John Locke but is "one of the salient characteristics of Western civilization as it has grown from the foundations laid by Christianity and the Greeks and Romans." Hayek also asserts that the rise of socialism represents an abandonment of "not merely nineteenth- and eighteenth-century liberalism but the basic individualism inherited by us from Erasmus and Montaigne, from Cicero and Tacitus, Pericles and Thucydides."[14] Neoliberals since Hayek often similarly ground their economic ideas in nineteenth-century philosophy while also routinely evoking a rhetorical linkage with even more distant pasts. Writing in the 1960s, Friedman calls "our" love of freedom and personal liberty "unchanging principles,"[15] and locates the emergence of "political freedom" in the free market thinking of the nineteenth-century liberals. However, he also goes much farther back in time to demonstrate how deeply the free market is rooted in the human experience. "Historical evidence speaks with a single voice on the relation between political freedom and a free market," he maintains. "I know of no example in time or place of a society that has been marked by a large measure of political freedom, and that has not also used something comparable to a free market to organize the bulk of economic activity." Noting that political freedom always comes along with a free market, Friedman goes on to cite ancient Greece as one of these "golden ages."[16]

These rhetorical evocations of past golden ages are meant to soothe anxieties about the disruption and inequality that free market principles seem inevitably to cause. If these principles governed the greatest eras of human achievement, then perhaps the social problems they engender can be more easily dismissed as the symptoms of too much rather than too little governmental regulation of our innate human instincts. Friedman presents capitalism as a necessary, intrinsic condition for political freedom throughout history, although in practice—as even his own example may illustrate, given that ancient Greece was a slave state—capitalism is not only founded on but actively requires some degree of systematized inequality to function successfully as a system. The principal tenet of modern capitalism is that those with capital must try to accumulate more, which can be done only by increasing the amount of surplus value generated by labor.[17] As Marx demonstrated, the system is predicated on the reality that some people have surplus money, which accumulates, while other people have none, and instead sell their physical labor to capitalists; this is fundamentally an unequal system, even leaving aside its more grotesque historical outcomes (like slavery). Whether or not all individuals have the legal right to better their own personal position within this system via hard work or luck does not change the basic inequality on which the system functions.

Thus, the neoliberal attempt to locate free market ideals in great eras of history must always remain a vague and general one, because any deeper study of history reveals that capitalism tends to worsen inequality rather than to ease it. Many scholars since Marx have attempted to outline the rise of capitalism in history, and to demonstrate how it was contingent on specific historical factors (such as the bubonic plague in medieval Europe and the expropriation of the peasantry from common lands), rather than emanating ahistorically from a basic expression of universal human nature. Such scholars have also been concerned with identifying how the capitalist system requires and maintains inequalities of various types, in every era. For example, the feminist Marxist Silvia Federici has spent her career demonstrating that race-, class-, and gender-based inequalities are ongoing *requirements* of capitalism, arguing that "the continuous expulsion of farmers from the land, war and plunder on a world scale, and the degradation of women are necessary conditions for the existence of capitalism at all times."[18] These are the brutal facts that so much lofty neoliberal rhetoric is designed to obscure, and they illustrate why neoliberals' grand claims to historical precedents provide so few dates or concrete details.

The Spirit of Neoliberalism

In *The Protestant Ethic and the Spirit of Capitalism*, Max Weber describes the ways that sixteenth-century Puritanism engendered a powerful new belief that amassing profits and participating in market competition were activities pleasing to God, despite the fact that the New Testament explicitly militates against such behavior. Weber quotes the great Puritan father Richard Baxter, who wrote:

> If God show you a way in which you *may*, in accord with His laws, acquire *more profit* than in another way, without wrong to your soul or to any other and if you refuse this, choosing the less profitable course, *you then cross one of the purposes of your calling. You are refusing to be God's steward, and to accept His gifts.*[19]

Over the next few centuries, these ideas became unmoored from their original religious foundations. By the time of Benjamin Franklin, Weber argues, the value of competing to earn profits had been secularized, and turned into simply a "maxim for the organization of life."[20] For Franklin and the other "bland deists" who propagated the spirit of modern capitalism, individuals simply have a duty to work hard and amass profits.[21] This duty is detached from any conception of an explicitly religious salvation, and thus, as Weber notes, it is somewhat strange. If amassing profits means an individual is more likely to go to heaven instead of hell, then it certainly makes sense to work hard to amass profits. If, however, we no longer believe that such activity is evidence of our divinely blessed status, there seems to be little reason for us to work so ceaselessly and compete so viciously with one another. For Weber, then, when we participate in profit-seeking behavior we are enacting a religious ritual that has been emptied of its religious content, which renders the ritual brittle and unsatisfying.

Future writers like Luc Boltanski, Eve Chiapello, Wendy Brown, and

David Harvey have interrogated the various ways that capitalism persuades us to continue participating in it. The condition Weber describes seems unbearable—why don't we revolt, or simply submit to despair and nihilism? Boltanski and Chiapello argue that despite its detachment from explicit religious ideas, contemporary capitalism remains nonetheless quite adept at supplying us with justifications for rallying to the system. Since the nineteenth century, these justifications have come largely from economic science, which uses data to "prove" the efficacy of certain policies or processes.[22] Boltanski and Chiapello maintain that although their foundation in empirical data allows such justifications to appear "non-ideological," they are nonetheless deployed as "powerful moral reasons" for the continuation of the capitalist system.[23] Neoliberal writers thus increasingly manifest a strange ambivalence, simultaneously insisting on the superiority of hard empirical data in justifying capitalism's continuing dominance and making grandly moralizing claims about things like "human nature" that are impossible to demonstrate or define empirically.

In light of work by writers like Federici and Thomas Piketty, reconciling statements about capitalism's wondrous ancient history with the effects of the system in practice is impossible. Even with so general a historical precedent as "ancient Greece," Milton Friedman reveals a basic and unavoidable contradiction between the neoliberal valorization of personal liberty and the unequal, unjust realities of a successful capitalist system. Since it is impossible to actually identify a time in the past when capitalism generated a better quality of life for everyone in a society, and since God and heaven no longer provide meaningful reasons for participating in capitalism, contemporary neoliberals must look to even vaguer justifications for their economic ideas, finding them in pseudoscientific formulations of human nature.

Neoliberals refer confidently to the fact that human nature is based on an instinctive desire to trade and barter, and to be self-interested and competitive in interactions with other individuals—a notion of individualism that is actually quite recent, and that emerged most prominently in the philosophical writings of thinkers like Thomas Hobbes and John Locke, as I discussed in chapter 2. Appeals to basic human nature should raise red flags to any critically engaged thinker, but for many neoliberals such a rhetorical maneuver offers the only means of justifying essentially antihumanist and certainly antisocial beliefs and practices. The neoliberal economist Deepak Lal's recent book advocating for a return to true classical liberalism is organized around the human nature fallacy; he begins by asserting that the basic model for all human nature is *homo economicus*, meaning that "human beings are self-interested and rational: maximizing utility as consumers and profits as producers."[24] In demonstrating this fact, Lal constructs a brief survey of human history beginning in "the Stone Age in Eurasia."[25] Stating that bartering "is part of our basic human nature," he argues that communalist social structures seek to repress this elemental expression of our species.[26] His historical survey is meant to prove that competitive capitalism is a more natural and moral system than socialism; along the way he compares Gandhi to Stalin, blames Chinese peasants' poor work ethic for the famine of the Great Leap Forward, and uses logic to prove that caring about the misfortunes of strangers is mere "sentimentality" that does nothing to better society.[27]

Neoliberals like Lal contribute to our widespread inability to conceive a postcapitalist world. Since capitalism appears to be inextricably bound up with our biological experience of life, and since we accept many of its tenets as natural expressions of our deepest instincts, it is indeed difficult to imagine some other way of organizing society. As senator Nancy Pelosi put it in a January 2017 town hall meeting, "We're capitalists, and that's just the way it is."[28]

The Idea of Classical Music

> If the classic has been defined in no small way by hinting at some inherently ethical quality, the question will arise at each invocation: whose classic and whose ethics?[29]

Theodor Adorno wrote that capitalist society "applies tradition systematically like an adhesive; in art, it is held out as a pacifier to soothe people's qualms about their atomization."[30] Classical music can serve as just such a soothing pacifier for neoliberal marketers to use on citizens, not only because of its obvious associations with *the classic*, a term that began being used in the eighteenth century to indicate timeless moral virtue, but also because of aspects of the new musical ideology that emerged in response to Beethoven's symphonies and that held those symphonies up as articulations of timeless, universal, idealized truth. The association of Beethoven—and specifically of the Fifth Symphony—with this kind of universal truth and virtue is one reason the work has become so well known. Orchestras feel compelled to program it year after year because audiences experience it as the ultimate work in the canon; its ubiquity and its perception as the classical symphony nonpareil (as well as the "van" in its composer's name) are surely why it was chosen for the LA Phil's VAN Beethoven marketing scheme.

In marketing campaigns like "Experience Amazing," classical music is often used as a generic stand-in for the idea of historical continuity. The tech strategist E. G. Nadhan, who writes regularly for Intel's *Peer Network* blog, wrote that the most powerful aspect of the Drone 100 event was "the synchronization between the classical audio music in the background with the dynamic visual technology in the foreground." For Nadhan, what makes this synchronization "even more symbolic" is the fact that this music is not new: "it is the time-tested classical music that continues to earn the respect of the connoisseurs with a refined taste for the arts. The same music would have drawn the appreciation of the crowds centuries back." The ultimate message Nadhan derives from Intel's whole campaign is that "the business of the enterprise has not really changed. The enabling technology has."[31] This kind of insistent dichotomy, which presents technological innovation as utterly new while also grounded in timeless historical precedent, is very common in the marketing and self-promotion of tech corporations.

The Intel marketing campaign's use of the symphony aligns the company with a very specific musical ideology that was born in the early nineteenth century. Within this ideology, large-scale instrumental works like Beethoven's symphonies became the means of bringing hidden universal ideals into the light—they enabled us to "look inside." An article about Intel's new commercial and marketing campaign says that the ad pairs Intel's mnemonic tone with Beethoven's symphony to show that "the chip manufacturer does more than just power computers."[32] The "Experience Amazing" ad, as well as Drone 100 and Brian Krzanich's keynote address, attempts to establish Intel at the center of humanity's most timelessly cherished ideals and as the reason products of immeasurable cultural value (like spaceships and Beethoven's Fifth) are born.

The genre of the symphony first emerged as a brief instrumental introduction played before the first act of an opera. From these undignified beginnings—as, essentially, music meant to quiet down a crowd before the main event—it evolved over a hundred years or so until, by the mid-nineteenth century, it had become the preeminent Western musical genre, the genre most associated with genius, artistry, and compositional mastery. Beethoven is strongly associated with this transition in the symphony's fortunes; beginning with his third, the "Eroica," he started writing symphonies that were fantastically long by then-conventional standards but that also exploited the generic form in interesting ways. Previously, the four movements of a symphony had been more or less discrete: four individual pieces bearing scant musical relationship to one another. But in the Fifth Symphony (which premiered in 1808), Beethoven linked all four movements together via the four-note "Fate motive." This motive recurs frequently throughout the symphony's first movement: one instrument passes it to the next, it rumbles in purely rhythmic form in the timpani, and even the cellos and basses take it up while all the other instruments are playing the movement's second theme, which, conventionally, is supposed to provide a moment of contrast. Not only does this simple motive tie the first movement intricately together, but it also provides the basis for the other three movements.

This compositional technique—dubbed "organicism"—became one of the signal goals of post-Beethoven nineteenth-century symphonic composition. As a structuring principle it fit in well with the cultural predilections arising in Europe during Beethoven's time. A persistent interest in organicism characterized the long nineteenth century, manifesting in many disparate realms of cultural production. In Darwin's theory of evolution, Hegel's and Marx's conceptions of historical progress, and the rise of the *Bildungsroman* (or "novel of development"), we can see deep interest in progressive development throughout the era. E. T. A. Hoffmann's famous essay on Beethoven's Fifth strongly foregrounded the organicism of the symphony as a primary reason for its historical superiority, even when compared with works by other, earlier greats like Mozart and Haydn. Hoffmann observed that for the sensitive and thoughtful listener, "there springs forth, issuing from a single bud, a beautiful tree, with leaves, flowers, and fruit," and described the way Beethoven's "simple but fruitful theme . . . forms the basis of each movement; all remaining subsidiary themes and figures are intimately related to the main idea." This extreme organicism—governing not only each movement but also the symphony as a whole—as well as the fact that the simple starting idea develops and evolves over time, is what lends the work its "unity."[33]

For Hoffmann, though, mere compositional complexity was not the real reason Beethoven's symphony was so superior to all previous compositions. For him, the unity that musical organicism generated was what enabled the work to go beyond the simple evocation of moods or feelings, instead leading the listener "imperiously forward into the spirit world of the infinite!"[34] Its ability to disclose to sensitive listeners the usually hidden realm of the infinite—a realm populated by ideal forms—was the aspect of Beethoven's instrumental music Hoffmann most prized. Mark Evan Bonds details the resurgence of Platonic idealism in German Romantic philosophy of the eighteenth and nineteenth centuries, noting that within an idealist framework, vagueness or lack of specificity (long considered weaknesses of instrumental music, in comparison with texted music) became transformed into great strengths.[35] For writers like Hoffmann, abstract symphonies like the ones Beethoven constructed were liberated from the tawdry concreteness of words, and from the realm of the merely human; thus liberated, such music attained the ability to reveal transcendent truths to individual listeners with the sensitivity and understanding necessary to accept them.

The conception of complex instrumental music as a vehicle for sublime revelation has colored Western music—its composition as well as its reception and historiography—in various ways ever since. Many German composers after Beethoven were haunted by this conception, feeling duty-bound to generate musical works of ever-increasing complexity and organic unity. Such an urge motivated Wagner's attempt to create the *Gesamtkunstwerk*, the "total work of art" in which every conceivable human art form would be combined in an epic and transcendent "music drama." Meanwhile, many twentieth-century French composers revealed their own entrapment within these dominating musical ideas by rebelling against them, creating instrumental music that self-consciously and often humorously deflated such overweening Germanic pretensions.[36] As recently as 2007, the musicologist Lawrence Kramer advocated for classical music's continuing relevance in contemporary society by putting forth the Hoffmannesque belief that such music enables the discovery of inner selves, and the realization that we are each unique.[37]

Theodor Adorno, too, was very interested in Beethoven's symphonies, and in what they revealed. However, where Hoffmann insisted that this music opened the realm of the infinite—that it transcended human reality and accessed the ideal—Adorno felt that it revealed specific truths about society and culture. For him, "authentic" works of art, like Beethoven's Fifth, articulated social reality, so careful analysis of these works could reveal that reality. Encoded in Beethoven's music are truths about the social relations governing his time and place, and thus good analysis will criticize the musical work and society simultaneously.[38] Given this understanding of Beethoven's music, it makes sense that Adorno was so disturbed by the transformations this music underwent in the growth of the culture industry.

In his essay "The Radio Symphony," Adorno assesses the Fifth Symphony and why it is meaningful, in the most literal sense—he seeks to reveal how the symphony imparts meaning. For Adorno, as for Hoffmann, the most meaningful aspect of the work is its organicism—the fact that the opening motive is not merely repeated often but is *developed*. Changing perpetually, the motive "gains structural perspective" by "wandering" from instrument to instrument, foreground to background, soft to loud.[39] This development is what enables the motive to be transformed from a "monad" to a "cell," the representative of the whole work. Adorno argues that this development—which comprises the work's ability to impart meaning—is possible only if we hear the transformation of the motive over time. Only in this gradual transformation does its repetition "become more than repetition."[40]

Adorno's essay has often been mischaracterized as simply a critique of the poor sound quality of early radio broadcasts, but what he is arguing is much deeper. Listening to the Fifth Symphony over the radio means not only that its quiet parts become inaudible and the subtle resonances between instruments are effaced; it also means listening while darning socks, chastising children, reading the newspaper, doing the dishes, or discussing the stock market. Such "atomized" listening—which Richard Leppert defines as "listening for the good parts"—reduces the intricate structure of the symphony to a series of sound bites, alienated from their context and incapable of generating meaning.[41]

In Walter Werzowa's remix of the Fifth, the aspects of the symphony that have caused everyone from Hoffmann to Adorno to hear the work as conveying meaning—its organic unity and the development of its main idea over time—are absolutely jettisoned, and replaced with mere repetition unattached to any notion of evolution or change. The remix simply alternates Beethoven's motive (the "good part" of the work) with Intel's mnemonic, back and forth. It also edits the movement drastically, interrupting transitions, cutting the second theme, moving directly from exposition to recapitulation, and ultimately condensing the entire movement from its original 502 measures down to a radically truncated collage of fifty-some measures, selected from various points in the movement. Finally, the remix transposes Beethoven's music, moving it up a half step, from C minor to C-sharp minor. The utility of this transposition is self-evident: the Intel mnemonic is in D-flat, and given the remix's role as an Intel commercial, as well as the centrality of the mnemonic to Intel's brand identity, it would not have made sense for Werzowa to transpose the mnemonic. The transposition also enables Beethoven's four-note opening motive (which here becomes G♯–G♯–G♯–E) to be answered by the Intel mnemonic (D–G♭–D♭–A♭), which, by ending on the same note Beethoven's motive begins on (G♯/A♭), creates the startling effect of "finishing" it, bringing Beethoven's motive full circle before the movement has properly begun.

The "atomized listening" that, Adorno argues, radio broadcasts both encourage and require shifts the meaning of the symphony "from the totality to the individual moment," because the *relation* of the individual moments to one another "is no longer fully affected." The symphony, once so inspiring for its ability to transform monads into cells, is reduced once more to a pastiche of unrelated and isolated utterances. In light of this, the widely held belief that radio compensates for its less desirable aural aspects by bringing the symphony to a wider audience is "hackneyed." For Adorno, broadcasting the symphony over the radio has both "trivialized and romanticized" it: "what is heard is not Beethoven's Fifth but merely musical information from and about Beethoven's Fifth."[42] In the intervening decades since Adorno wrote these words, both the Fifth Symphony and our listening habits have become exponentially more fragmented; the symphony has become a ringtone, a cultural touchstone detached from its original meaning, and we now listen to it on a plethora of devices, which allow us to pause, rewind, and skip sections we are tired of.[43]

Accordingly, Werzowa's composition goes much further in atomizing the symphony than simply broadcasting it over the radio ever could. In Beethoven's symphony, individual moments are meaningfully related to one another, changing, developing, and gaining momentum until ultimately their combination forms something much greater than the sum of its parts. The recomposed version presents only a few parts, not only detached from their appropriate context and thus prevented from making meaning, but also infiltrated by a totally alien idea (the Intel "bong") that slowly takes over; the end of Werzowa's version leaves Beethoven's "Fate motive" hanging on the dominant, and instead concludes with four repetitions of the Intel mnemonic, underneath text of the new slogan: Experience What's Inside.

The advertisement itself also visually detaches the symphony from its traditionally group-oriented mode of production, replacing that production with an atomistic conception of music-making. Although the live orchestral recording of Werzowa's recomposition provides the main soundtrack for the ad, the ad's visuals do not feature him or an orchestra. Instead, to represent the creation of what we are hearing on the soundtrack, the ad shows the Hawaiian musician Kawehi, who creates multilayered songs using the software Ableton Live and an array of technology. In a climactic moment in the advertisement, during the thunderous lead-up to what in

Beethoven's original would be the lyrical B theme, we see Kawehi triumphantly unleash a drum machine beat and a harmonized vocal iteration of the Fate motive that undergirds the rest of the ad's soundtrack.

The Intel advertisement attempts to sell a related set of ideas: by showing paralyzed people and amputees restored to full functioning via robotic prosthetics, the ad tells us that technology liberates individuals physically; by showing musicians and dancers interacting with computers and projection screens, the ad tells us that technology enables and enhances individual creativity; the space shuttle taking off tells us that technology can emancipate us from the earth itself. Finally, though, the ad tells us that technology can liberate us from others and enable us to be creative and innovative all by ourselves. Significantly, almost all the images in the Intel ad depict individuals working alone. With the exception of two shots of huge crowds (one watching a fireworks display; one at a rock concert) and one shot of several men playing video games together and screaming, the ad shows nothing but individuals performing tasks alone: one ballerina, one jogger, one skydiver, one BMX biker, one race car driver, one fashion model, one violinist, one face, one hand, one eyeball, one man hunched over in the dark, soldering a microchip. The ad does not depict the ninety-person orchestra that actually recorded the musical score; instead, it shows Kawehi, playing by herself.

Kawehi represents an ideal neoliberal individual. She uses Web 2.0 platforms like Kickstarter and YouTube to construct and maintain her career, and does not rely on the support of a label or any other kind of traditional employer. In addition, she uses technology to create innovative new musical sounds without the aid of other people, generating an impression of group music-making by splitting herself into multiple parts—using loops to accompany herself and to play her own guitar solos on top of her own drums and chordal accompaniment, and using a harmonizer to diffuse her voice into a multiplicity of voices.[44] In these ways, Kawehi represents the ideal individual to corporations like Intel.

Timothy Taylor concludes his *Music and Capitalism* with what he calls "an antidote to the technological triumphalism" that has now become so widespread in the discourse surrounding technological innovation and music. Noting that new technologies have made it easier for amateurs to record and disseminate their products—an arguably "democratizing" phenomenon—Taylor nonetheless also points out that the very ease of production has increased the workloads of professional musicians, because it enables their bosses "to demand more of them, faster, sooner."[45] Not only has the rise of digital technology changed musical labor formations and devalued musical expertise, but for many recording artists, "the absence of studio musicians has created a more sterile creative environment."[46] Where once the recording studio was filled with people—people smoking, talking, fighting, and listening together as well as contributing different skills and ideas to a given musical product—now the act of musical production is often a hermetic affair; Taylor argues that some of music's "sociality" is being lost.[47]

As this book has demonstrated, because of the threat to capital they rightly perceive in class consciousness and collective struggle, neoliberals undertake to destroy collective identity in a number of ways. Conservatives work to revoke all the government-funded programs that treat the poor and underemployed as a group with shared challenges and concerns, while progressives seek to maintain such a social safety net, though they do so in a way that similarly discourages collective identification and upholds the power structure: outlining a meritocratic strategy for helping individuals lift themselves out of poverty by dint of hard work and good morals. In neither case is capitalism itself identified as systemically causing inequality. Progressives and conservatives alike see poverty as an individual failing; the difference between them has mainly to do with the degree of sympathy they afford poverty's victims.

Of course, these moves are made not in the name of class warfare but rather with the goal of fostering independence and personal liberty in a given population. But in this formulation, *liberty* becomes attached to individuals' ability to care for themselves financially. Wendy Brown notes that anticollective processes break a citizenry down into individual units of human capital, and says that "a democracy composed of human capital features winners and losers, not equal treatment or equal protection."[48] Neoliberalism thus presents a marketized version of individualism, one in which the individual is all that matters, but all the things that contribute to constructing individuality—such as personal formative experiences, family life, education, race/gender/sexuality, and relations with others—are rendered unimportant in the face of the individual's market actions.

In previous eras of Western history, individualism was positioned as oppositional to society, but here it becomes one of society's requirements: the anticollective as collective value. Attempting to counter the prevalent view that liberal individualism is associated with "egotism and selfishness," Friedrich von Hayek argued in 1944 that in contrast with collectivism, individualism respects "the individual man *qua* man, that is, the recognition of his own views and tastes as supreme in his own sphere."[49] For Hayek, the possibility for individuals to shape their own spheres "is closely associated with the growth of commerce," a development he credits with having freed the individual "from the ties which had bound him to the customary or prescribed ways." Here, Hayek gestures toward creative destruction and the individual innovation on which modern liberal theory is founded, but by denigrating "customary" ways and "collectivism" he also seeks to establish the idea that social responsibilities serve to thwart individualism. The critical theorist Henry Giroux argues that neoliberalism is increasingly transforming our widespread understanding of freedom from the power of human beings to work together in shaping a functional collective society into "the right of the individual to be free of social constraints."[50] In the new world that corporations like Intel are helping to bring about, individuals are as radically discrete as they were for Thomas Hobbes. But where Hobbes envisioned social linkages in the form of laws imposed from above by an absolutist monarchy, in the Intel Leviathan we are linked together by the streams of data that carry our every experience and thought to the omniscient Cloud for sorting and monetizing.

Artists like Kawehi represent the Crusoe-esque individual fetishized by neoliberals, so it makes sense that the advertisement foregrounds her in its envisioning of music-making. Intel also emphasizes this notion in several short documentaries it produced about Kawehi, each of which glorifies how her use of technology frees her from conventional musical practices, most notably the need to rely on the musical labor of others.[51] In one video, Kawehi asserts that the Intel processor in her MacBook is the main thing that allows her to be a "one-woman band."[52] Similarly, Paul Tapp, Intel Marketing's technology director, says in an interview, "We chose Kawehi because she's a great poster-child for how modern musicians are disrupting the traditional production process. She effortlessly incorporates the sound of instruments in her songs that she has never even needed to learn."[53] No one in the videos or interviews about Kawehi talks about talent or skill (except to point out that computers alleviate our need to attain them); rather, it is technology that, according to Tapp, "is an enabler of creative arts and of new music."[54]

In its destruction of the meaningful relationships among individual musical ideas, Walter Werzowa's remix mimics neoliberalism's focused destruction of relations among individual human beings within society, and the way it replaces those individuals with units of "human capital" that encounter one another in purely transactional terms. Whereas Beethoven's symphonic music is organically deployed, conveying meaning via the structural development of musical ideas, this transformed version jettisons development and the relation of parts to whole, replacing these old-fashioned conveyors of meaning with the simple repetition of a brand.

This is what advertising does; in one sense, Intel's use of Beethoven is nothing special. The music critic Matthew Guerrieri has written an entire book about the first four notes of the Fifth Symphony and how they have suffused Western cultural history, infiltrating everything from disco to recorded answering machine greetings. Guerrieri demonstrates that the use of the "Fate motive" in commercials has been a commonplace for decades—after all, he wrote, "what better way to drill a name or a product or a slogan into the customer's head than to leash it to a tune that seemingly everybody already knew?"[55]

Guerrieri argues that these repetitions of the motive have slowly transformed it until it exists today only as "a neutered, omnipresent cultural artifact," valuable solely for its overwhelming familiarity. For example, the LA Phil's VAN Beethoven project presented only a four-minute snippet of the work, assuming—probably correctly—that it would be enough to give audience members the gist. However, examining Intel's "Experience Amazing" commercial along with the orchestral performance of the recomposed Fifth Symphony as accompaniment to Drone 100 reveals that Beethoven's motive is far from a neutered cultural artifact. On the contrary, its use in these marketing schemes conveys a very particular array of meanings. Certainly, its familiarity is part of why it was chosen to provide the sonic foundation for Intel's dramatic new campaign, but familiarity is not the only or even the most important reason for this choice. There are myriad widely familiar tunes in the public domain, but few of them convey the impression of sublime, timeless truth that Beethoven's motive has signified for two hundred years.

Conclusion: War and Conflict

Intel CEO Brian Krzanich introduced many innovations throughout his keynote address—including robots, unmanned drones, motion-sensing microchips, and sensors that can monitor the human body in various ways—applauding them all for "enabling creativity" and for "giving rise to an amazing new set of experiences."[56] The address, however, presented many moments of dissonance in which the qualities and capabilities attributed to a given innovation did not seem to match what was depicted on the stage.

For example, during the portion of the keynote address's "Creativity" section that focused on fashion, a woman modeled an "adrenaline dress":

a sexy cocktail dress that senses when its wearer's body is flooded with adrenaline and responds by extruding small plastic batwings. The audience applauded rapturously, but from a fashion perspective, what would be desirable about a dress that informed everyone around you that you were terrified? And what benefit did the plastic wings impart—were we to believe that they served as protection of some sort? Protection from what? Similarly, the musical innovations that A. R. Rahman demonstrated did not make sense from a musical perspective. Rahman's presentation was a progress narrative emphasizing the superiority of digitally generated music over old-fashioned acoustic music. It began with a live human drummer playing a series of rototoms with great skill and dexterity, but after a few seconds of this she pretended to accidentally drop her sticks, and began to mime confusion and embarrassment. The dilemma her fake clumsiness caused was solved by the introduction of the motion-sensing wristbands with which another performer began "drumming." The implication seemed to be that you can't drop the wristbands, because they are attached to your wrists; so wristband-wearing drummers are superior to error-prone acoustic drummers. But music the wristbands enabled was demonstrably inferior to the smooth, elegant complexity of what the live drummer had been playing before pretending to falter. The wristbands missed beats, lacked precision, and were unable to play multiple beats in quick succession, as even an untrained drummer holding two sticks can easily do. Again, it was unclear what was meant to be compelling, from a consumer's point of view, about such products. The Drone 100 project also manifested this dissonance. Are fireworks really a product begging to be innovated? Is it really necessary to generate fantastically complex, million-dollar drones in order to make the "smoke and dirt" of conventional fireworks displays a "thing of the past," as Krzanich claimed to desire? Who exactly is clamoring for drastic innovations in how we blow up fireworks a few times a year?

A visit to the "Military, Aerospace, Government" section of Intel's website helps untangle these confusions.[57] The patented RealSense technology that Krzanich's keynote address presented as enabling creativity in fashion and music is here praised for "transforming many activities carried out by Federal agencies and branches of the U.S. military."[58] These activities include monitoring and tracking a subject's "face and emotions," heightening the capabilities of surveillance and reconnaissance, and even "pattern matching of potential recruit tattoos," software that scans human bodies and compares their tattoos against a database of gang- and terrorist-related symbols. "The United States is continuing to invest in these proven platforms for intelligence collection," proclaims an article on the military website DefenseSystems.com, which also notes that the Air Force is spending more money every year on remote-piloted drones—with and without lethal capabilities—that are enhancing Washington's ability to navigate the challenging environments of its engagements in Syria, Iraq, Yemen, and Afghanistan.[59]

Now it is perhaps easier to imagine much more effective uses for the kinds of technology on display during Krzanich's keynote address. The motion-sensing wristbands, once their precision was improved (perhaps after a few years of perfecting in the consumer market), would be useful in remote-operating military robots; the adrenaline-sensing technology of the bizarre winged dress would make a lot more sense when applied to monitoring systems in the uniform of a soldier in combat (or perhaps when applied to the body of a suspected terrorist undergoing interrogation); and, of course, the fireworks drones that enable "unlimited creativity" are already a huge help in surveilling and killing enemies of the state, both at home and abroad.

The documentary Intel produced about the Drone 100 project quotes Horst Hoertner, director of the company that designed it, who notes that "as soon as you say 'drones,' people think 'dangerous,' but it isn't, really."[60] Yet Intel's own publicly accessible product descriptions demonstrate the falseness of this assertion; drones are indeed dangerous, and one of their most useful applications is in the arena of military engagement, where they are adept at silently placing civilians under surveillance, killing people, and blowing up buildings without putting valued personnel in danger. Intel's drone product manager, Natalie Cheung, is quoted in the same documentary as saying that "the reason why we decided to do Drone 100 is because we wanted to push the future of technology." Pouring immense financial resources into the development of unmanned drones capable of putting on a tepid fireworks display would not be a sound investment or a good way of "pushing the future of technology;" but generating innovations intended for mass purchase by the US military certainly would, especially today, when late capitalism has generated a condition of constant war requiring a ceaseless influx of soldiers and innovative new military products.

Ernest Mandel argued in 1972 that late capitalism generates a condition of endless war. Noting that a "permanent arms economy" represents one of the hallmarks of late capitalism, Mandel traced how arms expenditures create a stimulus for accelerating industrialization and extending the free market into new zones around the globe.[61] Endless war is financially lucrative for corporations, who can invest surplus capital into manufacturing an endless stream of weapons. It is also beneficial to the US government to be ceaselessly at war: once permanent war becomes normalized, the United States can constantly intervene in other countries in order to sculpt them into free markets amenable to US investment without raising undue alarm in the American citizenry, who have become conditioned to accept these interventions as simply the necessary, if unfortunate, result of the spread of freedom and safety.

While in some ways the Fifth Symphony may seem to be an odd piece for a contemporary tech corporation to link its products to—as I've suggested, in some senses the whole notion of "classical music" is incommensurable with the glorification of technological innovation—in other, perhaps more fundamental ways, the work is quite apropos. After all, the Fifth itself is a highly militaristic piece, one long understood as depicting victory in a battle (against fate, or against the Germans, or the Americans, or the Prussians—the Fifth has served many different nationalistic causes over its history).[62] The main motive was used for the letter *V* in Morse code (*V* for victory), which then became a trope of Allied resistance during World War II (for example, a BBC timpanist played the motive before every wartime broadcast). The symphony charts a narrative of violence, death, and transfiguration, from the main motive's brutal attacks throughout every moment of the first movement, to the overwhelming, bombastic conclusion of the fourth movement. Indeed, for two hundred years Beethoven's heroic period has often been understood in essentially warlike, violent terms.[63]

In addition to endless war, another thing we have been conditioned to accept is the notion that technological innovation is inevitable, automatically beneficial, and driven by the need to serve society (rather than by military or corporate interests). Scholars who study the military-industrial complex assess, among other things, the collaboration between the state and the technological corporations that produce the products it requires for surveillance activity. Julie Cohen describes this growing "surveillance-industrial complex," and charts the recent emergence of what she calls a newer "surveillance-innovation complex," which "casts surveillance in an unambiguously progressive light."[64] Since the Quantified Self movement that began in Silicon Valley in 2007, rhetoric has proliferated about the liberating and empowering capabilities that innovations in data accumulation bestow on us. In our efforts to better ourselves and become more connected to one another, we use devices and apps that harvest myriad data about our movements, preferences, purchases, social connections, work activity, and physical health.

In what is ostensibly our "free" time, we play games on our phones or through social media platforms that are also designed to collect our personal information. According to Cohen, such platforms provide a "method of behavioral conditioning," which teaches us that surveillance is an intrinsic aspect of life-changing technological innovations (like Apple watches, Facebook, Nike+, Google Maps, Uber and Lyft, and the various listening "pods" that have suddenly proliferated in everyone's homes). Thus, we learn to accept and even celebrate our participation in the expansion of the surveillance state. As Cohen points out, now that surveillance has been folded into the widely held cultural value of innovation, it has become "relatively impervious to regulatory restraint."[65]

This imperviousness also allows surveillance technology to penetrate the criminal justice system, in the form of "e-carceration" schemes that place convicted criminals (as well as immigrants, people with disruptive mental illnesses, and drug addicts) under constant monitoring via ankle bracelets or sweat-analyzing wristbands, as well as by license plate readers and facial recognition software deployed by drones. E-carceration is touted as potential "prison reform," because it could be used to release inmates from the brutal for-profit prisons in which they would otherwise be housed. However, such a transformation of incarceration not only continues to profit corporations—the ones who innovate, produce, and maintain the technologies e-carceration requires—it also widens the dystopic zone of surveillance and intensifies the policing of poor people and people of color. Critics of e-carceration note that these technologies are used not only to harvest valuable data from prisoners but also to strengthen existing policing strategies that prevent "undesirable" types of people from moving freely throughout the city. GPS tracking devices may be used to keep a sex offender away from schools; they could also be used to prohibit African American people from entering upscale white neighborhoods or to make it impossible for poor people to congregate in public spaces. Such devices are already being used to monitor people as they await trial, and immigrants who have not committed any crime; soon they may start being attached to the bodies of people arrested for acts of political protest, or poor parents whose child rearing is being monitored by Social Services, or homeless people whose presence disturbs affluent homeowners and shoppers.

"This journey never really ends . . . new products are always on the horizon, and areas of conflict will always exist."[66] The word *conflict* indicated Brian Krzanich's transition into a segment on Intel's progress in "reforming the supply chain" by which minerals mined in countries like the Democratic Republic of Congo get sold and manufactured into Intel microchips. Since many African nations like the DRC have been destabilized by foreign intervention meant to open their natural resources to corporations like Intel, this supply chain has conventionally been characterized by extreme violence and horror; the mines are often run by warlords and maintained by brutally enforced slave labor. The products of such supply chains have become euphemistically known as "conflict minerals," and Krzanich acknowledged that the challenges they present are "complex." Nonetheless, since it is Intel's goal "to improve the lives of everyone on the planet through their experiences with technology," the company decided to make every Intel product "conflict free" by 2015.[67]

Although countries like the DRC descend into social chaos partly because of foreign interventions meant to open a cheap supply of resources for multinational corporations, the acceptance of endless war and the increasing displacement of political action onto consumer choices enable corporate undertakings like Intel's to seem benevolent. Krzanich ended this section of his keynote address by emphasizing the empowering role consumption can play in bringing about social equality: "And you can look for the conflict free symbol on our products to be confident that you're doing your part to improve the human experience." Intel's corporate responsibility page similarly informs us that "our choices can impact the lives of millions."[68] Consumers are invited to show their disapproval of slave labor, not by protesting the foreign interventions that have generated such labor formations in countries like the DRC, but rather by purchasing the products that those interventions make possible—products now made using less slave labor than they relied on before, and marketed via this statistic.[69] Thus, the desire to end corporate oppression worldwide becomes reconfigured as an imperative to purchase the products of those corporations.

Increasingly, capital seeks to infiltrate every sphere of life, including not only free time, social interactions, work, and war but also sleep. In a harrowing essay, Jonathan Crary explores how the US military is experimenting with drugs that would enable soldiers to remain alert for days or even weeks without sleeping, so that the condition of war would become uninterrupted even by soldiers' natural circadian rhythms.[70] It is easy to imagine the integration of this kind of goal with the physical, emotional, and mental monitoring systems Intel is developing. Discussing the growing prevalence of the kind of smart technology that is moving our society toward universal connectivity, Krzanich noted that we can see this connectivity expanding every day, "whether it's our thermostats, our refrigerators, our cars, our bodies, they're becoming smart and connected." He said that the next step is for computing to "gain senses" so that it can "become an extension of you. It's integrated into you, you *want* it, it's part of your daily routine."[71]

Inserting its products into the military-industrial complex is not enough, however. From a marketing standpoint, to attain true global dominance Intel must find ways of capturing the consumer market—as noted above, this has long been a concern of the company, which for decades has been outpaced in this regard by corporations like Apple and Microsoft. The military will purchase only so many drone processors and motion-sensing chips; to truly corner the tech market a corporation must also be successful in selling cheaper versions of those products to individual consumers. By parading technological innovations primarily intended to aid the military and the surveillance state as enabling individual consumer creativity, Intel effectively kills two birds with one stone: early adopters will purchase the music-producing wristbands or the adrenaline dress or the consumer drone because they are cool and new, while Intel can also supply the military-industrial complex with the tools it needs to maintain American global dominance and advance Western corporate interests abroad. Meanwhile, our use of Intel's products also serves to generate vast amounts of free data for that corporation, which it uses to further monetize our movements, habits, and private lives. Thus, for Intel—or for Google, or for all the other massive corporate conglomerates who use classical music in their marketing campaigns—appropriating the associations of moral virtue, timeless grandeur, and fundamental human rights that vaguely adhere to the idea of classical music is crucial if they are to make capitalist globalization, the surveillance state, and drone warfare seem like inspiring features of humanity's highest nature.

For two hundred years, Beethoven's instrumental music has served as a metaphor for all that is most exalted and transcendent. This vague but deeply felt perception is one that can be used to promote neoliberalism very effectively. Neoliberals evoke transcendent human nature and the great golden ages of the past in arguing for free market principles, but they do so without specificity—they never provide dates, primary source evidence, or even the kind of scientific proof they otherwise claim to value so highly. Neoliberal belief is about gut feelings, not facts or intellectual understanding. We feel in our gut that liberty and personal choice are morally right and thus that entrepreneurial success is an indication of virtue, but we must be careful not to bring these vague ideas into the light of intellectual understanding. If we did, we would see how fraught, ambivalent, and historically contingent they really are.

Whether Beethoven's Fifth does reveal to us the infinite world of the spirit realm is not my main concern here. Rather, I want to show that the scraps of this idea that cling tenaciously to Beethoven are what make his music attractive to people who believe (or who want to believe, or who want others to believe) that there are such things as transcendent, universal truths. Among such people are neoliberals, who believe not only that free market principles are the reason for every great advancement in human history, but even that they are encoded into the very DNA of our species. Given this faith, it makes sense that the marketing departments of tech corporations would look to Beethoven, and other "classical" music, to underscore ad campaigns selling neoliberal ideas as timeless truths. And by emphasizing that this music constitutes a "fundamental human right" that is just as vaguely conceived as the great golden ages of the free market that neoliberals cite, many classical music institutions' marketing campaigns fall right into step with attempts to naturalize and spiritualize the products and processes of corporate globalization.

Conclusion: Music against Capitalism

The new music projects and products I have discussed in this book can appear revolutionary because their makers are rebelling against both a two-hundred-year-old conception of musical transcendence and the quaint notion that art should be critical of society. They are refusing the idea—present in Theodor Adorno's thinking as well as in the much older criticism of E. T. A. Hoffmann—that music that is immediately comprehensible and pleasing to a wide variety of people is necessarily fraudulent or inauthentic. By rejecting this idea, the artists and production companies examined here, and the critics and institutions that support their work, have been successful in widening the appeal of certain kinds of art music. This result seems to emphasize that classical music is "for everyone" and that it can thus continue to be "relevant" in today's world. In this sense, these discursive practices are resisting the kind of intellectual elitism that manifests in both Hoffmann's and Adorno's writing, and that has continued to inform the perspectives of many fans, critics, and scholars to the present day.

This book has demonstrated some of the ways these practices are conditioned by (and supportive of) neoliberalism. Neoliberal values continue to shape the composition, performance, reception, and remuneration of many musical projects in the United States today. However, in recent years some have argued that neoliberalism is in its death throes, thanks to decades of deregulation, privatization, and outsourcing, and the growing inequality and precarity they have generated. In many respects, contemporary phenomena like Trump and Brexit (as well as the recent upsurge in socialist and communist organizations' memberships) have emerged from the growing fissures riddling neoliberal ideology; accordingly, some economists and pundits have declared that neoliberalism is dead or dying.[1] There is, then, a great irony in the fact that just as neoliberal thinking has penetrated classical music practice so effectively, it has come under direct attack in the wider world. However, contradictions in Trump's policy alignments and fan base, and the persistence of neoliberal assumptions that both his supporters and his critics make, demonstrate that this formulation of capitalism is far from defeated, and is in some respects stronger than ever.

Crises occur regularly in the history of capitalism. So far, the system has always emerged from them renewed and reconsolidated. It does so by seeming to grant concessions to its critics while continuing to maintain the primary goal of strengthening elite power. We can see that this dynamic remains constant today in that corporations like Apple, Amazon, Dell, US Steel, and Ford were quick to announce their willingness to collaborate with Trump on tax repatriation deals, deregulation plans, and various other forms of corporate subsidy in exchange for bringing a token number of jobs back into the United States.[2] Even though some of these corporations—Apple, for example—have long publicized their passionate commitments to diversity and global social justice, they nonetheless swiftly began collaborating with a white nationalist administration to ensure that the conditions for accumulation would remain secure.[3]

Neoliberalism continues to dominate US discourse in other, subtler ways as well. For example, despite the rage toward CEOs and bankers that many Trump voters expressed during the 2016 election, the neoliberal notion that the country "should be run like a business" still widely persists; indeed, Trump represents the apotheosis of this idea. Also, though Trump's popularity stems in part from a widespread rebuke of globalization, and though his administration's nationalist, xenophobic policy positions seem to run counter to neoliberalism's envisioning of a vibrant global community, in many ways Trump's reformulation of globalization represents not an abandonment of neoliberal principles but rather an intensification of them. His former national security adviser, H. R. McMaster, describes the president's "clear-eyed outlook that the world is not a 'global community' but an arena where nations, nongovernmental actors and businesses engage and compete for advantage."[4] Trump abandons the fiction that deregulated corporate free marketeering makes everyone in the world more equal and free, and instead embraces the reality of brutal market competition that actually characterizes contemporary globalization. This view is simply neoliberalism stripped of its pretense of virtue.

More alarming, perhaps, is that progressive attacks on Trumpism often fall prey to neoliberal assumptions and values. Democrats' attempts to discredit the GOP's repeal of the Affordable Care Act often relied on data showing that such a repeal would hurt the economy, rather than criticizing the repeal as a tactic of class warfare intended to further disenfranchise the working class and the poor (many self-identified progressives also argue against universal healthcare because implementing it would be too expensive).[5] Similarly, passionate critics of white nationalism sometimes start from basic neoliberal precepts, by replacing moral considerations with economic ones. During the widespread protests against the 2017 "Muslim ban" that prohibited people from certain Middle Eastern countries from entering the United States, many critics of the ban sought to delegitimize it by pointing out that some immigrants go on to do great things and contribute to the economy. "Steve Jobs Was Son of Syrian Migrant," proclaimed an indignant headline in the *Independent*; the article went on to quote the entrepreneur David Galbraith, who described his rage at seeing the famous photo of three-year-old Syrian refugee Aylan Kurdi washed up dead on a beach, saying it made him "wonder what little boys like him could have achieved if they had been given the chance."[6] Anti-Trump arguments like these, which explain the value undocumented immigrants contribute to the US economy, proliferated in response to the Muslim ban.[7] Such liberal critiques effectively replace moral considerations about human dignity or shared rights with a rhetoric of meritocratic exceptionalism that upholds capitalist values. In such formulations, the dead child on the beach is not tragic for his own sake but rather because he might have become Steve Jobs one day. Do people other than great billionaires deserve to live, and are there ways individuals can contribute to society other than by contributing to the economy? Such defenses do not provide any grounds for believing or saying so, and thus they are no help as we cast about wildly for adequate vocabulary to counter the horror of what we are seeing.

So neoliberalism is not dead; rather, the fact of its current crisis offers it the possibility of reconsolidating and strengthening itself. Racist, authoritarian nationalism presents many grave dangers to human rights, but one of these dangers is that it will frighten us into doubling down on the bland free market platitudes that contemporary liberals offer. Indeed, we can already see neoliberal common sense being positioned as the sane, healthy "center" in our disruptive partisan battles. Milquetoast centrism certainly looks better in comparison with white pride marches, state-sanctioned lynch mobs, and Muslim bans (although it's worth pointing out that that's not saying much). Additionally, since capitalism has always been adept at transforming itself to seem to give its critics what they demand, another real danger is that this crisis will simply lead to a more nationalistic form of capitalist globalization, in which corporations pay lip service to bringing back US jobs while continuing to impose structural adjustments on foreign nations and accumulating capital on a gigantic scale.

All these rhetorical, political, and corporate trends—as well as the fact that our country's educational system has been neoliberalized, with profound social ramifications we will be negotiating for decades—demonstrate that it remains important to continue rigorously criticizing these values and assumptions wherever they rear their heads, especially, I would argue, when they are put to work in the service of resistance to Trumpism. After all, it was during just such a crisis that neoliberalism first emerged as a powerful set of ideas: the Chicago school economists who originally propagated neoliberalism positioned it explicitly as the only viable means of warding off fascism and safeguarding individual freedoms. Today, this same positioning is under way. The investment banker Emmanuel Macron's successful campaign to become the president of France also explicitly proposed neoliberalism as the only alternative to fascism, among other advantages, and American pundits and politicians began making similar moves immediately after Trump's election.[8]

Since the election, the rhetorical positioning of some of the artists I have discussed here has changed along the lines just described. In the past, The Industry's promotional rhetoric was optimistic in its celebration of currently existing reality. This opera company praised the innovation that makes Los Angeles such a vibrant city; the multicultural diversity of its streets and neighborhoods; and the technology that allows everyone to take part in performances of opera. Such rhetoric was in step with the marketing materials of corporations like Google and Intel, as well as with the self-promotion of US political propaganda. Now, however, The Industry's celebratory tone has been replaced with a more somber one. Its 2016 promotional email (titled "Opera Post-Fact") begins with a quote from Bertolt Brecht: "In the dark times, will there be singing? There will be singing—about the dark times." The email promises that the company's 2017 projects "will speak directly to the fear and despair in this 'post-fact' era." Because of Trump's assault on the values of diversity and tolerance, The Industry can now market its espousal of neoliberal imperatives like technological innovation and personalization, along with its formulation of elite-centric multiculturalism, as part of "the resistance" to Trump. Indeed, many have already noted how "the hashtag resistance" has become merely another branding strategy that commodifies dissent.[9]

But what might real alternatives look and sound like? And in what ways might they be figured as politically oppositional to the reigning ideologies that have shaped our world and lives in such destructive ways? This book has been a critical project, but in concluding it I sketch some general suggestions for alternative ways of making and thinking about music that might help construct more genuinely oppositional ideas—ideas that might resist the ideologies of both neoliberalism and resurgent white nationalism.

Oppositional Musics

Obviously, one approach to a critical music-making would be to make music that simply can't be commodified. Phil Ford discusses this possibility in *Dig*, in his examination of John Benson Brooks, who spent decades constructing a vast and indecipherable archive in a wholly idiosyncratic approach to art-making. Although Brooks himself did not intend his work to resist commodification—he wanted to make money, and was crestfallen when he didn't—Ford nonetheless uses this example to explore the features that make an art practice impenetrable by market logic. Brooks's actual product—an album of music and recorded soundscapes called *Avant Slant*—was just one odd combination of ideas from his lifetime of archival work and, Ford argues, thus could not be understood by anyone but Brooks himself. *Avant Slant* illustrates Ford's thought experiment about what art would be like if it were only practice—for Ford, as for Marx, all versions of the commodity form are future oriented, and thus everyone engaged in producing commodities is "imprinted" with a relentless drive to innovate. Because of this, Ford suggests considering what a radically present-oriented ethos would mean for musical practice. Instead of orienting music production to the future—its eventual sale in some sort of marketplace, hence its ability to "reach" or "speak to" audiences—we might imagine a music that has no future, a music that exists only in the moment of its creation. This would mean that there would be no music world, no music institutions or schools, no music journalism (and no musicologists).

Thinking along the lines suggested by *Avant Slant* certainly generates one way of rejecting a money orientation, and Ford's thought experiment depicts a version of artistic autonomy that could indeed be more or less free of market logic. However, his utopian model is also highly individualistic—as Ford himself says, "practice will not give us a new, radical, unco-optable subculture; it merely gives us back our own lives, in all their smallness and unimportance."[10] This is a vision of individual artistic autonomy that shares features with the autonomous ideal of the nineteenth century that so many musicologists have been at pains to dismantle. It is focused on the self rather than the collective. It envisions a musical practice that is geared not outward, toward the community, but rather only inward, toward the inscrutably personal and individual. This, I think, represents a fallback position, with respect to the fight against capitalism's totalizing drive to commodify all human experience. Retreating to our own private, individual realms of practice represents an extreme version of the kind of "localism" that many leftists decry for its impotence and lack of real collective politics. Even worse, it resembles Adorno's pessimistic insistence that "what is objectively, socially required is now preserved exclusively in hopeless isolation."[11] Consciously reclaiming an individual, internal space separate from commodity culture can be a life-affirming move, but a more fully realized revolutionary approach would have to incorporate a powerful collective identification into its demands for autonomy.

Yet many of today's self-described composer "collectives" are oriented toward financial sustainability, in the form of branding and market competition as well as competing for grants and donations. But there are others that do try to eschew this orientation. For example, the Frog Peak publishing collective is committed to what it calls "the idea of availability over promotion," and makes available via its catalogue a fantastically diverse array of experimental artworks, from scores and recordings to theoretical treatises to experimental collaborative open-access projects undertaken collectively online. It makes no distinction between relatively famous or marketable artists in its catalogue—the premise of the group is that every artist helps and supports every other artist, simply by pursuing individual activities and being listed together in the catalogue. Frog Peak also does not play much of a curatorial role; there is no picking and choosing of individual pieces with an eye toward marketability. The organization collects no payments except when composers choose to donate them, it maintains no copyrights over the works it publishes, and its directors are unpaid. It also avoids a money orientation by refusing to take part in the ecosystem of grants and donations that supports many other arts organizations—while it refuses to engage in market competition, it has also never incorporated as a nonprofit. On Frog Peak's website, its founders proclaim, "If something doesn't sell for 20 years, we don't care."[12] It does not turn a profit, but it is sustainable in the sense that it has endured for thirty years, and in fact its roster of artists has grown over that time. Artists are drawn to it for political, rather than promotional, reasons. But Frog Peak is not a lone oddity; the musicologist Giacomo Fiore locates that collective in a time-honored and complex genealogy of experimental art practices and communities that are explicitly oriented away from the market. Perhaps surprisingly, Fiore argues that the very sustainability and success of Frog Peak "is due to a steadfast adherence to its twin anti-editorial and noncommercial principles."[13]

Approaches like Frog Peak's are interesting because they ask us to confront some of the assumptions we may make about art production in contemporary culture. One of the first questions that arises concerning such outsider approaches to art is, How do these people make a living? Such a question reveals the degree to which our ideas about art-making—and even about artistic autonomy—are tied to financial reward; conventional notions concerning artistic sustainability focus on the types of artworks that generate their own income by being attractive to corporations or broad fan bases, or that are supported by state or philanthropic funding. But presumably, artists whose practices explicitly reject this kind of money orientation make their living in myriad ways, working in a variety of employment sectors, just like everyone else. By not expecting or wanting their art to earn them a living, they are able to attach art-making to a different set of values and priorities than those of the artists examined in this book. On the one hand, this approach may come dangerously close to articulating the kind of "do what you love" ethos I criticized in chapter 1. However, this ethos is always directed at the end goal of financial profitability; self-help books and business advice formulate it as an if-then statement: "Do what you love, and the money will follow." This orientation is very different from Frog Peak's, in which financial profit is explicitly not a goal of art production itself. If sustainability—making a living—is contingent on binding art production to the dynamic of market exchange or elite sponsorship, then a given artwork's very sustainability renders lifeless its ability to criticize power.

This may suggest a different kind of rhetorical tactic from the one the artists discussed in my previous chapters deploy in advocating for what they do. What if we stopped thinking of musical production as "work" requiring adequate remuneration from the market or from institutions? The musician and writer Jean Smith exemplifies an artist who has rigorously maintained a gap between "art" and "work" in her own life while also remaining oriented toward the world rather than toward a radical personal autonomy. Smith is part of Mecca Normal, an experimental musical duo that played a major role in the first wave of Pacific Northwest indie rock in the late 1980s. In an essay outlining her thoughts on art and work, Smith describes Mecca Normal as a band "that has never intended to be famous, rich or even liked." She notes that "the activity of not attempting to get somewhere in terms of what already exists presents an opportunity to make things up as we go along,"[14] and then discusses the many day jobs she has had throughout her life:

> I thrive while turning customer service in a clothing store into perfor-
> mance art, or reading sections of my manuscript to clients while I worked at
> Curves—the gym for women who hate gyms. I use jobs as a source of songs
> and stories, and as a sort of abstract comparative study—how conventional
> people live. A part-time job takes pressure off my creativity. I'm not thinking
> about how well a song will sell. I make songs for other reasons, including
> happiness.[15]

Smith seems to be describing something akin to the intense engagement with "everyday life" insisted on by the historical avant-garde, a goal
quite different from the imperative to "communicate with audiences" that
I've diagnosed in contemporary classical music culture. Smith also doesn't
think of such day jobs as beneath her or as stymying her "real" work. When
she says that "it is possible to take something you care about and make it
your life,"[16] she is using the term *life* as an index of something much larger
than merely "making a living."

Though it may be conceptually inspiring, a lifestyle like Smith's is also
precarious and financially unstable. She chooses jobs according to a complex personal ethic that prohibits her from working for certain corporations or in certain sectors that she perceives as more socially destructive
than others; this ethic further limits her opportunities to make money. She
goes long periods without health insurance and often worries about paying
the rent. If she becomes sick or disabled or once she is too old to work, her
ability to survive will become uncertain. Smith's situation in this regard is
frightening and unnecessary and should be unacceptable to society, and
yet it is no different from the lives of millions of people in this country—
and billions around the world—about whose sufferings nothing is done.
She insists on remaining a part of this vast multitude and using her art
practice to engage honestly with the world as it is, rather than working to
chain her art to the very marketplace that immiserates everyone else.

One of the musical issues Adorno returns to again and again is the way
capitalism limits the potential for experiencing and expressing subjective
freedom. He argues that in the Western tradition, "art had always imagined that it could locate its enduring core and substance in the subject."[17]
Because currently existing reality is so unequivocally bad, and the condition of late capitalism so universal, however, the individual subject has become ephemeral and problematic. This condition has undermined "art in

which subjectivity asserts itself as a positive good." But as Adorno himself admits, it is difficult to imagine a music bereft of subjectivity; in fact he criticizes composers like John Cage for "abdicating" subjectivity in favor of a misguided celebration of "the music itself"—a compositional approach he scathingly describes as "transform[ing] psychological ego weakness into aesthetic strength."[18]

How might music articulate or at least suggest a productive formulation of subjectivity despite the degraded condition of the individual in contemporary culture? Such a music would have to challenge the timeworn centrality of radical individualism to our conception of artistic authenticity and of life itself. The music theorists Bryan Parkhurst and Stephan Hammel discuss the "musical consequences of bourgeois society's atomic conception of individuality and individual agency," noting that, for example, rounded and closed song forms articulating a single perspective might be contrasted against collective forms like baroque ritornello that are more open to improvisatory group musicking. Such forms are governed by norms of a "collective vision of agency" which might be potentially "counterhegemonic" under capitalism.[19] Perhaps in music that experimented with articulating many perspectives simultaneously we might hear a sound that more productively gestured toward an actually free world, and a more just formulation of diversity than the Western-centric, market-friendly one that neoliberals propagate. The anthropologist Anna Tsing uses a musical metaphor to underscore her envisioning of the countless "entanglements" that constitute life and from which we have all been alienated by capitalism's history of turning everyone and everything into resources for investment.[20] Tsing uses the term *polyphonic assemblage* to describe how different lifeworlds contain all sorts of life—not only different human beings but also animals, trees, insects, bacteria, and so on—some that are related to one another, and some that are not. Comparing this assemblage to a fugue or madrigal, in contrast with "music with a single perspective," Tsing asks that we learn to once again appreciate "multiple temporal rhythms and trajectories."[21]

Music and musical practices that explore entanglements instead of celebrating discrete, individualist, or otherwise teleological perspectives might help us envision more humane and communal tactics for survival than the ones currently articulated in mainstream classical musical discourses. According to the journalists, institutions, and artists I've examined in the previous chapters, if classical music is to survive, it must innovate, it must leave the stuffy confines of traditional opera houses and concert halls, it must learn to compete in the marketplace on its own merits. Musicians and composers must become entrepreneurs: adaptable, self-managing individuals who compete with one another to disrupt old ways of doing things. This discourse presents a version of survival that is common to American fantasies—as Tsing puts it, this formulation means "saving oneself by fighting off others," and thus "survival" ultimately becomes "a synonym for conquest and expansion."[22] Indeed, as I discussed in chapter 4, the powerful belief in healthy competition between individuals is one enshrined in the "spirit of capitalism" itself—Max Weber observed that the Puritans felt that the opportunity to compete with others in order to accumulate wealth is an opportunity given by God, one that we shirk at our souls' peril. However, it is becoming increasingly evident that surviving in any meaningful sense will be contingent on more than our ability to conquer others. Music seeking to awaken a radically new sense of collectivity—one based not just on like-minded individuals' recognition of one another, but on our shared recognition of the intrinsic worth and meaning of every life on earth, human and otherwise—would contribute to the process of reorienting us away from the competitive ethos that is destroying our world.

This represents a very different envisioning of connectivity from the one articulated by corporations as they attempt to connect us all via data and smart technology. The Cisco Systems marketing rhetoric I discussed in chapter 1 at first seems like Tsing's idea of entanglements ("we are all connected . . . one universe . . . one planet"). But Tsing insists that in order to survive, we must abandon all the unified progress narratives inherited from the Enlightenment, and instead recognize the earth as a vast system of lifeworlds, some of which overlap and some of which are discrete, some of which have shared goals and some of which do not. By contrast, Cisco emphasizes that "we" are "working with one purpose" and that this unified goal orientation makes us "amazing together."

Another way artists might productively challenge the values of capitalism could be to reject, refuse, or otherwise critique the imperative toward uniqueness and originality, which lend themselves so well to competitive individualism. There are artists like the Irish composer Jennifer Walshe whose work seems to oppose the cult of original genius. In one project, Walshe spent two years presenting and publishing under nine different pseudonyms. She created complex backstories for these alter egos, using the internet to disperse intentionally contradictory information about them and to plant false information and fictitious news events concerning "their" work. When reading about this art collective—called Grúpat—it becomes hard to discern who "Jennifer Walshe" is: in some articles or reviews, her real name may never even appear, as the author of the review in question may be unaware of her many personae; the author may even be Walshe herself, writing under yet another pseudonym. Speaking to the ephemerality of individual subjectivity, she notes, "I must say that Jennifer Walshe is a persona as much as [her many alter egos], in terms of being a social construct and being regarded in a certain way."[23] The artist and theorist eldritch Priest (lowercase intentional) points out that Walshe does all this self-consciously in the realm of Western art music, a realm hostile to anonymity and pseudonymity, because namelessness is associated more with folk and oral traditions than with those of high art.[24] By experimenting with identity in this way, and by intentionally spreading out her artistic self over many separate "people," Walshe rejects values like originality, genius, individuality, and uniqueness that have been so important to Western art music and to bourgeois progress narratives. Her project also might be figured as a critique of the doctrine of flexibility that conditions labor—including artistic labor—today. She seems almost to parody this condition, by literally splitting herself into multiple selves, each with its own personality, appearance, mode of speaking, and artistic process. In this way she riffs puckishly on the "fragmentation" of the self that Ilana Gershon identifies as a signal feature of neoliberal subjectivity.[25]

Conceptual music in general might be figured as offering the possibility of resistance to various kinds of commodification as well as new ways of constructing ideas about life and the world. Conventional descriptive tools are inadequate for explaining such art, and often these works resist materiality in such a way as to be completely ephemeral. Walshe, for example, often works with imaginary sounds—one of her pieces entails the performer visualizing the inside of their own body as a diamond mine and then using the voice to "pulverize" diamonds—and with processes rather than products. Tim Rutherford-Johnson describes one of her more well-known pieces, "THIS IS WHY PEOPLE O.D. ON PILLS / AND JUMP FROM THE GOLDEN GATE BRIDGE" (2004), the "score" for which instructs the performer to "learn to skateboard" and then create a mental image of a skateboarding route that is then somehow realized in sound. For Rutherford-Johnson, such dematerialized music "turns our attention to the nature of mediation itself."[26]

Such music not only resists aspects of commodification; it also solicits performers and audiences into the imaginative, theoretical work of artistic creation outside currently normative parameters. Everyone involved must try to do the impossible work of envisioning the skateboard route or the internal diamond mine of the singer, and such work creates spaces for envisioning different ways of thinking, being, and making. When we encounter art or music that we cannot make sense of, it can cause us to question what we think we know, and why and how we know it: What is "music," and why do I think it ought to sound a certain way? Who told me that music ought to sound in such a way, and why? These kinds of questions can start the critical ball rolling, simply by confronting us with the many received wisdoms via which we thoughtlessly operate. The musicologist Stephen Graham argues that strange, experimental, "fringe" artistic gestures or musical sounds can invoke a kind of "aesthetic counter-magic" by "offering to audiences the chance to experience new ways of organizing sound and thus of experiencing the world."[27]

Music is, by its nature, highly variable. Raymond Williams points out, for example, that while some artworks exist in space as objects, music does not—even canonical classical music exists only as "notations" in varying scores and performances, and thus in some fairly crucial ways "there is no Fifth Symphony."[28] For Williams, this lack of tangibility points to a powerful difference between viewing an artwork as an object and viewing art as a practice. When we talk about art only in terms of objects, he argues, we merely articulate a theory of consumption—how to "profitably or correctly" consume a given work of art. By contrast, when we recognize the shifting, ephemeral nature of notational arts like music, and the fact that they exist in multiple forms whenever we generate them, we can "break" from our cherished theories of consumption to gain insight into music as "a complex of extending active relationships."[29] In *Dig*, Phil Ford discusses music's enigmatic essence, which can be used to serve any purpose. At the same time, he insists, something exists in all music—bad or good—that can't be captured, assimilated, or used, simply because it is *sound*.[30] Because it refuses to link the idea of musical autonomy to any given set of musical techniques or processes, such a formulation of music's ephemerality perhaps widens our ability to perceive and appreciate that idea and the powerful work it can do for our critical imaginations. This ungraspable aspect of music might provide a fruitful object for contemplation as we struggle to untangle our deeply felt assumptions about individualism and freedom, hoping to find some aspect of those values that is not contingent on market logic.

Art and the World

The preceding discussion may raise some questions. Each of the above examples still interacts with capitalism in some way—Jean Smith is paid wages for labor she gives to capitalists; Jennifer Walshe wins awards and is written about in the arts press; Frog Peak relies on the internet, and so on—so we might ask, Is music doomed to be simply a product of culture conditioned by the base of the economy and unable to be anything else, even when it tries? Is music capable of being truly oppositional, or do the previous examples merely indicate the impossibility of getting "outside" the system completely? Worse, do these examples perhaps reiterate capitalist logics in some way we just can't see yet? Finally, does (or can) music even affect social reality in the first place? If so, how does it do this, and how might it do it differently? If not, then what's the point of making music at all?

The question of art's potential to affect the social world has interested Marxists (as well as pseudo-Marxists like Jacques Attali) for decades. Luc Boltanski and Eve Chiapello's *The New Spirit of Capitalism* pursues the question of whether, and if so how, cultural production can affect the social realm. Their object of study is the revolutionary struggle of 1968, in which both workers and university students participated. The authors point out that while the collective critique articulated by workers posed a genuine threat to capitalism, the individualist one posed by students—the "artistic critique"—was easily incorporated into the system. Capitalism was transformed in order to grant individual workers certain kinds of personal freedoms, but it did not change in terms of the collective injustice it wreaks; indeed, meeting the demands of the artistic critique actually worsened the system's collective injustice in several ways, as the new freedoms it allowed ultimately generated new labor formations (like the gig economy) that intensified exploitation and labor precarity. For Boltanski and Chiapello, this example illustrates the fact that ideas produced by knowledge workers can indeed affect the social realm, albeit not always in a revolutionary manner. The authors assert that artists could perhaps play a small role in opposing capitalism, but only if they seek out radical new demands to make of power, ones that are not grounded in the desire for personal expression and individual freedom of choice.

Theodor Adorno, on the other hand, generally foreclosed on this possibility. He argued that "the role of music in the social process is exclusively that of a commodity; its value is that determined by the market."[31] Music serves no direct purpose and is no longer even able to accurately depict the contemporary condition; thus, "the alienation of music from man has become complete." Furthermore, the very music that seeks to address this alienation by striving to embody it—as in works by Schoenberg and Webern—is in turn rejected by a society that cannot make sense of this gesture. In his essay on the fetish character in music, Adorno notes an irony in the widespread rejection of early serialist music on the basis that it is incomprehensible:

> The terror which Schoenberg and Webern spread, today as in the past, comes not from their incomprehensibility but from the fact that they are all too correctly understood. Their music gives form to that anxiety, that terror, that insight into the catastrophic situation which others merely evade by regressing. . . . [Their music is] a single dialogue with the powers which destroy individuality.[32]

All the artists my previous chapters examine have identified the source of music's alienation in the very musical gestures (those of early modernism) that Adorno argues opposed or at least revealed it. Accordingly, they attempt to resolve this alienation not by standing apart but by reaching out to audiences and by generating friendly, tuneful, or otherwise "accessible" music and performances. Adorno calls these kinds of affirmative discourses about music and audiences "deceptions" that serve as "an apology for music which has allowed itself to be intimidated economically."[33] In short, such artists have decided that music's alienation from society is music's fault, not society's. Accordingly, Adorno argues, they attempt to change music, "with no change in society." He leaves open the question of whether music itself could aid the necessary changes in society that would resolve the alienation of the individual (although he remains pessimistic on the subject); regardless, he argues that music's effect will only ever be negligible if all it does is work to establish "immediacy."[34]

If Adorno (rhetorically, at least) leaves open the question of music's ability to effect social change, other post-Marxists developed much more rigid refutations of this notion, arguing that music can have no emancipatory potential whatsoever—all it can do, in all its many forms, is reaffirm capitalism. A recent article by Bryan Parkhurst and Stephan Hammel seeks to challenge this argument, which is crystallized in writings by the contemporary music theorists Henry Klumpenhouwer and Adam Krims. Parkhurst and Hammel want to bring back the commitment to praxis that is at the core of Marx's political economy but that (they argue) has been effaced by so much post-Marxist thinking.[35] Is it true, they ask, that cultural commodities, simply by virtue of being commodities, must "monolithically" serve capital? Probably in most cases the answer is yes. However, they point out that Marx's *Capital*, for one, can and does take the form of a commodity (when it is mass produced and sold at bookstores or on Amazon), and yet the book—meaning the ideas and analyses it contains—nonetheless continues to also serve the interest of the oppressed class, "even if the oppressors have found an occasional use for it, too."[36] They focus on how ideas of agency emerge and are developed, and how musical praxis can encourage or inhibit particular types of agency. Parkhurst, Hammel, Klumpenhouwer, and Krims (as well as Adorno) seem to agree that music can function to show us reality; what is at issue here is whether we can learn from and be changed by that display, and then change the real world accordingly. For Parkhurst and Hammel, by reflecting reality back at us music "can also be efficacious in upholding or modifying that conception: what we see in the mirror can lead us to change what we show to the mirror, but it can also play a reinforcing role by confirming our sense that things should remain as they are."[37]

In this sense, then, music and musical analysis, by "making explicit" our norms of musicking, can develop new awareness of how we conceive agency, which could lead us to developing new norms, new conceptions of agency, which could—at least in theory—affect the economic base. Therefore, according to Parkhurst and Hammel, music (and music criticism) can (sometimes) be a "political instrument."[38] Our struggle against capitalism obviously demands the creation of counterhegemonic thinking, and making normative an alternative view of society that might contest and replace the one we currently hold. The construction of musical norms is one small but real aspect of how these changes could begin to happen. Will we allow musical norms to be created that reinforce capitalist ideologies, like the ones diagnosed in this book? Or will we insist on showing those norms for what they are while seeking out real alternatives?

The reader at this point may still be wondering how useful such artistic gestures really are, though. After all, none of the examples of oppositional music I've described really "propose solutions" to our current predicament, and most of them are so niched that hardly anyone has even encountered them—obviously, Frog Peak is not going to bring about the end of global capitalism, so what's the point? Furthermore, by being so rigorously anti-market, don't some of these artists foreclose on the possibility of attaining the kind of widespread visibility that makes it possible to really spread political messages? And don't we have to make political compromises in order to attain such visibility?

These are fair questions, to which I can only offer my still-unshaken belief that the project of imagining differently continues to remain vitally important, perhaps more important now than ever before. The imaginative project is not political action—it can never stand in for direct action—but surely it is what plants the seeds for action. If we are unable to even imagine what a different world could look like, then we truly have resigned. Frog Peak artists or Jean Smith may not be proposing the kind of technocratic, chartable solutions that liberals require before they will even consider addressing a social problem. But at least they are trying to think, to envision alternatives, to squirm out from under the various ideologies of capitalism, and to challenge various aspects of the artistic and social status quo. This endeavor—to think and imagine differently—remains a necessary one.

Utopian Imaginaries

Such imaginative critics of capitalism are often accused of "utopian" thinking, and utopian thinking, as we all know, is a futile gesture, at best naïve and at worst dangerous. In a review of a book about communism, Stanford University research fellow Jennifer Roback Morse tackles communist utopianism, and asks the question "that surely must haunt any friend of liberty—indeed, any honest person," which is, "What made the communist idea appeal to so many people?"[39] Morse discusses the "criminal empire" of Stalinist Russia as well as of China, North Korea, and Cuba, and claims that their "strategies" continue to serve as "the mainstay of the radical left in the United States."[40] Similarly, in an extensive book review assessing recent scholarship on utopianism, the journalist Akash Kapur discusses the failure of utopian efforts to remake society, associating this failure with the personal and philosophical failings of the utopians themselves—their "egoism, acquisitiveness, [and] competitiveness" and the "ills of human flesh" they always fall prey to.[41]

Kapur cites many examples of failed historical utopias to demonstrate the impossibility of challenging capitalism or remaking society in any radical way. However, he does not note that because of the threat many utopian efforts present to existing power hierarchies, the coercive behavior of Western democracies has often had more of a negative impact on these efforts than their own internal ideas have. For example, many critics of communism hold up Cuba's poverty as a case study of why communism doesn't work, but they fail to acknowledge that the oppressive sanctions the United States and other Western capitalist democracies have enacted against Cuba for decades have surely played a part in that country's impoverishment.

Even more obviously, the states these utopian efforts challenge tend to violently crush serious utopian projects. Silvia Federici examines the fates of the many anticapitalist heretical communities that flourished in the sixteenth century, comprised of peasants who fled the imposition of wage labor and the enclosure of the commons to establish communal, nonmonetary, often matriarchal social structures in the woods and hills of Western Europe. Because of the threat these communities posed to hereditary and merchant-class power and to the growing consolidation of a capitalist money economy, armies of the state ruthlessly hunted their members down with dogs and horses, burned their homes and lands, and publicly tortured their leaders to death.[42] In 1871 the French army lined the members of the Paris Commune up against a wall and shot them—a conclusion to the communist experiment that we can hardly chalk up to a philosophical or moral failure on the part of the Communards themselves. More recently, the activists who took part in the Occupy movement were forcibly removed from the nominally public lands they were trying to lay claim to; militarized police officers arrested them, sprayed them with tear gas, confiscated their belongings, and drove weaponized vehicles into their encampments. Nonetheless, in explaining the "failure" of the Occupy movement, many commentators pointed to inherent flaws in the movement itself, like the fact that it lacked strong leadership and concrete goals, as though a statement of demands would somehow have stopped the policing of private property that is a foundational requirement of capitalism.

Returning to Morse's question about why communism appeals to people when it so obviously generates "criminal empires," we might just as easily ask why so many people continue to find the idea of capitalism so appealing. While state communism certainly engendered horrific conditions in the bounded times and places in which it has existed, the depredations of capitalism are global and ongoing. The utter, irreversible devastation of the environment, the for-profit prison system, the imposition of debt peonage on entire populations, the expansion of a dystopic and oppressive surveillance state, mass displacement and genocide, and the use of slave labor are features of capitalist accumulation both in the United States and around the world, features intentionally implemented by governments and corporations. Why are these conditions not also perceived as constituting a reprehensible "criminal empire"?

In the general acceptance of capitalism as a normative and unchangeable system—and in the widespread ability to discount or excuse the previously mentioned horrors the system generates—we can see how capitalist logics have worked themselves into our fundamental assumptions and conventional wisdoms. Critics like Kapur and Morse fail to see that capitalism itself is a profoundly utopian idea, in the sense that it continuously promises to deliver us into a perfect society that never actually materializes. In fact, this is a foundational belief of modern economics. Commentators on the left have pointed out how economists treat the processes of capital as natural laws, despite their actual emanation from a specific—and surprisingly recent—time and place. Geoff Mann analyzes college economics textbooks to demonstrate that mainstream economics treats the market "like one of the fundamental forces of the universe, as independent of human desires as gravity."[43] In dismantling the utopianism that lies at the heart of contemporary economics, Mann notes the vast number of variables that shape actual life on earth but in unquantifiable or unpredictable ways—variables like love and hate, extreme weather events, communal identification, language mixes, degrees of social peace, religious beliefs, and countless other factors whose impact on the economy cannot be empirically measured or accurately predicted. Because these factors cannot be plotted on a graph, economic modeling cannot take them into account when assessing how or whether markets function. In short, economics cannot comprehend myriad real-world conditions or events except as external "disturbances" of an idealized pure market. Partly because of all these unquantifiable variables, Mann concludes that there could never be a real-world market that functioned exactly in accordance with economic models. Amazingly, economists know this, but instead of adjusting their models to account for reality, they instead call reality itself a "second-best" variation on a mythical perfect model.[44] As Mann puts it, in economics— supposedly an empirical science—"the real world is never taken in its own actuality as the basis for understanding."[45] This is utopian thinking at its most insidious; indeed, it is much more starry-eyed than communism, which at least starts from the recognition of inequality and suffering, conditions that actually exist. Capitalism has continuously promised us a degree of equality and freedom that has yet to materialize and that currently seems further out of reach than ever before. It has not expanded the zone of freedom globally; it has simply accumulated a relative degree of comfort for the few by exploiting the labor of the many, all the while assuring us that our participation in this system is the only viable way to generate peace and prosperity for all. This cultish logic continues to condition US political and social discourse, even as cracks in its current iteration have begun to appear.

Critique in the World

Although I have concluded by trying to reclaim the urgent necessity of utopian thinking, this book has not explored examples of such thinking in any depth. Rather, it has been a critical project directed at dissecting some examples of capitalist ideology in contemporary musical practice. But critique itself is not political action—like the oppositional gestures briefly charted in these pages, critique remains a small, imaginative process rather than a concrete political act. We might, then, wonder what the point of this book is, and indeed, as with musical practice, we might wonder whether the critical project holds any real social value at all.

Like the oppositional musics discussed above, critique is perhaps most unsatisfying for its refusal to offer grand, easily implementable solutions—the literary critic Rita Felski argues that the critic's fundamental stance is one of "againstness," and this stance can make it hard to do anything *but* criticize.[46] Is everything always only bad, as the critic seems to insist? If so, what are we supposed to do? How (and why) are we supposed to go on living? For the critic, systematically dismantling the weak ideas and nonsense jargon characterizing mainstream discourses of all kinds—and even attacking our own poorly formulated thoughts or bad values—can feel clarifying, like polishing a filthy window and looking through it at last. Yet it's true that this negating practice can sometimes start feeling less like a window than like a barred door: what is beyond the critique?

At the same time, I think that it is unjust to assert that the act of criticism is always only a negation, an act of taking away something that seems good and replacing it with the awareness of false consciousness. On the contrary, in my experience critical thinking and writing play an important role in keeping hope alive. Felski calls critique "a style of interpretation driven by a spirit of disenchantment," and it may seem counterintuitive to suggest that actively seeking disenchantment can be a hopeful project.[47] But living under late capitalism means living in a miasma of false advertising that attests to the impossibility of there being any other way to live than this. These messages come from everywhere, not only from the media we consume and from the politicians and corporations that run our country, but from our teachers, our friends and family, artists and writers and scholars, even people who believe they are oriented against power. We are tightly wrapped in a shroud of late capitalism's self-perpetuating logics. Undertaking a critique of all this—seeking to become disenchanted by it—means trying to peel back a corner of this shroud and peer beneath it. What's under there? Who could we be, were we not entangled in this moldering network of ideology? In this sense, criticism can be a ray of light that penetrates the darkness. If we are still able to think through, beyond, or around capitalist logic, even if minutely or imperfectly, it must mean that such logic is not all there is. This belief allows the possibility of hope, and hope is what wards off the socially useless conditions of nihilism and despair. Despite his reputation for extreme pessimism, Theodor Adorno's deeply moving statement on the value of critical thought speaks to the practice's grounding in hopefulness:

> The happiness that dawns in the eye of the thinking person is the happiness of humanity. The universal tendency of oppression is opposed to thought as such. Thought is happiness, even where it defines unhappiness: by enunciating it. By this alone happiness reaches into the universal unhappiness. Whoever does not let it atrophy has not resigned.[48]

At the same time, as Felski notes, critique itself isn't automatically rigorous or intrinsically radical. Climate change skeptics perform critiques of scientific evidence, for example; and police officers, like critics, operate via a "hermeneutics of suspicion" that we would not call radical in the progressive political sense of the word. Furthermore, as Felski puts it, "the imagined location of critique" is always "*elsewhere*: outside, below, in the margins, or at the borders," when in reality of course there is no "outside."[49] We are all inside. I earn my living in the American university system, a system that has undergone rapid neoliberalization over the past few decades. I can and do hold on to the aspects of my work that still feel socially beneficial in some way, but the fact remains that with my labor, I uphold a system of profound exploitation. I celebrate education as a public good even as my students are shackled and sold into lifelong debt peonage by predatory lending institutions. I strive desperately to achieve tenure, knowing that the casualization of academic labor means many of my colleagues and friends will never even make it onto the tenure track. My retirement funds are safeguarded for me by the state, which invests them in a stock market whose amoral machinations are literally destroying the world. Criticism on its own will not solve any of this, nor is the critic absolved simply by pointing it out.

Finally, it may be true that in some fundamental sense critique today has "run out of steam," as Bruno Latour puts it.[50] In the 1960s, it may have been a radical act to deconstruct texts and demonstrate that there are no such things as "facts." Today, however, we live in a "post-fact" era, in which respect for scientific evidence or logical argument has ebbed to catastrophically low levels. Latour points out that in a sense, everyone is a postmodernist now, each of us staking our own objective claim on truth and deciding what to believe based on our own idiosyncratic system of gut feelings and news feeds curated for us by algorithms based on our shopping habits. Both Latour and Felski address the fact that for many people, then, critique is fundamentally unsatisfying. We want truth, and critique gives us ambiguities. We want to know what is good and what is bad, and critique gives us only contradictions.

Latour accuses critique of stripping away the "thingy" qualities from everything: the critic insists that nothing is real, and yet of course some things are real, and we can and should care about such real things deeply. There is truth to this portrait of the critic, and yet I have experienced my critical project in precisely the opposite terms. I have sought to insist on what is real, in the face of marketing gestures that present a falsely positive vision of capitalist processes. Against musical ideas that promote techno-utopian corporate visions of multicultural collaboration or urban renewal, I have tried to impose the realities of inequality, violence, mass displacement, and gentrification that such visions disguise. Into the widespread belief that entrepreneurialism and competitive individualism promote social justice, I have tried to insert the realities of precarity, commodification, and labor intensification that such formations impose. Against the glorified visions of the "human creativity" technology enables, I have insisted on the realities of surveillance dystopia and drone warfare that are radically remaking our actual lived experience. Like most fictions, the promotional fantasies I criticize all have aspects of truth to them, but they function only by rigorously masking other, perhaps more pressing, truths. More troubling is the fact that although the projects I've addressed in this book are often critically unreflective, historically uninformed, and philosophically or even aesthetically insipid, they have nonetheless won Pulitzers, MacArthurs, and Guggenheims. They have received millions of dollars in corporate, municipal, and institutional sponsorship. They are widely celebrated in the arts press and widely performed at major venues all over the country. They are upheld as the "saviors" of classical music, and for this reason they are also playing a major role in reshaping how music is taught and studied in academic institutions. The very fact that so many people seem to find these fantastical promotional rhetorics inspiring and worthy of mass subsidy and support demands critical attention; this belief is what generated this book.

I have discussed the ideal of autonomy throughout this study, positioning it as a fraught, often deeply philosophically flawed attempt to get outside market logic. I've examined what happens to this ideal when it is taken into the service of capitalism, as in Intel's reinvention of Beethoven's Fifth, but more importantly, I've tried to understand the reasons that so many contemporary music practitioners and scholars have ceased yearning for it. The autonomous ideal, in one form or another, has played a major role in determining how we make and value music for nearly two centuries. I am not concerned with whether this ideal has ever actually existed; rather, what interests me is that so many have yearned for it so evidently and for so long. The chipping away of even the *desire* for a noncommodified space is capitalism's most urgent project, and the musical products, practices, and discourses examined in this book demonstrate the ongoing success of that project. By critiquing such phenomena, I want to try to reawaken our desire to escape capitalism.

Crises in capitalism are frightening. Depressions, recessions, waves of bankruptcies and forced migrations, and mass unemployment and immiserization generate social instability and despair, which can provide openings for nihilistic political movements to come marching through. At the same time, these crises show us that capitalism is not inevitable, that it can be assailed and, potentially, destroyed. While the present political, social, and environmental landscape is a bleak and ruinous one, the cracks that are forming in capitalist logic might also provide purchase for alternatives to take root. For these alternatives to flourish, we need to think critically about our goals, our values, the rhetoric we repeat, and the survival techniques we practice, as well as how we work to justify those practices to ourselves.

ACKNOWLEDGMENTS

A million thanks to Elizabeth Branch Dyson, who shepherded this project with much kindness, encouragement, and good advice. I also thank Dylan Joseph Montanari and the editorial and marketing teams at Chicago, Sandra Hazel for her rigorous copyediting, and the three anonymous reviewers whose generous engagement powerfully transformed the book. I am grateful to Kathleen Kearns, the "Book Coach," who helped me hammer out the first draft of the manuscript. Finally, my thanks to John Nolan, who put together the musical examples in chapter 1.

I extend my gratitude to my colleagues in the UMass Department of Music and Dance, whose lively community I am happy to be a part of. Special thanks to my music history colleagues Ernest May, Erinn Knyt, and Emiliano Ricciardi, and my colleague and chair, Roberta Montemorra Marvin, for their tireless support and encouragement. I am also deeply grateful to UMass for providing a pretenure research leave, during which I wrote the entire first draft of this book; to say that this leave made my life easier would be a vast understatement. Thanks also go to the UMass Interdisciplinary Studies Institute, which granted me a yearlong fellowship during which I benefited from workshops with colleagues in multiple disciplines. Parts of chapter 1 were first published as an article in *Music and Politics*, and I am grateful to its publishers for allowing me to republish here.

I have always been lucky when it comes to mentors. I am so grateful to my undergraduate adviser Eleonora Beck not only for the guidance and friendship she has given me over the past twenty-three years but also simply for the example she set, from the very beginning, of joyful, engaged teaching and of how to lead a balanced, happy life. My luck with mentors continued to hold at UCLA. The faculty I studied with—Susan McClary, Raymond Knapp, Elizabeth Upton, Robert Fink, Elisabeth Le Guin, Olivia

Bloechl, Mitchell Morris, Timothy Taylor, Tamara Levitz, and Robert Walser —were uniformly wonderful and gave their time unselfishly. I didn't know it then, but the very first class I took at UCLA would resonate far into my future: Robert Fink's seminar "The Death of Classical Music" introduced many of the debates, texts, and concepts I find myself grappling with in my work today, and the first paragraph of my introduction was also inspired by the series of stage-setting vignettes that open his *Repeating Ourselves*. Two mentors at UCLA deserve special thanks. I am so grateful to Raymond Knapp, from whose skillfully designed independent studies and firm editing hand I learned so much, and who was unfailingly kind during the sometimes difficult early years of grad school. I am deeply indebted as well to Susan McClary for the warmth and generosity she has always shown me, for her incredible gift as a teacher, and for the brilliance of her example as a writer and intellect. She has indelibly shaped how I think and write about music.

I'm grateful to the community of fellow grad students at UCLA that has nurtured me as a teacher and scholar in countless ways; our support network and friendship continue to mean the world to me. Thank you especially to Phil Gentry, Julianne Lindberg, Jessica Bissett Perea, Marcie Ray, Elizabeth Morgan, Joanna Love, Hyun Kyong Chang, Kariann Goldschmitt, Pete Broadwell, Lindsay Johnson, and Eric Wang.

The ideas in this book developed over several years of reading and talking with smart people. Parts of chapters 1, 2, and 4 were presented at meetings of the American Musicological Society and the Society for American Music; the book has benefited greatly from feedback I received from conference attendees. Roger Mathew Grant probably isn't aware of the transformative role he played in the development of my critical orientation, but I thank him for it anyway. My colleague Jason Hooper has provided indispensable advice and solidarity as I've worked on this project and started my career at UMass. A million thanks to James Currie for his generous engagement with the manuscript. Thank you to Kirsten Leng, for long talks about culture, power, feminism, and comedy. I'm also deeply grateful for the friendship and collaboration cohering around the study of neoliberalism and new music; I especially thank John Pippen, Will Robin, and David Blake, as well as Anne Shreffler and Judy Lochhead, for their mentorship and encouragement. Many of these friendships began at iterations of the "Musicology and the Present" conference series I coordinate with the brilliant Andrea Moore, whom I cherish as an interlocutor and a friend.

Many people outside academia have supported me in profound ways. Thank you first and foremost to my beautiful family: my parents, Mike and Susan Ritchey, and my brother, Buck Ritchey, who was my first friend and is still my best. I celebrate their adventurous spirits, their openness to life and to other people, their commitment to reading and writing, and their abiding curiosity. Thank you to Steve Schroeder and all my lifelong friends in Portland (and the Portland diaspora) for teaching me about collective loyalty; I love the community we have built. Thank you to Elizabeth Gramm and Burke Hilsabeck for maintaining our far-flung friendship over the years and for engaging in utopian thought exercises that have given me hope. Thank you to Lucas Small and Sarah Habeck for their inspiring construction of and commitment to alternative kinship networks, and for game nights and dog care. Thank you to Jessica Hopper and Mike Merrill for encouraging my writing in so many weird ways over the years. Regarding the formulation of some of my ideas about capitalism and art, several friendships have proved especially important. I cannot read certain passages of the book without thinking of Geneviève Castrée, who was slowly dying as I was writing the first draft; I hope something of her fierce idealism has made it into the final version. Thank you to Jae Choi for her close attention to and interest in language and semantics, for tolerating my many rants, and for alerting me to my overreliance on em dashes. Thank you also to my ride-or-die Katy Davidson for their incredible kindness and friendship, for transforming my musical life, for making me laugh the hardest, and for their unique ability to express the woeful, sublime experience of life (and death) in the Anthropocene.

Finally, I am grateful to my husband, Andrew Ritchey (né Peterson), who sees things as they are. He has spent years talking with me about these ideas, reading countless drafts, and listening to run-throughs of conference papers. It is impossible that this book would exist without his generous, sustained intellectual labor, or without the joyful foundation of his partnership in my life. I admire his wisdom and insight, his gift for the absurd, his powerful political rage, and his extraordinary gentleness with people and other creatures. Thank you, old man, for refusing to despair. This book is for you.

NOTES

INTRODUCTION

1. See Ferris, *Silent Urns*. Michael Long specifically addresses the ethical dimension of the term *classic* in *Beautiful Monsters*, 31.

2. Metzer, *Musical Modernism at the Turn of the Twenty First Century*.

3. Brown, *Edgework*, 40. The idea of rationality as a central feature of capitalist conditioning was first seriously examined by Max Weber, in *The Protestant Ethic and the Spirit of Capitalism*. For Weber, modern capitalism requires the rationalization of work. To survive within the system, individuals must methodically, rigorously systematize their work by taming their natural instincts and desires. Doing this on a grand scale, Weber argues, requires bureaucracy. Wendy Brown's notion of neoliberal rationality extends this discussion, and positions the US government itself as a large-scale bureaucracy that "manages" its citizens much like a business manages its employees. Brown's theory of neoliberal rationality builds on Foucault's notion that neoliberalism represents a new form of "governmentality," within which individuals no longer have to be coerced or forced into following neoliberal principles, but rather are trained to govern themselves in accordance with those principles. Brown asserts that this dehumanizing replacement of governance with bureaucratic management requires citizens to "rationalize" not only their approach to their work but their participation in democracy on a grand scale. See Weber, *The Protestant Ethic*; Foucault, "Governmentality"; and Brown, *Undoing the Demos*.

4. Brown, *Undoing the Demos*, 22.

5. In particular, see "The 'One-Man Band' and Entrepreneurial Selfhood in Neoliberal Culture," Dale Chapman's 2013 article relating the contemporary boom in live solo multi-instrumental performances to neoliberalism's insistence that citizens become wholly self-reliant. See also Martin Scherzinger's revival of Theodor Adorno and Max Horkheimer's approach to understanding capitalist structures through analyzing music in "Music, Corporate Power, and Unending War." James Currie has undertaken several critiques of academic musicology's failure to address its own complicity in furthering capitalist logic and neoliberal values. See "Music after All," and *Music and the Politics of Negation*. In "Musicological Omnivory in the Neoliberal University," David Blake assesses how the musicological privileging of "interdisciplinarity" is conditioned by neoliberalism.

6. Yuval Sharon, quoted in Lanz, "'Invisible Cities' Opera Moves from Union Station to Your Listening Device."

7. Moore, "Neoliberalism and the Musical Entrepreneur." Three other recent works that examine certain aspects of neoliberalism with regard to classical music or musicology have also influenced the present study: Blake, "Musicological Omnivory in the Neoliberal University"; Robin, "A Scene without a Name"; and Pippen, "Toward a Postmodern Avant-Garde."

8. Hoffmann, "Beethoven's Instrumental Music," 35 and 37.

9. Babbitt, "The Composer as Specialist," 53 and 54.

10. Sanna Pederson argues that the recent history of the concept can be understood only via comprehending the cultural context of German musicology in the 1970s, when musicologists from opposite sides of the Berlin Wall were engaged in a battle over musical meaning and the relationship between music and culture. Pederson, "Defining the Term 'Absolute Music' Historically."

11. Jameson initially laid out this notion in a 1984 article; the full exploration of his ideas came in 1991 with the publication of *Postmodernism: Or, the Cultural Logic of Late Capitalism*.

12. Taylor, *Music and Capitalism*, 2.

13. Taylor, 4.

14. Taylor, 2; Attali, *Noise*.

15. Drott, "Rereading Jacques Attali's *Bruits*."

16. Drott, 736.

17. Drott, 742.

18. Boltanski and Chiapello, *The New Spirit of Capitalism*.

19. See also Mauro, "The Death and Life of the Avant-Garde."

20. Zaslaw, "Mozart as Working Stiff."

21. Zaslaw, 107.

22. Taruskin, "The Musical Mystique."

23. Taruskin, 338.

24. Currie, "Music after All," 161.

25. Meiksins Wood, *Democracy against Capitalism*, 2.

26. See Williams, "Base and Superstructure in Marxist Cultural Theory."

27. Federici, *Caliban and the Witch*.

28. Weber, *The Protestant Ethic*.

29. Boltanski and Chiapello, *The New Spirit of Capitalism*, 9.

30. Boltanski and Chiapello, 20.

31. Brown, *Edgework*, 11 and 15.

32. Micro loans have proved to have a negligible impact on poverty, and have even been linked to waves of suicides (in India, for example) committed by people unable to pay back their loan or even keep up with the interest, which in some cases can be exorbitant. The economist Jason Hickel writes that "microfinance has become a socially acceptable mechanism for extracting wealth and resources from poor people." See "The Microfinance Delusion."

CHAPTER 1

Portions of this chapter first appeared as an article in *Music and Politics*, and I am grateful to the editors for permission to republish them here. See Ritchey, "Amazing Together."

1. See the Boston Symphony Orchestra's database of seasonal statistics on American

orchestras: http://bsomusic.org/stories/the-orchestra-season-by-the-numbers-data base.aspx (accessed October 4, 2018).

2. A video of this complete performance was once available on YouTube but has since been taken down. Video montages (emphasizing the Amazing Together theme) from the rest of the partner summit are still up on Cisco's website at the time of this writing: https://blogs.cisco.com/partner/cisco-partner-summit-day-3-thats-a-wrap (accessed October 4, 2018).

3. The partner summit is held in a different city each year; Cisco makes a one-time donation—which it calls a "local giveback"—to a local organization in each city, often a youth and/or music organization (for example, the 2013 local giveback was to the Boston Children's Chorus).

4. The Yahoo Finance listing for Cisco details its bewildering array of holdings in every sector of business related to internet connectivity: https://finance.yahoo.com/q/pr?s =CSCO+Profile (accessed October 4, 2018).

5. See Born, *Rationalizing Culture*; and Niebur, *Special Sound*.

6. See Taruskin, *The Oxford History of Western Music*, 5:495.

7. In *Rationalizing Culture*, Born paints a detailed portrait of IRCAM as a nation-building project, and provides a comprehensive explanation of its sources and amounts of funding.

8. Quoted in Tiee, "Bay Area Composer Mason Bates to Create New Steve Jobs Opera."

9. For this profile, see http://www.heinzawards.net/recipients/mason-bates (accessed October 4, 2018).

10. Midgette, "A Composer Offers the Field Just What It Needs."

11. See Michael Tilson Thomas's website, https://michaeltilsonthomas.com/2016/03/14/mason-bates-works-for-orchestra/ (accessed October 4, 2018).

12. The entire YTSO Sydney performance is viewable on the YTSO's YouTube channel: https://www.youtube.com/watch?v=LnKJpYGCLsg, 2:22:11, posted March 20, 2011.

13. The live paintings were mostly produced by Obscura Digital, a design company that often works with Google. The YTSO performance was the first time that images were projected onto the exterior of the opera house, although since then this has become routine.

14. Michael Tilson Thomas, remarks during the YTSO Sydney performance, https://www.youtube.com/watch?v=LnKJpYGCLsg, 2:22:11, posted March 20, 2011. Quote occurs at 46:35:00.

15. Friedman and Friedman, *Free to Choose*, 265.

16. Friedman, *Capitalism and Freedom*, 4.

17. Friedman and Friedman, *Free to Choose*, 147.

18. Harvey, *A Brief History of Neoliberalism*, 68.

19. See Dosi and Nelson, "An Introduction to Evolutionary Theories in Economics." For a study of innovation that positions it as a central feature of evolutionary economics, see Audretsch, *Innovation and Industry Evolution*.

20. Marx and Engels, *The Communist Manifesto*, 38.

21. Schumpeter, *Capitalism, Socialism, and Democracy*, 82.

22. Schumpeter, 132.

23. Clayton Christensen established the theory of "disruptive innovation" in 1995, in "Disruptive Technologies: Catch the Wave."

24. Two recent examples of books by academic economists who optimistically explore

innovation's role in successful economic policy are Atkinson and Ezell, *Innovation Economics*; and Janeway, *Doing Capitalism in the Innovation Economy*.

25. LaBarre, "Who's the Best at Innovating Innovation?"

26. See Elazar, "Federal/Confederal Solutions to the Israeli-Palestinian-Jordanian Conflict"; Hickman, "You Can Innovate while You Meditate"; Billingham, "Is There Any Place for Innovation in the Funeral Industry Today?"; Ewait, "Reuters Top 100: The World's Most Innovative Universities"; Wagner, *Creating Innovators*.

27. See Lebrecht, *Who Killed Classical Music?*; Johnson, *Who Needs Classical Music?*; Kramer, *Why Classical Music Still Matters*. See also Mark Vanhoenacker's article "Requiem" and William Robin's retort, "Classical Music Isn't Dead."

28. Moore, "Neoliberalism and the Musical Entrepreneur," 35.

29. See Brookes, "Missy Mazzoli Has a Different Take on Classical Music—and People Are Listening."

30. Sandow elaborates on these themes and ideas regularly on his blog, *Sandow*, at http://www.artsjournal.com/sandow/ (accessed October 11, 2018). See for example his discussion of ways the Metropolitan Opera might enter "the real world": http://www.artsjournal.com/sandow/2007/11/dumbing_it_down.html (accessed October 4, 2018). See also John von Rhein's article about Sandow in the *Chicago Tribune*, "What Can Be Done to Make Classical Music More Relevant to Today's Culture?"

31. Ricker, "YouTube Symphony—Year Two Coming."

32. "YouTube Announces Launch of 'YouTube Symphony Orchestra 2011," YouTube media release, October 12, 2010, https://sites.google.com/site/ytso2011press/media -release-finale-event-3-20.

33. "Mothership" is scored for full orchestra, plus harp, piano, and electronica. My discussion of this piece refers to the published score (San Jose, CA: Aphra Music, 2012) and the live version that was performed by the YTSO in Sydney.

34. I don't provide a link because the videos are always being taken down for copyright infringement, but searching for Major Lazer live videos on YouTube will bring up many examples.

35. Bates, "The Mechanics of Musical Narrative."

36. This is not meant to be an insult; film scoring has traditionally relied on such tropes as a primary tactic for helping construct narrative coherence among the disparate images comprising a film.

37. Friedman and Friedman, *Free to Choose*, 265.

38. See Taylor, *Music and Capitalism*, chap. 2.

39. Today, according to Aubrey Anable, "leisure time has shifted from being a counterpart to labor time to being another modality of productive work available for the temporal calculus that capital loves." Anable, "Labor/Leisure," 193.

40. "Do what you love" rhetoric and the widespread acceptance of free labor both resonate with Max Weber's idea of "the calling" in the Protestant ethic. Even though the explicitly religious connotations of the Puritans' ideas about constant, devoted work within a vocation have fallen away over the centuries, we are nonetheless still conditioned by these ideas; we believe work to be a source of personal fulfillment and that working hard and diligently is an expression of moral virtue.

41. Applebaum, "Multiculturalism and Flexibility," 309.

42. The project's creators have never revealed how much the event cost, but from piecing together information in various interviews and reviews of both YTSO performances it seems that Google paid for musicians' airfare and visa costs—as well as,

presumably, room and board—and also paid normal performance fees to Tilson Thomas, Bates, and the star soloists featured throughout the program.

43. Michael Tilson Thomas, remarks during the YTSO Sydney performance, https:// www.youtube.com/watch?v=LnKJpYGCLsg, 2:22:11, posted March 20, 2011. Quote occurs at 15:00:00.

44. Bates wrote solos in the score for "Mothership," but he notes that solos can be improvised whenever a performer is comfortable doing so. He includes lead sheets in the back of the score, giving harmonic information and suggested groups of notes to improvise around in each solo section.

45. For a brief and illuminating history of multiculturalism from 1911 through the 1990s, see Gordon and Newfield, introduction to *Mapping Multiculturalism*, 1–18. They cite for example an influential 1981 book by the Republican economist George Gilder, who argued that there is no need for governmental assistance of African Americans because no one in a position of power is racist any longer.

46. Friedman, *Capitalism and Freedom*, 15.

47. Friedman, 109.

48. Friedman, 109.

49. See Federici, *Caliban and the Witch*.

50. Jodi Melamed argues that official multiculturalisms serve as "unifying discourses for U.S. state, society, and global ascendancy and as material forces for postwar global capitalist expansion." *Represent and Destroy*, 1. See also the sociologist Jon Cruz's identification of multiculturalism as "part of a *social logic* of late capitalism" that conflates capitalist imperatives with humanistic ones like tolerance and justice ("From Farce to Tragedy," 19 [emphasis in original]).

51. In the rise of white supremacist nationalism that helped sweep Donald Trump into the White House in 2016, we can perhaps see some of the complicated fallout from this decades-long process of attaching antiracist values to free market principles. Trump's campaign successfully married the desire for economic renewal to racist xenophobia; in light of the US government's similar tradition of attaching issues of race and ethnicity to the workings of the market, the success of his racist campaign perhaps makes more sense.

52. Friedman, *Capitalism and Freedom*, 110.

53. After a two-year legal battle, for example, Google at last released its workforce demographic data—data which prove that the company is the least culturally and gender diverse of any in Silicon Valley, with a workforce that is overwhelmingly male, and white or Asian. See Harkinson, "Silicon Valley Firms Are Even Whiter and More Male Than You Thought."

54. Llopis, "Diversity Management Is the Key to Growth."

55. See Bersin, "Why Diversity and Inclusion Will Be a Top Priority for 2016."

56. Apple's "diversity" page can be viewed at www.apple.com/diversity (accessed October 4, 2018).

57. See Hamde et al., "Diversity and Diversity Management in Business and Organisation Studies."

58. Quoted in Davis, "Rethinking 'Race' Politics," 46.

59. Davis, 46. It is also worth noting that the business world is not unaware of the alarming contradiction between "utilitarian" and "ethical" reasons for valuing corporate diversity. See for example van Dijk, van Engen, and Paauwe, "Reframing the Business Case for Diversity."

60. See the YTSO announcement video: https://www.youtube.com/watch?v=LCFtKX nrbio, 1:13 (accessed October 4, 2018).

61. "The 'Internet Symphony' Global Mash Up" video, https://www.youtube.com/watch?v=oC4FAyg64OI, 4:46 (accessed October 4, 2018).

62. In 2014, Bates caused a scandal when he similarly accessorized cultural difference in his personal life. On October 31, he tweeted a picture of himself, his wife, and their two children dressed up in stereotypical Native American costumes for Halloween. Many of his followers criticized him, and pointed out that he was engaging in cultural stereotyping as well as dressing up in "redface," a racist practice. Instead of apologizing, Bates doubled down, tweeting, "Ok, I will now dress up as Casper the friendly ghost and try not to offend the bed sheets." The composer Alex Temple responded: "You do know that Native Americans are, like, actual humans who exist, right?"

63. Boltanski and Chiapello, *The New Spirit of Capitalism*, chap. 6.

64. For example, in *Race and the Chilean Miracle*, the anthropologist Patricia Richards dissects how contemporary mainstream Chilean society prizes multicultural tolerance and inclusivity, except in the case of Chile's indigenous population, many of whom choose to remain separated from the mainstream of urban life, instead practicing traditional tribal customs and maintaining a barter economy. Richards reveals that Chileans who otherwise advocate for multicultural tolerance resort to racist language and accusations of "backwardness" when discussing the isolationism of Chile's indigenes. See also Hale, "Neoliberal Multiculturalism" and *Más Que un Indio*.

65. Hale, "Neoliberal Multiculturalism," 12.

66. See the video of the YTSO final performance: https://www.youtube.com/watch?v=LnKJpYGCLsg, 2:22:11, posted March 20, 2011. Baskin's introduction occurs at 1:44:55.

67. The ethnomusicologist Bonnie Wade makes a similar observation about the development of Japan's classical music culture during the early part of the twentieth century. One of the many ways Japan sought to quickly modernize itself was via the musical education of its children; by teaching these children to perform and appreciate Western classical music, Wade argues, the Japanese government sought to quickly inculcate "the idea that the culture of the colonizer was superior." She identifies this acceptance of classical music as one of the means by which Japan displayed its acceptance of Western values and thus avoided being physically colonized by the United States. *Music in Japan*, 13.

68. Michael Tilson Thomas, remarks during the YTSO Sydney performance, https://www.youtube.com/watch?v=LnKJpYGCLsg, 2:22:11, posted March 20, 2011. Quote occurs at 1:05:00.

69. See the YTSO full performance: https://www.youtube.com/watch?v=LnKJpYGCLsg, 2:22:11, posted March 20, 2011. Barton's performance occurs at 1:06:55.

70. Newfield and Gordon, "Multiculturalism's Unfinished Business," 79.

71. For further information, see the exposés on Apple factories published by the nonprofit organization China Labor Watch, including Li Qiang, "Apple Should Not Profit at the Expense of Low-Wage Workers." See also Duhigg and Barboza, "In China, Human Costs Are Built into an iPad."

72. Tsing, *The Mushroom at the End of the World*, 29.

73. For an optimistic alternate history of the internet, see Evans, *Broad Band*.

74. Boltanski and Chiapello, *The New Spirit of Capitalism*, 14.

75. Wilkie, *The Digital Condition*, 58.
76. Lesbian separatist movements also emerged in the 1970s, comprising groups of women who came to believe that there was no way to live a life within the capitalist United States without capitulating to patriarchy in some way. Consequently, they pooled their resources and established self-sustaining, explicitly anticapitalist farms around the country, where men (often including the residents' male children) were literally not allowed to set foot. See Levy, "Lesbian Nation."
77. From King's report to the SCLC staff, May 1967, accessible online at http://www .thekingcenter.org/archive/document/mlk-speech-sclc-staff-retreat# (accessed October 4, 2018).
78. See Gage, "What an Uncensored Letter to M.L.K. Reveals."
79. See Ahmed, *On Being Included*.
80. Sandow, "YouTube (Sigh) Symphony."
81. Tommasini, "YouTube Orchestra Melds Music Live and Online."
82. Wakin, "Getting to Carnegie via YouTube."
83. Description on Mason Bates's blog: masonbates.com/work/work-garages.html (accessed October 4, 2018).
84. See Ritchey, "The (R)evolution of Steve Jobs."
85. Bates, video interview.
86. My discussion is based on the score (Aphra Music, 2014). "The Rise of Exotic Computing" is scored for a flute, oboe, B-flat clarinet, bassoon, F horn, C trumpet, harp, piano, violin, viola, cello, bass, and a single percussionist who alternates between marimba, glockenspiel, and cymbals. There is also an "electronica" part consisting of a performed drum machine beat that is mostly notated in the score (meaning: not improvised), and indications for triggering various synthesized sounds by using a laptop. The piece has not been officially recorded, although a live recording of the introduction alone is available in snippet form on Bates's blog (https://www .masonbates.com/listen/ [accessed October 4, 2018]).
87. In Robert Fink's *Repeating Ourselves*, he makes a related claim, arguing that whereas critics and composers positioned early pulse-pattern minimalism as music that resisted commodification, in actuality the music is fully imbricated within the type of meaningless repetition that became the vehicle for consumer capitalism in the postwar United States. For Fink, the early minimalism of composers like Reich is organized by rhythmic flow, and teaches its listeners to "surf" the waves of repetition characterizing the advertising language and much of the media content of the 1960s. I take up Fink's ideas in more detail in chapter 2.
88. Marx and Engels, *The Communist Manifesto*, 38.
89. For a book-length examination of the way technological awe has reformulated the aesthetic category of the sublime, see Nye, *American Technological Sublime*.
90. Harvey, *A Brief History of Neoliberalism*, 157–59.
91. For further reading on neoliberalism and Big Data, see Day, *Indexing It All*. For an extensive critique of the ways individual participation in social media contributes unpaid labor to the corporate construction and maintenance of the surveillance state, see Fuchs, *Reading Marx in the Information Age* and *Internet and Surveillance*.
92. Endler, "CES 2014."
93. Huyssen, *After the Great Divide*, 11.
94. This advertisement is widely available on YouTube.
95. See Goehr, *The Imaginary Museum of Musical Works*.
96. Heussner, "YouTube Orchestra."

97. Leppert, "The Musician of the Imagination," 47.
98. See Boltanski and Chiapello, *The New Spirit of Capitalism*; McGuigan, *Neoliberal Culture*; and Ford, *Dig*.

CHAPTER 2

1. Greenstein, "The Extraordinary Musician."
2. Greenstein was one of the originators of the term, initially calling his and his friends' approach to music-making an "indie classical" one, and dubbing his label (New Amsterdam Records) an "indie classical" label. The musicologist William Robin's 2016 dissertation, "A Scene without a Name," is currently the definitive study of the indie classical community. Robin provides an extensive etymology of the term and describes the debates that swirled around it from its first use. See also his "The Rise and Fall of 'Indie Classical.'"
3. For an in-depth critique of the musical entrepreneurship Chase promotes, see Moore, "Neoliberalism and the Musical Entrepreneur."
4. William Robin notes for example that while the indie classical scene actually comprises a relatively small number of artists and musicians, and is almost totally confined to New York City, the arts press nonetheless presents it as "the new generation" of classical music practitioners in the United States, letting this small group stand in for the myriad young composers and artists across the nation who represent a much more diverse array of musical styles and career practices. Robin attributes this to the "feedback loop" between the self-descriptions on New York–based composers' blogs and websites, and the uncritical propagation of those descriptions in reviews and profiles in New York–based publications, which are then approvingly cited on composers' blogs and websites ("A Scene without a Name," 88).
5. Robin, "A Scene without a Name," 91.
6. It's worth noting, though, that in some key respects neoliberalism represents a fairly dramatic reconfiguring of the Enlightenment ideals it claims to hold so dear. For example, classical liberals like Smith strongly believed that individuals were socially constituted and bore a responsibility to society; Smith wrote that the "perfection of human nature" is constituted by "feeling much for others and little for ourselves." Although he tended to share the view that humans are selfish, and that organizing society via a free market would be a better guarantee of egalitarianism than relying on individuals to act benevolently, at the same time Smith would never have agreed with Margaret Thatcher that "there is no such thing as society." Neoliberals, on the other hand, are suspicious of empathy and collective identification, and tend to view any demand for social responsibility as placing untenable constraints on individual freedom. See Smith, *The Theory of Moral Sentiments*, 30.
7. Gilbert, *Common Ground*.
8. Friedman, *Capitalism and Freedom*, 3.
9. Friedman, 18.
10. Friedman was not the first political economist to associate the free market's freedom with Crusoe—Karl Marx made this connection in the 1850s—although he may have been the first to consider this association a positive one. In the introduction to the *Grundrisse*, Marx sneers at the depiction of the individual as "an isolated hunter and fisherman," associating this fantasy with "the unimaginative conceits of the eighteenth-century Robinsonades," meaning Adam Smith and David Ricardo. Marx, *Grundrisse*, 83.
11. Quoted in Keay, "Aids, Education, and the Year 2000!," 10.

12. See Harvey, *A Brief History of Neoliberalism*, in particular his examination of the CIA takeover of Chile, in which every form of communal organization was disrupted, including free health clinics in poor neighborhoods.

13. Hochschild, *The Commercialization of Intimate Life.*

14. For example, today we outsource all kinds of "care" by breaking the concept up into isolated fragments that can be quantified and monetized. Bathing, feeding, and medicating the elderly are all tangible, economizable aspects of care that someone can be paid to perform; loving, intently listening to, thinking about, and sympathizing with old people are intangible, noncommodifiable aspects of care, and thus we ignore them in our definitions of what constitutes "elder care." It is via this kind of fragmentation of "care" that we become amenable to the idea of developing robots to take care of the elderly.

15. Gershon, "Neoliberal Agency."

16. Gershon, 539.

17. Hochschild, *The Commercialization of Intimate Life,* 29.

18. Brown, *Edgework,* 42.

19. Brown, *Undoing the Demos,* 37.

20. Brown, *Edgework,* 43.

21. See Hearn, "Brand Me 'Activist.'" See also Humphreys and Thompson, who argue that "the market aligns these myriad consumer goals with the economic interests of producers catering to a particular market segment," and that these alignments thus "reinforce neoliberal ideological values that support individuated, market-based solutions over collective and political ones." "Branding Disaster," 880.

22. Greenstein, "Milton Babbitt's Birthday."

23. Sheridan, "Judd Greenstein."

24. Brookes, "Missy Mazzoli Has a Different Take on Classical Music—and People Are Listening."

25. Babbitt, "The Composer as Specialist," 48 and 51.

26. Babbitt, 54.

27. For a more detailed analysis of the kind of "portfolio careers" musicians and composers in the United States are increasingly required to develop, see Moore, "Neoliberalism and the Musical Entrepreneur."

28. For a brief history of this transition, see Clarke, "What in the F——'s Name Is Fordism."

29. This process of dismantling labor reforms is what leads some commentators to argue that we are returning to a state of feudalism. However, I would point out that even under feudalism, the nobility had certain agreed-on obligations to the serfs who worked their land and to the knights who fought their battles. Today's corporations recognize no such obligations to the impoverished people around the globe who manufacture their products. See Federici, *Caliban and the Witch.* Federici discusses the mutually obligatory nature of the relationship between lords and serfs, noting that it was so important to medieval society that it was ritually consecrated in vassalage ceremonies that were similar to marriage rites. Another crucial difference between feudal Europe and the social formations of contemporary capitalism is that serfs had access to the wilderness areas that were owned by no one ("the commons"), upon which they could fish, hunt, cut firewood, pick fruit, and even live, if dispossessed of their homes. Today's worker lacks even this rudimentary safety net—indeed, enclosing the commons and preventing the people's use of them were major tactics in wealthy nobles' and merchants' war to consolidate a

money economy in sixteenth-century Europe. This is the issue that contemporary protest movements like Occupy seek to draw attention to, by literally occupying public spaces (parks, squares) that supposedly belong to everyone but that are in reality treated like private property, and protected as such by militarized police.

30. Hayek, *The Road to Serfdom*, 55.

31. Friedman, *Capitalism and Freedom*, 144.

32. See Philip Mirowski's critique of Wikipedia: "Postface: Defining Neoliberalism." Mirowski demonstrates that neoliberals operate via a "double truth doctrine," which presents one truth for the masses and another truth for those at the top.

33. Friedman, *Capitalism and Freedom*, chap. 6, "The Role of Government in Education."

34. William Robin addresses the rhetoric of boundarylessness in "A Scene without a Name"; see also my essay, "New Music in a Borderless World." For a recent analysis of the role genre plays in indie classical discourse, see Metzer, "Sharing a Stage."

35. Howe, review of Nico Muhly, *I Drink the Air before Me*.

36. Pippen, "Toward a Postmodern Avant-Garde."

37. Blake, "Musicological Omnivory in the Neoliberal University."

38. Blake, 353.

39. See Robin, "A Scene without a Name"; Gendron, *Between Montmartre and the Mudd Club*; and Gann, *Music Downtown*.

40. In the 1990s Kyle Gann referred to this tendency toward stylistic eclecticism and boundary pushing as "totalism," a new compositional trend he declared to have a "populist-yet-intellectual spirit." While the term didn't really catch on, Gann's diagnosis of this trend and his predictions are trenchant. *American Music in the Twentieth Century*, 355. See also Jeremy Grimshaw's essay on Philip Glass's "Bowie" symphonies (composed throughout the 1990s), in which he argues that the success of these works depended on their being widely perceived as crossing the boundary "between the canonical and the heretical," because Glass used tracks from David Bowie's art-rock albums as symphonic material. Grimshaw calls this focus on boundary crossing "the inevitable product of a musical arena in which the crossover is no longer an anomaly but an ideal." "High, 'Low,' and Plastic Arts," 473.

41. Robin, "A Scene without a Name," 15; Ritchey, "New Music in a Borderless World."

42. Fink, *Repeating Ourselves*, 3.

43. From Greenstein's comments about "Sing Along" on his website, www.juddgreenstein.com/sing-along/ (accessed October 5, 2018).

44. Boltanski and Chiapello, *The New Spirit of Capitalism*.

45. See Harvey, *A Brief History of Neoliberalism*, chap. 1.

46. See McRobbie, *Be Creative*.

47. NPR staff, "Missy Mazzoli."

48. Moore, "Neoliberalism and the Musical Entrepreneur," 43.

49. "The idea of an 'obligation to search for and then accept a vocational calling' now wanders around in our lives as the ghost of beliefs no longer anchored in the substance of religion." Weber, *The Protestant Ethic*, 124.

50. See Florida, *The Rise of the Creative Class*.

51. Nico Muhly writes and speaks often about this issue, for example arguing that critics should restrict themselves to "talking about notes and rhythms" rather than try to locate composers in a historical lineage" ("Lots of Things").

52. It is worth noting that Greenstein (like many contemporary commentators) mischaracterizes the avant-garde—the historical avant-garde was both politically motivated and socially oriented. Indeed, until the middle of the twentieth century

"avant-garde" was synonymous with radical political activism. What Greenstein means to characterize as "inward-looking" is actually the postwar modernist school of composition: people like Milton Babbitt, who were in many ways rebelling against the historical avant-garde's injunction to communicate with audiences and contribute to the reshaping of society. See Bürger, *Theory of the Avant Garde*; and see Huyssen's exegesis of the dialectical relationship between the historical avant-garde and mass culture (and his assertion that modernism severs this dialectic) in literature and the arts, *After the Great Divide*.

53. Metzer, *Musical Modernism at the Turn of the Twenty First Century.*
54. Gann, "Judd Greenstein."
55. *Politico*, "'Indie Classical' Goes Uptown."
56. Johnson, "Judd Greenstein."
57. See Brown, *Edgework* and *Undoing the Demos.*
58. Sirota, "New Music Fight Club."
59. See Fink, *Repeating Ourselves*; and Gopinath, "The Problem of the Political in Steve Reich's *Come Out.*"
60. Adorno, "The Aging of the New Music," 196.
61. Robin, "A Scene without a Name," 75.
62. Sheridan, "Judd Greenstein."
63. "There are many consumer-related factors that have contributed to DIY's spike in popularity," writes an editor of *Business News Daily* in an article that goes on to note that DIY methods help entrepreneurs "get up and running more quickly and cheaply." *Bloomberg* reports on a "growing DIY economy" that relies on "self-employed workers." Guides like *The Creative Entrepreneur: A DIY Visual Guidebook for Making Business Ideas Real* have proliferated in recent years, promising "less stress, more joy" as well as tips for "thinking like a CEO." Fallon, "Do It Yourself"; and Matthews, "The Do-It-Yourself Economy Just Hired 1 Million American Entrepreneurs."
64. Weininger, "Flute Genius Claire Chase Brings Entrepreneurial Spirit to Boston."
65. For an extensive cultural history of DIY, see Azerrad, *Our Band Could Be Your Life.*
66. See Eileraas, "Witches, Bitches & Fluids." Michael Azerrad also discusses the ways bands like K Records's Beat Happening—known for silly dancing and twee lyrics about ice cream and candy—were nonetheless considered punk, and played and toured with hard-core bands (like Fugazi and Black Flag) that had very different sounds. Azerrad quotes a member of the scene who explains this phenomenon: "They came from similar standpoints about how they felt about themselves and independence and freedom . . . so then you could perform together because you were coming from the same places in your heart. You may not make the same music, but you feel about music the same way." *Our Band Could Be Your Life*, 470.
67. Jim McGuigan succinctly observes that "capitalism has been brilliant at responding to disaffection, criticism, and opposition by stealing the enemy's clothes and flaunting them cynically on the catwalk as a means of refashioning an exploitative system; in effect, of denying genuine entitlement and, indeed, liberation." *Neoliberal Culture*, 41.
68. Some might assert that communities like those that cohered around this kind of punk ethos were still participating in capitalism—they certainly accepted money for performing, and sold their music as commodities—and in some senses it may be true that such localized forms of resistance merely represent a "kinder, gentler" form of capitalism. At the same time, it is worth distinguishing *capitalism* from the mere exchange of money for goods or services—after all, such money exchange

has existed for millennia, and all over the world, while the system of capitalism is only a few centuries old. What makes capitalism different is its accumulative principle, via which owners of capital accumulate profit for its own sake (rather than for its exchange value). Perhaps even more important, this system of accumulation is effected by an exploitative relationship between producers and the owners of capital—those who own the means of production profit from the labor of others by paying workers a lower wage than the market value of the commodity those workers produce. These features distinguish capitalism from previous historical examples of money economies. This understanding of capitalism derives obviously from Marx. See also Weber, *The Protestant Ethic*.

69. See Wendy Brown's statement, that neoliberal subjects become "rational, calculating creatures whose moral autonomy is measured by their capacity for 'self-care'— the ability to provide for their own needs and service their own ambitions" (*Edgework*, 42). For a book-length study of self-care under neoliberalism, see Hochschild, *The Commercialization of Intimate Life*.

70. McRobbie, *Be Creative*, 58 and 11.

71. McRobbie, 3.

72. Tommasini, "Claire Chase Invites Young Musicians to Create New Paths." Chase's address to the Bienen School is viewable on the school website: http://www .pickstaiger.org/video/2013-bienen-school-music-convocation-address-claire-chase (accessed October 4, 2018).

73. Moore, "Neoliberalism and the Musical Entrepreneur," 47.

74. See Eileraas, "Witches, Bitches & Fluids." For a history of K Records, see Baumgarten, *Love Rock Revolution*.

75. Quoted in Press and Reynolds, *The Sex Revolts*, 264.

76. Davidson, "A New New York School."

77. Quoted in *Politico*, "'Indie Classical' Goes Uptown."

78. Muhly, "Think Fast."

79. See Azerrad, *Our Band Could Be Your Life*; Taylor, *Music and Capitalism*; Taylor, *The Sounds of Capitalism*, chap. 8; and Mylonas, "Amateur Creation and Entrepreneurialism."

80. Weston, "Going between the Notes with Nico Muhly." See also Muhly's blog entry about indie classical, in which he points out that the term *indie* connotes sloppy musicianship and amateurism, which the indie classical scene does not display or endorse: "One final thing, though, and I hope that some people will join me in this; can we stop saying Indie-Classical? At least about me, for starters? The next person who says that has to come over and sight-sing through my complete unrecorded liturgical music from high school which consists of *multiple* Te Deums and Jubies-late, sets of responses, to say nothing of a fifty minute long Reproaches and then we're going to solfège Ockeghem together, transposed with clefs, followed by luncheon, and then at the end of all that we can talk about 'Indie.'" Muhly, "Lots of Things."

81. Broyles, *Mavericks and Other Traditions in American Music*.

82. Muhly, "Hindi Classical."

83. Muhly, "Hindi Classical."

84. See Mylonas, "Amateur Creation and Entrepreneurialism." Mylonas argues that the entrepreneur is a central concept for understanding the transformation of today's artist, who represents and propagates "the narcissistic, post-political self" as the ideal neoliberal subject (p. 1). See also Jen Harvie's study of participatory art, *Fair*

Play, in which she coins the term "artrepreneur" in her argument about how contemporary artists' embrace of neoliberal flexibility puts the value of being an artist at "serious ideological risk" (p. 62).

85. Currie, "Music and Politics," 76.

CHAPTER 3

1. Promotional copy advertising *Hopscotch* on the opera's website, www.Hopscotch Opera.com (accessed October 8, 2018).
2. This phrase appears in most statements The Industry makes about itself on its website. See https://theindustryla.org/about/ (accessed October 8, 2018).
3. See Robin, "'Hopscotch' Takes Opera into the Streets," and Farber, "Car Hop."
4. Marlow, "Is This the Opera of the Future?"; Broverman, "One Last Chance to See L.A.'s Wildly Innovative Car Opera"; submission page for The Industry's *Good* Maker proposal, http://maker.good.is/myLA2050create/projects/HOPSCOTCH.html (accessed October 8, 2018).
5. Bexel press release, https://bexel.com/news/worlds-first-large-scale-opera-for-wire less-headphones-invisible-cities-premiering-at-los-angeles-union-station/ (accessed October 8, 2018).
6. Sharon, "Invisible Cities."
7. Quoted in Hart, "Traffic Jam." Sumanth Gopinath and Jason Stanyek discuss the way mobile performances like the ones examined here often foreground their engagement with each city in which they take place. However, Gopinath and Stanyek point out that while marketing and promotional materials often describe such works as "duets" between performers and the city or between audiences and the city, these works also evoke an elided "third partner," which is the tech gear that actually enables the piece. This gear is *"arguably more important than the city itself."* Gopinath and Stanyek, "The Mobilization of Performance," 15 (emphasis in original).
8. Sennheiser, "Invisible Cities: An Opera for Headphones Receives Emmy for KCET Documentary of Landmark Headphone Opera Production," press release, July 30, 2014, https://en-us.sennheiser.com/news-invisible-cities-an-opera-for-headphones -receives-emmy-for-kcet-documentary-of-landmark-headphone-opera-production (accessed October 8, 2018).
9. Ross, "Opera on Location."
10. For a history of alternative venues for classical music in New York City, see Robinson, "Chamber Music in Alternative Venues in the 21st-Century U.S."
11. See Levine, *Highbrow/Lowbrow.*
12. For a canonical early theorization of this artistic turn, see Bourriaud, *Relational Aesthetics.*
13. Lanz, "'Invisible Cities' Opera Moves from Union Station to Your Listening Device"; Farber, "Car Hop."
14. Megan Steigerwald's dissertation "Bringing Down the House" uses extensive fieldwork to explore The Industry's productions and transformations of musical labor.
15. The curator and art theorist Claire Bishop says that such art should ideally be "entirely beholden to the contingencies of its environment and audience," and that moreover, "this audience is envisaged as a community," one with the power to engage with art and with each other. "Antagonism and Relational Aesthetics," 54.
16. Crane, "Moving Parts."
17. See Waleson, "'Hopscotch, a Mobile Opera in 24 Cars": *"Hopscotch* has broken the fourth wall with a vengeance."

18. Bishop, "Antagonism and Relational Aesthetics," 52. See also Harvey, *The Condition of Postmodernity*.

19. Quoted in *National Post*, "Why the Boston Orchestra Is Giving Its Patrons iPads."

20. Harvie, *Fair Play*.

21. This term was coined by the futurist Alvin Toffler, in his book *The Third Wave*.

22. For example, YouTube is a corporation whose product is video content that is up-loaded for free by YouTube's users; YouTube does not pay for this content, but is able to generate massive amounts of advertising revenue based on it. The same is true of Facebook, Twitter, Instagram, and most other "Web 2.0" platforms. See My-lonas, "Amateur Creation and Entrepreneurialism"; Fuchs, *Internet and Surveillance*; and Mirowski, "Postface: Defining Neoliberalism."

23. See for example Heise, "Opera for Everyone"; Black, "Opera for the Masses."

24. From The Industry's *Good* Maker submission for *Hopscotch*, http://maker.good.is/myLA2050create/projects/HOPSCOTCH.html (accessed October 8, 2018).

25. Quoted in Crane, "Moving Parts."

26. The budget for *Hopscotch* was several million dollars—most of it donated from foundations, businesses, and individuals, and only around three hundred thou-sand dollars of it coming from ticket sales. https://theindustryla.org/a-60k-pledge-towards-hopscotch/ (accessed October 8, 2018).

27. Crane, "Moving Parts"; Ross, "Opera on Location"; Lanz, "'Invisible Cities' Opera Moves from Union Station to Your Listening Device"; Farber, "Car Hop."

28. See Kim, "All Roads Lead to Boyle Heights."

29. See Eric Avila's history of racial segregation in Los Angeles, which details how the Home Owners' Loan Corporation's race-based grading criteria factored significantly in 1930s Los Angeles in determining property values in white as opposed to pre-dominantly nonwhite neighborhoods. "Invariably, neighborhoods that sheltered even a few black families received a D rating and were redlined." *Popular Culture in the Age of White Flight*, 35.

30. For more on the ethnic/racial history of Boyle Heights as well as the role finan-cial institutions have played in constructing the area's demographics over time, see Avila, *Popular Culture in the Age of White Flight*; and Sanchez, "'What's Good for Boyle Heights is Good for the Jews.'" For 2011 census data on the area, see http://maps.latimes.com/neighborhoods/neighborhood/boyle-heights/ (accessed Octo-ber 8, 2018). Although it's important to note that these demographics are changing yet again, now that a steady influx of wealthy white people is moving into the area thanks to the gentrifying processes discussed here.

31. Marx, *Capital*, 1:812.

32. Federici, *Caliban and the Witch*; Harvey, *A Brief History of Neoliberalism*. The contem-porary phenomenon of mass home foreclosures that precipitate huge bonuses for Wall Street, for example, represents what Harvey calls "a very stark contemporary case of predation and legalized robbery typical of accumulation by dispossession." *A Companion to Marx's Capital*, 313.

33. Glass, "Introduction: Aspects of Change." My understanding of gentrification has been informed by the work of several urban studies scholars, most notably Billing-ham, "The Broadening Conception of Gentrification"; Smith, "Toward a Theory of Gentrification"; Lees, Slater, and Wyly, *Gentrification*; and Slater, "The 'Eviction' of Critical Perspectives from Gentrification Research."

34. Taylor, *Toxic Communities*.

35. See Chapple, "From Central Avenue to Leimert Park"; Estrada, "If You Build It, They Will Move"; Mohl, *The Interstates and Cities*; and Schwartz, "Urban Freeways and the Interstate System."

36. Since at least the early 1980s, scholars and researchers have widely observed the role of artists in this second wave of gentrification. See the National Endowment for the Arts' commissioned study: Grodach, Foster, and Murdoch, "Gentrification and the Artistic Dividend"; Cole, "Artists and Urban Redevelopment"; and Zukin, *Loft Living*.

37. See Flew, *Global Creative Industries*; see also Townley and Beech, eds., *Managing Creativity*, in which the editors present a heartfelt argument that "managerialism" is an overlooked creative field (at one point they compare an Excel spreadsheet to a musical score).

38. Katharina Bodirsky demonstrates that the "Florida effect" has been widely influential in city planning policy across the world, in "Culture for Competitiveness."

39. See Jamie Peck's justifiably famous critique of Florida, in chapter 5 of *Constructions of Neoliberal Reason*.

40. Billingham, "The Broadening Conception of Gentrification."

41. See Murray, "Hollenbeck Station Celebration"; construction is under way on the Regional Connector Transit Project. See https://www.metro.net/projects/connector/ (accessed October 9, 2018); construction is also under way on the Sixth Street Bridge, which will be completed by the end of 2020. See Barragan, "Taking a Look at the Under-Construction Sixth Street Bridge."

42. Xia and Goffard, "6th Street Bridge, Spanning Much of LA's Past, Finally Starts to Fall to Demolition Crews."

43. See Lovett, "Los Angeles Bridge's Demolition Is a Sign of Changes Sweeping the City."

44. For more on the alienation and community disruption gentrification causes, see Slater, "The 'Eviction' of Critical Perspectives from Gentrification Research."

45. See Fifteen Group's explanation of the Wyvernwood proposal on its website: https://fifteengroup.com/company/011108_wyvernwood.htm (accessed October 9, 2018).

46. Avila, *Popular Culture in the Age of White Flight*, 35.

47. This conflict has been widely covered in the press; see for example Carroll, "'Hope Everyone Pukes on Your Artisanal Treats'"; and Barragan, "Boyle Heights Freaks Out about Being Sold as the Next DTLA." Moses Kagan, the owner of Adaptive Realty, also responded to the protests, and critically engaged with his own role in gentrification, in a post on his blog: http://kagansblog.com/2014/05/boyle-heights/.

48. Serve the People LA, "Against Art."

49. Defend Boyle Heights, "Destroy the Boyle Heights Arts District One Gallery at a Time, One Landlord at a Time."

50. See for example Jones, "Artwashing," in which he derides local activists, declares that art is good for the world, and notes that "there is such a thing as civilisation—and it has a way of looking a bit like gentrification."

51. For an influential historical study demonstrating that city planning has been driven by the profit motive, see Fairfield, *The Mysteries of the Great City*.

52. Defend Boyle Heights, "Statement about the Self Help Graphics Accountability Session and Beyond."

53. Local activists allege that The Industry did consult with one Boyle Heights art gallery, Self Help Graphics and Art. This alleged collaboration has drawn fierce and on-

going community protests. The gallery has denied having had any communication with The Industry, but it is thanked on the Support page of the *Hopscotch* website.

54. Serve the People LA, "Against Gentrification, Against Bourgeois Art."

55. As of this writing, The Industry has not responded publicly to the Boyle Heights protests. Music director Marc Lowenstein was quoted in one review as saying that he had been "shaken" by the physical intimidation of the protesters, who he said yelled "This park is for brown people" over and over despite his efforts to engage them in conversation (quoted in Carroll, "'Hope Everyone Pukes on Your Artisanal Treats'"). Descriptions of the protests appear on many Boyle Heights activist blogs, but in articles related to gentrification published in LA news outlets and on tenants' rights blogs; I have not found a review of *Hopscotch* that discusses it in detail. For an activist perspective on the protest, see Serve the People LA, "Against Gentrification, Against Bourgeois Art."

56. Serve the People LA, "The Youth Will Lead the Revolutionary Struggle."

57. The Industry, *Hopscotch*, 2017, by The Industry Records, Los Angeles, compact disc, track 2, 0:00–0.15.

58. Mohl, *The Interstates and Cities*, 4.

59. Estrada, "If You Build It, They Will Move," 304–6.

60. Avila, *Popular Culture in the Age of White Flight*, 189.

61. The promotional video for *Hopscotch* can be viewed at https://www.youtube.com/watch?v=LivzsddPn-Q (accessed October 9, 2018).

62. For an intense dissection of the way media narratives have shaped American understandings of poverty and the inner city, see Macek, *Urban Nightmares*. See also Wacquant, *Punishing the Poor*.

63. Friedman, *Capitalism and Freedom*, 34.

64. Lees, Slater, and Wyly, *Gentrification*, 165.

65. Blomley, *Unsettling the City*.

66. Slater, "The 'Eviction' of Critical Perspectives from Gentrification Research," 751.

67. See for example Carroll, "'Anti-white' Graffiti in Gentrifying LA Neighborhood Sparks Hate Crime Debate."

68. Miles, *Limits to Culture*, 36.

69. Quoted in Gelt, "'Hopscotch,' the World's First Mobile Opera, Will Take to L.A.'s Streets in 24 Cars."

70. Harvie, *Fair Play*, 108.

71. Yuval Sharon, quoted in Lanz, "'Invisible Cities' Opera Moves from Union Station to Your Listening Device."

72. Major support for *Hopscotch* was provided by wealthy individual donors as well as the National Endowment for the Arts, the Colburn Foundation, Bloomberg Philanthropies, the Getty Foundation, and many departments and offices of the city of Los Angeles.

73. Philharmonic CEO Deborah Borda noted that Sharon's appointment represented the organization's search "for new ways to stretch our boundaries." Sharon said that he hopes to use his new role to undertake "a complete disruption of a conventional trajectory for an organization." See the LA Philharmonic's press release: https://www.hollywoodbowl.com/press/releases/1515/ (accessed October 9, 2018).

74. Fragoza, "Art and Complicity." Ultra-Red has collaborated with the Boyle Heights public housing activist group Union de Vecinos on housing-related artworks. See Leavitt, "Art and the Politics of Public Housing."

75. Smith, "Toward a Theory of Gentrification," 82.

CHAPTER 4

1. See Intel's documentary video and more information about the project: https://iq
.intel.com/100-dancing-drones-set-world-record/ (accessed October 9, 2018). See
also http://www.guinnessworldrecords.com/news/2016/1/intel-stuns-during-ces-key
note-with-record-for-most-drones-airborne-simultaneousl-411677 for Guinness's
coverage of the record set (accessed October 9, 2018).

2. Beethoven's friend Anton Schindler published the first biography of the composer
in 1840, and it was used as a primary source in Beethoven studies for at least one
hundred years. Later scholarship, however, has revealed that Schindler simply invented many of the details and anecdotes his biography attributed to the composer;
his assertion that Beethoven referred to the first four notes of the Fifth Symphony as
"fate knocking at the door" has been widely propagated but is probably false.

3. Musicologists have been interested in how Beethoven used silences. See for example
Cooper, "Beethoven's Uses of Silence"; see also *The First Four Notes*, Matthew Guerrieri's cultural history of the Fifth Symphony, in which he examines the resonant
and "invisible" silence with which the work opens (the first thing we "hear" in the
Fifth is actually an eighth rest).

4. Identifying corporations with these short musical tags has become a commonplace
in advertising (think of the start-up sounds for the Macintosh or for Microsoft Windows, single chords that instantly identify the brand) and is obviously derived from
the older musical advertising model of the jingle. Sumanth Gopinath provides a
brief explanation of this kind of "sonic branding" in *The Ringtone Dialectic*, 187.

5. The video of the complete Consumer Electronics Showcase 2016 keynote address has been taken off YouTube, but as of this writing a full transcript is available: https://singjupost.com/intel-ceo-brian-krzanich-keynote-at-ces-2016-full-tran
script/8/?singlepage=1 (accessed October 9, 2018). Intel also hosts a highlights
reel from the keynote on its YouTube channel: https://www.youtube.com/watch?v=
BslGBBYsi8c (accessed October 12, 2018).

6. See Gopinath, *The Ringtone Dialectic*, 97–98, on the prevalence of mallet instruments in sonic branding.

7. See the Consumer Electronics Showcase 2016 keynote address transcript.

8. This quotation was taken from a video presentation aired during the keynote address, and is not represented in the full transcript.

9. See the Consumer Electronics Showcase 2016 keynote address transcript.

10. Harvey, *The Condition of Postmodernity*, 292.

11. *Economist*, "Virtual Reality and Beethoven."

12. For more on the Creators Project, see https://www.vice.com/en_us/topic/the
-creators-project (accessed October 9, 2018). Huang, "NovaTrio Brings Live Visual
Technology to Classical Music."

13. See McGuigan, *Neoliberal Culture*; and Clarke, "What in the F——'s Name Is
Fordism."

14. Hayek, *The Road to Serfdom*, 13.

15. Friedman, *Capitalism and Freedom*, 5.

16. Friedman, 9. See also Burgin, *The Great Persuasion*, 178, in which he notes that
Friedman "valorized an idealized version of the nineteenth century and then lever-
aged that vision to lambast the administrative practices of the present day."

17. Both Marx and Weber discussed the compulsory nature of capitalism. Marx noted
how even capitalists are forced to constantly compete ("one capitalist always strikes
down many others"), and described "the entanglement of all peoples in the net of

the world market." Weber formulated modern capitalism as a "cosmos" that "determines the style of life of all individuals born into it." Marx, *Capital*, 1:929; Weber, *The Protestant Ethic*, 123.

18. Federici, *Revolution at Point Zero*, 12.

19. Quoted in Weber, *The Protestant Ethic*, 109 (emphasis in original).

20. Weber, 16. Cultivating the qualities of honesty, punctuality, diligence, and thrift—which, for the earlier Puritans, were all evidence of spiritual virtue—becomes, for Franklin, merely useful, because an individual who manifests these qualities is more likely to persuade others to extend lines of credit. In discussing Franklin's famous maxims for how to lead a good and useful life via diligently amassing profits, Weber wrote, "The frame of mind apparent in the cited passages from Benjamin Franklin that met with the approval of an entire people would have been proscribed in the ancient world, as well as in the Middle Ages, for it would have been viewed as an expression of filthy greed and completely undignified character" (p. 20).

21. Weber, 18.

22. Boltanski and Chiapello, *The New Spirit of Capitalism*, 12.

23. Boltanski and Chiapello, 9.

24. Lal, *Reviving the Invisible Hand*, 151.

25. Lal, 153.

26. Lal, 154.

27. Lal, 168.

28. See the clip from this portion of the Town Hall, which is posted on CNN's YouTube channel: https://www.youtube.com/watch?v=MR65ZhO6LGA (accessed October 12, 2018).

29. Long, *Beautiful Monsters*, 31.

30. Adorno, "On Tradition," 376.

31. Nadhan, "Drones Align the Business of Music with the Technology of Information."

32. Slefo, "Intel Mixes Beethoven with Its Iconic Mnemonic in Spot about 'Amazing Experiences.'"

33. Hoffmann, "Beethoven's Instrumental Music," 38–39. For a compelling history of the German philosophical ideas that influenced Hoffmann and the German reception of Beethoven, see Bonds, *Music as Thought*.

34. Hoffmann, "Beethoven's Instrumental Music," 38.

35. Bonds, *Music as Thought*.

36. See for example Debussy's piece for solo piano, "Golliwog's Cakewalk," in which he incorporates the famous diminished seventh chord that begins Wagner's *Tristan und Isolde* into a jaunty ragtime tune, clearly as a joke. Emmanuel Chabrier similarly punctured Wagnerian pretensions, for example in his set of variations on themes from *Tristan und Isolde* for piano four hands, *Souvenirs de Munich*.

37. Kramer, *Why Classical Music Still Matters*.

38. For more on Adorno's thoughts about authentic art and society, see Paddison, "Authenticity and Failure in Adorno's Aesthetics of Music"; Richard Leppert's first "Commentary" in his edition of Adorno's *Essays on Music*, 85–112; and Keller, "Adorno and the Dialectics of Mass Culture."

39. Adorno, "The Radio Symphony," 258.

40. Adorno, 259.

41. Leppert, "Commentary," in *Essays on Music*, 226.

42. Adorno, "The Radio Symphony," 262.

43. Sumanth Gopinath discusses how ringtone selection in the late 1990s was "a veritable primer in some of the most overplayed melodies in the history of Western music." The opening motive from Beethoven's Fifth was a popular early ringtone (*The Ringtone Dialectic*, pp. 69 and 90).

44. Dale Chapman analyzes the proliferation of "one-man bands" and the way the discourses promoting them deploy neoliberal values. "The 'One-Man Band' and Entrepreneurial Selfhood in Neoliberal Culture."

45. Taylor, *Music and Capitalism*, 152.

46. Taylor, 151.

47. Taylor, 151–53.

48. Brown, *Undoing the Demos*, 36.

49. Hayek, *The Road to Serfdom*, 14.

50. Giroux, *The Terror of Neoliberalism*, 62.

51. See IntelCanada, "Symphony of One"; IntelDeutschland, "Inside the Tech"; Intel, "The Human Radio."

52. Intel, "The Human Radio."

53. Quoted in Landau, "Kawehi Harnesses Tech, Creates One-Woman Orchestra."

54. IntelDeutschland, "Inside the Tech."

55. Guerrieri, *The First Four Notes*, 239.

56. See the Consumer Electronics Showcase 2016 keynote address transcript at https://singjupost.com/intel-ceo-brian-krzanich-keynote-at-ces-2016-full-transcript/8/?singlepage=1 (accessed October 9, 2018).

57. For the "Military, Aerospace, Government" section of Intel's website, go to https://www.intel.com/content/www/us/en/government/products/programmable/overview.html (accessed October 10, 2018).

58. See https://www.intel.com.tr/content/dam/www/public/us/en/documents/solution-briefs/realsense-powers-machines-that-can-see-brief.pdf.

59. See Pomerleau, "How Technology Has Changed Intelligence Collection."

60. See the video documenting the making of Drone 100: https://iq.intel.com/100-dancing-drones-set-world-record/ (accessed October 10, 2018).

61. Mandel, *Late Capitalism*, 303. In 2004 Michael Hardt and Antonio Negri extended Mandel's ideas, arguing that in contemporary capitalism, the state of warfare is no longer an exception but rather "an interminable condition" and "a permanent social relation," constituting a primary organizing principle of society. *Multitude*, 12.

62. See Watkins, *Proof through the Night*.

63. For example, while Susan McClary was widely and hatefully excoriated for daring to point out, in 1987, that the first movement recapitulation of the Ninth Symphony evokes the rage of a thwarted sexual assault, in reality commentators have understood this musical moment in precisely these terms for two centuries. In his defense of McClary's comments, Robert Fink charts this history, noting that "an entire line of male critics have grasped at metaphors of (often sexualized) violence to situate this passage." All that was different in McClary's account was that, unlike E. T. A. Hoffmann, she suggested such moments of musical violence might be upsetting rather than transcendent. Fink, "Beethoven Antihero," 111.

64. Cohen, "The Surveillance-Innovation Complex," 208.

65. Cohen, 208.

66. See the Consumer Electronics Showcase 2016 keynote address transcript at https://singjupost.com/intel-ceo-brian-krzanich-keynote-at-ces-2016-full-transcript/8/?singlepage=1 (accessed October 9, 2018).

67. At the time of this writing, Intel states that it has met its goals of manufacturing all its microprocessors using conflict-free minerals, and that it is "continuing [its] pursuit of conflict-free supply chains" for manufacturing its "broader product base." See Intel's white paper, "Intel's Efforts to Achieve a 'Conflict-Free' Supply Chain."

68. Intel's corporate responsibility page can be found at https://www.intel.com/content/www/us/en/corporate-responsibility/conflict-free-minerals.html (accessed October 10, 2018).

69. See Mukherjee and Banet-Weiser, *Commodity Activism*.

70. Crary, *24/7*.

71. See the Consumer Electronics Showcase 2016 keynote address transcript at https://singjupost.com/intel-ceo-brian-krzanich-keynote-at-ces-2016-full-transcript/8/?singlepage=1 (accessed October 9, 2018).

CONCLUSION

1. Martin, "Nobel Prize–Winning Economist Stiglitz Tells Us Why 'Neoliberalism Is Dead.'"

2. See Biddle, "There's Nothing Apple's CEO Cares about More Than Not Paying Taxes."

3. We can also see in some of Trump's economic proposals the continuing process by which capital seems to concede to its critics while maintaining elite power. Examples include his plans to privatize air traffic control and allow private firms like Goldman Sachs to purchase public assets, as well as his plan to make $274 billion in cuts to welfare and other social programs to subsidize tax cuts for the wealthy. These sorts of policies, if enacted, would entail an enormous upward redistribution of wealth, a prime goal of neoliberal capitalism since the 1970s. See Keefe and Sirota, "Trump Administration Conflicts of Interest"; and Wagner, "The Pontiff versus the Mogul."

4. McMaster and Cohn, "America First Doesn't Mean America Alone."

5. See Drum, "Health Care Systems Are Expensive. Deal with It." Drum says that a universal health care system in the United States would require an additional $1.5 trillion in government spending, and notes, regarding a single-payer system, that "nobody serious is going to buy it."

6. Walker, "Donald Trump's Muslim Ban."

7. See Chen, "Undocumented Immigrants Contribute Over $11 Billion to Our Economy Each Year"; and Furman and Gray, "Ten Ways Immigrants Help Build and Strengthen Our Economy."

8. Macron vowed to run France "like a start-up," and has developed an economic policy focused on technological innovation and the state subsidization of the tech industry. See Alderman, "Macron Vowed to Make France a 'Start-Up Nation.' Is it Getting There?" See also "Centrism Takes on the Extremes," in which Noah Smith praises neoliberalism and argues that it represents the only surefire means of combating "the dangerous forces of extremism," represented by "communism, fascism, or militarism." Warning readers that this benevolent ideology is "under assault from both sides," Smith says that for progressives, "'Neoliberalism: Mend it, don't end it' should be the slogan of the day." See also Reixeira, "What Right-Wing Populism?"; and Bowman, "Coming Out as Neoliberals."

9. See Hess, "The Trump Resistance Will Be Commercialized"; and Monllos, "This Creative Agency Is Trying to Brand the Anti-Trump Movement."

10. Ford, *Dig*, 224.
11. Adorno, "Why Is the New Art So Hard to Understand?," 200.
12. See Frog Peak's website at http://www.frogpeak.org/fpfaq.html (accessed October 10, 2018).
13. I am grateful to Giacomo Fiore for sharing some of his research and archival materials on Frog Peak with me. The quotation is taken from "'A Home for Artists' Work,'" the paper he delivered in 2017 at the meeting of the Society for American Music.
14. Smith, "Surviving the Underground."
15. Smith, "Surviving the Underground."
16. Smith, "Surviving the Underground."
17. Adorno, "Vers une musique informelle," in *Quasi una Fantasia*, 280.
18. Adorno, 283.
19. Parkhurst and Hammel, "On Theorizing a 'Properly Marxist' Musical Aesthetics," 52.
20. Marx used the term *alienated* to describe the separation of the worker from the processes of production; Tsing in *The Mushroom at the End of the World* stretches the term to include the separation of nonhumans from "their livelihood processes" (p. 290). This means that for Tsing, animals and plants are also alienated.
21. Tsing, 23.
22. Tsing, 27.
23. Quoted in Gray, "Jennifer Walshe Spins a Fine Tale."
24. Priest, *Boring Formless Nonsense*.
25. Gershon, "Neoliberal Agency."
26. Rutherford-Johnson, *Music after the Fall*, 97–98.
27. Graham, *Sounds of the Underground*, 53.
28. Williams, "Base and Superstructure in Marxist Cultural Theory," 16.
29. Williams, 15.
30. Ford, *Dig*, 222. See also Currie, "Music after All."
31. Adorno, "On the Social Situation of Music," 391.
32. Adorno, "On the Fetish-Character in Music and the Regression of Listening," 315.
33. Adorno, "On the Social Situation of Music," 391.
34. Adorno, 392.
35. Parkhurst and Hammel, "On Theorizing a 'Properly Marxist' Musical Aesthetics."
36. Parkhurst and Hammel, 40. This is a much more focused argument than the one that generally affirms commodity culture by simply pointing out that different commodities can mean different things to different people. I don't think Parkhurst and Hammel are saying that *all* or *any* music can generate real political praxis; such music would have to be constructed with that goal in mind, just as *Capital* was.
37. Parkhurst and Hammel, 49.
38. Parkhurst and Hammel, 47 and 50.
39. Morse, "The Appeal of the Empire of Lies," 283.
40. Morse, 284.
41. Kapur, "Couldn't Be Better," 71.
42. Federici, *Caliban and the Witch*.
43. Mann, *Disassembly Required*, 77.
44. Economists use the term *second best* to describe real-life situations in which totally optimal conditions for economic processes cannot be met.
45. Mann, *Disassembly Required*, 88.

46. Felski, *The Limits of Critique*, 129.
47. Felski, 2.
48. Adorno, "Resignation," 293.
49. Felski, *The Limits of Critique*, 119.
50. Latour, "Why Has Critique Run out of Steam?"

BIBLIOGRAPHY

Adorno, Theodor W. "The Aging of the New Music." In *Essays on Music*, 181–202.

———. *Essays on Music*. Edited by Richard Leppert. Translated by Susan H. Gillespie. Berkeley: University of California Press, 2002.

———. "On the Fetish-Character in Music and the Regression of Listening." In *Essays on Music*, 288–317.

———. "On the Social Situation of Music." In *Essays on Music*, 391–436.

———. "On Tradition." Telos 94 (Winter 1993-94): 75–82.

———. "The Radio Symphony." In *Essays on Music*, 251–70.

———. "Resignation." In *Critical Models: Interventions and Catchwords*, translated by Henry W. Pickford, 289–94. New York: Columbia University Press, 1998.

———. "Vers une musique informelle." In *Quasi una Fantasia: Essays on Modern Music*, translated by Rodney Livingstone, 269–322. London: Verso, 1998.

Ahmed, Sara. *On Being Included: Racism and Diversity in Institutional Life*. Durham, NC: Duke University Press, 2012.

Alderman, Liz. "Macron Vowed to Make France a 'Start-Up Nation.' Is It Getting There?" *New York Times*, May 23, 2018.

Anable, Aubrey. "Labor/Leisure." In *Time: A Vocabulary of the Present*, edited by Joel Burges and Amy J. Elias, 192–208. New York: New York University Press, 2016.

Applebaum, Richard P. "Multiculturalism and Flexibility: Some New Directions in Global Capitalism." In Gordon and Newfield, *Mapping Multiculturalism*, 1–18.

Atkinson, Robert, and Stephen Ezell. *Innovation Economics: The Race for Global Advantage*. New Haven, CT: Yale University Press, 2012.

Attali, Jacques. *Noise: The Political Economy of Music*. Translated by Brian Massumi. Minneapolis: University of Minnesota Press, 2006.

Audretsch, D. B. *Innovation and Industry Evolution*. Cambridge, MA: MIT Press, 1995.

Avila, Eric. *Popular Culture in the Age of White Flight: Fear and Fantasy in Suburban Los Angeles*. Berkeley: University of California Press, 2004.

Azerrad, Michael. *Our Band Could Be Your Life: Scenes from the American Indie Underground 1981–1991*. New York: Little, Brown, & Company, 2001.

Babbitt, Milton. "The Composer as Specialist." In *The Collected Essays of Milton Babbitt*, edited by Stephen Peles, Stephen Dembski, Andrew Mead, and Joseph N. Straus, 48–54. Princeton: Princeton University Press, 2003.

Banet-Weiser, Sarah. *Authentic: The Politics of Ambivalence in Brand Culture*. New York: New York University Press, 2012.

Barragan, Bianca. "Boyle Heights Freaks Out about Being Sold as the Next DTLA." *Curbed Los Angeles* (newsletter), May 28, 2014. http://la.curbed.com/2014/5/28/10094384/boyle-heights-freaks-out-at-being-sold-as-the-next-downtown.

——. "Taking a Look at the Under-Construction Sixth Street Bridge," *Curbed Los Angeles* (newsletter), March 16, 2018. https://la.curbed.com/2018/3/16/17129192/la-sixth-street-bridge-construction-101-freeway.

Bates, Mason. "The Mechanics of Musical Narrative." *Mason Bates* (blog), 2011. http://www.masonbates.com/blog/the-mechanics-of-musical-narrative/.

——. "Mothership." Scored for full orchestra, plus harp, piano, and electronica. San Jose, CA: Aphra Music, 2012. Distributed through Bill Holab Music, www.billholabmusic.com (accessed October 10, 2018).

——. "The Rise of Exotic Computing." Scored for a flute, oboe, B-flat clarinet, bassoon, F horn, C trumpet, harp, piano, violin, viola, cello, bass, and a single percussionist who alternates between marimba, glockenspiel, and cymbals. San Jose, CA: Aphra Music, 2014. Distributed through Bill Holab Music, www.billholabmusic.com (accessed October 10, 2018).

——. Video interview about "The Rise of Exotic Computing." Chicago Symphony Orchestra, "CSO Sounds and Stories," September 24, 2014. http://csosoundsandstories.org/mason-bates-on-the-rise-of-exotic-computing/.

Baumgarten, Mark. *Love Rock Revolution: K Records and the Rise of Independent Music*. Seattle, WA: Sasquatch Books, 2012.

Bersin, Josh. "Why Diversity and Inclusion Will Be a Top Priority for 2016." *Forbes*, December 6, 2015. https://www.forbes.com/sites/joshbersin/2015/12/06/why-diversity-and-inclusion-will-be-a-top-priority-for-2016/#576eda8b2ed5.

Biddle, Sam. "There's Nothing Apple's CEO Cares about More Than Not Paying Taxes." *The Intercept*, May 4, 2017. https://theintercept.com/2017/05/04/theres-nothing-apples-ceo-cares-about-more-than-not-paying-taxes/.

Billingham, Chase M. "The Broadening Conception of Gentrification: Recent Developments and Avenues for Future Inquiry in the Sociological Study of Urban Change." *Michigan Sociological Review* 29 (Fall 2015): 75–102.

Billingham, Peter. "Is There Any Place for Innovation in the Funeral Industry Today?" *Death Goes Digital* (blog), August 2, 2016. http://www.deathgoesdigital.com/blog/digital-strategy-funeral-directors-innovation.

Bishop, Claire. "Antagonism and Relational Aesthetics." *October* 110 (2004): 51–79.

——. *Artificial Hells: Participatory Art and the Politics of Spectatorship*. London: Verso, 2012.

——. "The Social Turn: Collaboration and Its Discontents." *ArtForum* 44, no. 6 (2006): 178–83.

Black, Ezrha Jean. "Opera for the Masses." *Artillery Magazine*, January 7, 2014. http://artillerymag.com/media-opera/.

Blake, David. "Musicological Omnivore in the Neoliberal University." *Journal of Musicology* 34, no. 3 (Summer 2017): 319–53.

Blomley, Nick. *Unsettling the City: Urban Land and the Politics of Property*. New York: Routledge, 2004.

Bodirsky, Katharina. "Culture for Competitiveness: Valuing Diversity in EU-Europe and the 'Creative City' of Berlin." *International Journal of Cultural Policy* 18, no. 4 (2012): 455–73.

Boltanski, Luc, and Eve Chiapello. *The New Spirit of Capitalism*. Translated by Gregory Elliott. London: Verso, 2005.

Bonds, Mark Evan. *Absolute Music: The History of an Idea*. Oxford: Oxford University Press, 2014.

———. *Music as Thought: Listening to the Symphony in the Age of Beethoven*. Princeton, NJ: Princeton University Press, 2006.

Born, Georgina. *Rationalizing Culture: IRCAM, Boulez, and the Institutionalization of the Musical Avant-Garde*. Berkeley: University of California Press, 1995.

Bourriaud, Nicolas. *Relational Aesthetics*. Translated by Simon Pleasance and Fronza Woods. Dijon: Les Presses du Réel, 2002.

Bowman, Sam. "Coming Out as Neoliberals." Blog post, Adam Smith Institute, October 11, 2016. https://www.adamsmith.org/blog/coming-out-as-neoliberals.

Brookes, Stephen. "Missy Mazzoli Has a Different Take on Classical Music, and People Are Listening." *Washington Post*, May 7, 2011. https://www.washingtonpost.com/entertainment/music/missy-mazzoli-has-a-different-take-on-classical-music—and-peopleare-listening/2011/05/03/AFxMPV9F_story.html?utm_term=.7fdf823eda98.

Broverman, Neal. "One Last Chance to See L.A.'s Wildly Innovative Car Opera." *Los Angeles Magazine*, November 5, 2015. http://www.lamag.com/driver/one-last-chance-to-see-l-a-s-wildly-innovative-car-opera/.

Brown, Wendy. *Edgework: Critical Essays on Knowledge and Politics*. Princeton, NJ: Princeton University Press, 2005.

———. *Undoing the Demos: Neoliberalism's Stealth Revolution*. New York: Zone Books, 2015.

Brown-Saracino, Japonica. *The Gentrification Debates*. New York: Routledge, 2010.

Broyles, Michael. *Mavericks and Other Traditions in American Music*. New Haven, CT: Yale University Press, 2004.

Burchell, Graham, Colin Gordon, and Peter Miller, eds. *The Foucault Effect: Studies in Governmentality*. Chicago: University of Chicago Press, 1991.

Bürger, Peter. *Theory of the Avant Garde*. Translated by Michael Shaw. Minneapolis: University of Minnesota Press, 1984.

Burgin, Angus. *The Great Persuasion: Reinventing Free Markets since the Depression*. Cambridge, MA: Harvard University Press, 2012.

Carroll, Rory. "'Anti-white' Graffiti in Gentrifying LA Neighborhood Sparks Hate Crime Debate." *Guardian* US edition, November 4, 2016. https://www.theguardian.com/us-news/2016/nov/04/boyle-heights-art-gallery-vandalism-hate-crime-gentrification.

———. "'Hope Everyone Pukes on Your Artisanal Treats': Fighting Gentrification, LA Style." *Guardian* US edition, April 19, 2016.

Chapman, Dale. "The 'One-Man Band' and Entrepreneurial Selfhood in Neoliberal Culture." *Popular Music* 32, no. 3 (October 2013): 451–70.

Chapple, Reginald. "From Central Avenue to Leimert Park: The Shifting Center of Black Los Angeles." In *Black Los Angeles: American Dreams and Racial Realities*, edited by Darnell Hunt and Ana-Christina Ramon, 60–80. New York: New York University Press, 2010.

Chen, Michelle. "Undocumented Immigrants Contribute Over $11 Billion to Our Economy Each Year." *Nation*, March 14, 2016. www.thenation.com/article/undocumented-immigrants-contribute-over-11-billion-to-our-economy-each-year/.

Christensen, Clayton. "Disruptive Technologies: Catching the Wave." *Harvard Business Review* (January–February 1995). https://hbr.org/1995/01/disruptive-technologies-catching-the-wave.

Clarke, Simon. "What in the F——'s Name Is Fordism." In *Fordism and Flexibility: Divisions and Change,* edited by Nigel Gilbert, Roger Burrows, and Anna Pollert, 13–30. New York: St. Martin's Press, 1992.

Cohen, Julie E. "The Surveillance-Innovation Complex: The Irony of the Participatory Turn." In *The Participatory Condition in the Digital Age,* edited by Darin Barney, Gabriella Coleman, Christine Ross, Jonathan Sterne, and Tamar Tembeck, 207–26. Minneapolis: University of Minnesota Press, 2016.

Cole, David B. "Artists and Urban Redevelopment." *Geographical Review* 77, no. 4 (October 1987): 391–407.

Cooper, Barry. "Beethoven's Uses of Silence." *Musical Times* 152, no. 1914 (Spring 2011): 25–43.

Crane, Dan. "Moving Parts." *California Sunday Magazine,* October 4, 2015. https://story.californiasunday.com/hopscotch-roving-opera.

Crary, Jonathan. *24/7: Late Capitalism and the Ends of Sleep.* London: Verso, 2013.

Crawford, Richard. *The American Musical Landscape: The Business of Musicianship from Billings to Gershwin.* Berkeley: University of California Press, 1993.

Cruz, Jon. "From Farce to Tragedy: Reflections on the Reification of Race at Century's End." In Gordon and Newfield, *Mapping Multiculturalism,* 19–39.

Currie, James. "Music after All." *Journal of the American Musicological Society* 62, no. 1 (Spring 2009): 145–203.

———. "Music and Politics." In *The Routledge Companion to Philosophy and Music,* edited by Theodore Gracyk and Andrew Kania, 546–56. New York: Routledge, 2011.

———. *Music and the Politics of Negation.* Bloomington: Indiana University Press, 2012.

Davidson, Justin. "A New New York School." *New York Magazine,* March 20, 2011. http://nymag.com/arts/classicaldance/classical/reviews/new-composers-davidson-review-2011-3/.

Davis, Angela. "Rethinking 'Race' Politics." In Gordon and Newfield, *Mapping Multiculturalism,* 40–48.

Day, Ronald E. *Indexing It All: The Subject in the Age of Documentation, Information, and Data.* Cambridge, MA: MIT Press, 2014.

Defend Boyle Heights. "Destroy the Boyle Heights Arts District One Gallery at a Time, One Landlord at a Time." *Defend Boyle Heights* (blog), April 6, 2018. http://defendboyleheights.blogspot.com/2018/04/destroy-boyle-heights-arts-district-one.html.

———. "Statement about the Self Help Graphics Accountability Session and Beyond." *Defend Boyle Heights* (blog), July 6, 2016. http://defendboyleheights.blogspot.com/2016/07/defend-boyle-heights-statement-about_6.html.

Dosi, G., and R. Nelson. "An Introduction to Evolutionary Theories in Economics." *Journal of Evolutionary Economics* 4, no. 3 (1994): 153–72.

Drott, Eric. "Rereading Jacques Attali's *Bruits.*" *Critical Inquiry* 41, no. 4 (Summer 2015): 721–56.

Drum, Kevin. "Health Care Systems Are Expensive. Deal with It." *Mother Jones,* May 24, 2017. http://www.motherjones.com/kevin-drum/2017/05/health-care-expensive-deal-it.

Duhigg, Charles, and David Barboza. "In China, Human Costs Are Built into an iPad." *New York Times,* January 25, 2012.

Economist. "Virtual Reality and Beethoven: Dimension no. 3," October 3, 2015. http://www.economist.com/news/united-states/21669956-technology-could-help-classical-music-attract-new-audiences-dimension-no-3.

Eileraas, Karina. "Witches, Bitches & Fluids: Girl Bands Performing Ugliness as Resistance." *TDR* 41, no. 3 (Autumn 1997): 122–39.

Elazar, Daniel J. "Federal/Confederal Solutions to the Israeli-Palestinian-Jordanian Conflict: Concepts and Feasibility." Jerusalem Center for Public Affairs, accessed October 4, 2018, http://www.jcpa.org/dje/articles/fedconfed-sol.htm.

Endler, Michael. "CES 2014: Cisco's Internet of Everything Vision." *Information Week*, January 11, 2014. http://www.informationweek.com/strategic-cio/executive-insights-and-innovation/ces-2014-ciscos-internet-of-everything-vision/d/d-id/1113407.

Estrada, Gilbert. "If You Build It, They Will Move: The Los Angeles Freeway System and the Displacement of Mexican East Los Angeles, 1944–1972." *Southern California Quarterly* 87, no. 3 (Fall 2005): 287–315.

Evans, Claire L. *Broad Band: The Untold Story of the Women Who Made the Internet.* New York: Portfolio, 2018.

Ewait, David. "Reuters Top 100: The World's Most Innovative Universities." Reuters, September 28, 2016. http://www.reuters.com/article/amers-reuters-ranking-innovative-univers-idUSL2N1C406D.

Fairfield, John D. *The Mysteries of the Great City: The Politics of Urban Design, 1877–1937.* Columbus: Ohio University Press, 1993.

Fallon, Nicole. "Do It Yourself: 4 Tips for DIY Entrepreneurs." *Business News Daily*, November 18, 2014. http://www.businessnewsdaily.com/7472-diy-industry-tips.html.

Farber, Jim. "Car Hop: The Industry's Mobile Opera *Hopscotch* Takes to the Streets." *San Francisco Classical Voice*, October 27, 2015. https://www.sfcv.org/preview/the-industry/car-hop-the-industry's-mobile-opera-hopscotch-takes-to-the-streets.

Federici, Silvia. *Caliban and the Witch: Women, the Body, and Primitive Accumulation.* New York: Autonomedia, 2004.

———. *Revolution at Point Zero: Housework, Reproduction, and Feminist Struggle.* Oakland, CA: PM Press, 2012.

Felski, Rita. *The Limits of Critique.* Chicago: University of Chicago Press, 2015.

Fenlon, Iain, ed. *Music in Medieval and Early Modern Europe: Patronage, Sources and Texts.* Cambridge: Cambridge University Press, 1981.

Ferris, David. *Silent Urns: Romanticism, Hellenism, Modernity.* Stanford, CA: Stanford University Press, 2000.

Fink, Robert. "Beethoven Antihero: Sex, Violence, and the Aesthetics of Failure, or Listening to the Ninth Symphony as Postmodern Sublime." In *Beyond Structural Listening? Postmodern Modes of Hearing*, ed. Andrew Dell'Antonio, 109–53. Berkeley: University of California Press, 2004.

———. *Repeating Ourselves: American Minimal Music as Cultural Practice.* Berkeley: University of California Press, 2005.

Fiore, Giacomo. "'A Home for Artists' Work': Experimental Publishing by Frog Peak Music since 1982." Paper presented at the annual meeting of the Society for American Music, Montréal, March 25, 2017.

Flew, Terry. *Global Creative Industries.* Cambridge: Polity Press, 2013.

Florida, Richard. *The Rise of the Creative Class, and How It's Transforming Work, Leisure, Community and Everyday Life.* New York: Basic Books, 2002.

Ford, Phil. *Dig: Sound and Music in Hip Culture.* Oxford: Oxford University Press, 2013.

Foucault, Michel. *The Birth of Biopolitics: Lectures at the Collège de France 1978–1979.* Translated by Graham Burchell. New York: Palgrave MacMillan, 2008.

———. "Governmentality." In *The Foucault Effect: Studies in Governmentality*, edited by Graham Burchell, Colin Gordon, and Peter Miller, 87–104. Chicago: University of Chicago Press, 1991.

Fragoza, Carribean. "Art and Complicity: How the Fight against Gentrification in Boyle

Heights Que the Role of Artists." *ArtBound*, July 20, 2016. https://ww.kcet.org/shows/artbound/boyle-heights-gentrification-art-galleries-pssst.

Friedman, Milton. *Capitalism and Freedom*. Chicago: University of Chicago Press, 1962.

Friedman, Milton, and Rose Friedman. *Free to Choose: A Personal Statement*. San Diego: Harcourt, 1980.

Fuchs, Christian. *Internet and Surveillance: The Challenges of Web 2.0 and Social Media*. New York: Routledge, 2011.

———. *Reading Marx in the Information Age*. New York: Routledge, 2016.

Furman, Jason, and Danielle Gray. "Ten Ways Immigrants Help Build and Strengthen Our Economy." Blog post, July 12, 2012. Obama White House archives. https://obamawhitehouse.archives.gov/blog/2012/07/12/ten-ways-immigrants-help-build-and-strengthen-our-economy.

Gage, Beverly. "What an Uncensored Letter to M.L.K. Reveals." *New York Times*, November 11, 2014.

Gann, Kyle. *American Music in the Twentieth Century*. New York: Schirmer, 1997.

———. "Judd Greenstein." *Chamber Music*, January/February 2010. http://www.juddgreenstein.com/press/AmericanComposer_Greenstein.pdf.

———. *Music Downtown: Writings from the Village Voice*. Berkeley: University of California Press, 2006.

Gelt, Jessica. "'Hopscotch,' the World's First Mobile Opera, Will Take to L.A.'s Streets in 24 Cars." *Los Angeles Times*, September 9, 2015. http://www.latimes.com/entertainment/arts/la-ca-cam-fall-arts-hopscotch-opera-la-20150913-story.html.

Gendron, Bernard. *Between Montmartre and the Mudd Club: Popular Music and the Avant Garde*. Chicago: University of Chicago Press, 2002.

Gershon, Ilana. "Neoliberal Agency." *Current Anthropology* 52, no. 4 (August 2011): 537–55.

Gilbert, Jeremy. *Common Ground: Democracy and Collectivity in an Age of Individualism*. New York: Pluto Press, 2014.

Giroux, Henry. *The Terror of Neoliberalism: Authoritarianism and the Eclipse of Democracy*. Boulder, CO: Paradigm, 2004.

Glass, Ruth. *London: Aspects of Change*. Centre for Urban Studies. London: MacGibbon and Kee, 1964.

Goehr, Lydia. *The Imaginary Museum of Musical Works: An Essay in the Philosophy of Music*. Oxford: Clarendon Press, 1992.

Gopinath, Sumanth. "The Problem of the Political in Steve Reich's *Come Out*." In *Sound Commitments: Avant-Garde Music and the Sixties*, edited by Robert Adlington, 121–44. Oxford: Oxford University Press, 2009.

———. *The Ringtone Dialectic: Economy and Cultural Form*. Cambridge, MA: MIT Press, 2013.

Gopinath, Sumanth, and Jason Stanyek. "The Mobilization of Performance: An Introduction to the Aesthetics of Mobile Music." In *The Oxford Handbook of Mobile Music Studies*, edited by Gopinath and Stanyek, 2:1–42. Oxford: Oxford University Press, 2014.

Gordon, Avery F., and Christopher Newfield. Introduction to *Mapping Multiculturalism*, 1–18. Minneapolis: University of Minnesota Press, 1996.

———, eds. *Mapping Multiculturalism*. Minneapolis: University of Minnesota Press, 1996.

———. "Multiculturalism's Unfinished Business." In *Mapping Multiculturalism*, 40–48.

Graham, Stephen. *Sounds of the Underground: A Cultural, Political and Aesthetic Mapping of Underground and Fringe Music*. Ann Arbor: University of Michigan Press, 2016.

Gray, Louise. "Jennifer Walshe Spins a Fine Tale." *MusicWorks* 116 (Summer 2013). https://www.musicworks.ca/featured-article/profile/jennifer-walshe-spins-fine-tale.

Greenstein, Judd. "The Extraordinary Musician." *21CM Magazine*, February 2015. http://21cm.org/magazine/state-of-the-art-form/2015/02/22/the-extraordinary-musician/.

———. "Milton Babbitt's Birthday." *Judd Greenstein* (blog), May 11, 2006. http://www.juddgreenstein.com/milton-babbitts-birthday/.

Grimshaw, Jeremy. "High, 'Low,' and Plastic Arts: Philip Glass and the Symphony in the Age of Postproduction." *Musical Quarterly* 86, no. 3 (Autumn 2002): 472–507.

Grodach, Carl, Nicole Foster, and James Murdoch III. "Gentrification and the Artistic Dividend: The Role of the Arts in Neighborhood Change." *Journal of the American Planning Association* 80 (2014): 21–35.

Guerrieri, Matthew. *The First Four Notes: Beethoven's Fifth and the Human Imagination.* New York: Alfred A. Knopf, 2012.

Guldbrandsen, Erling E., and Julian Johnson, eds. *Transformations of Musical Modernism.* Cambridge: Cambridge University Press, 2015.

Hale, Charles R. *Más Que un Indio: Racial Ambivalence and Neoliberal Multiculturalism in Guatemala.* Santa Fe: School of American Research, 2006.

———. "Neoliberal Multiculturalism: The Remaking of Cultural Rights and Racial Dominance in Central America." *PoLAR* 28, no. 1 (May 2005): 10–28.

Hamde, Kiflemariam, Maddy Janssens, Koen Van Laer, Nils Wåhlin, and Patrizia Zanoni. "Diversity and Diversity Management in Business and Organisation Studies." In *Diversity Research and Policy: A Multidisciplinary Exploration*, edited by Steven Knotter, Rob de Lobel, Lena Tsipouri, and Vanja Stenius, 159–79. Amsterdam: Amsterdam University Press, 2011.

Hardt, Michael, and Antonio Negri. *Multitude: War and Democracy in the Age of Empire.* New York: Penguin Press, 2004.

Harkinson, Josh. "Silicon Valley Firms Are Even Whiter and More Male Than You Thought." *Mother Jones*, May 29, 2014. https://www.motherjones.com/media/2014/05/google-diversity-labor-gender-race-gap-workers-silicon-valley/.

Hart, Hugh. "Traffic Jam: 'Hopscotch' Orchestrates Opera on Wheels in Los Angeles." FastCoCreate.com, October 29, 2015. http://www.fastcocreate.com/3052501/traffic-jam-hopscotch-orchestrates-opera-on-wheels-in-los-angeles.

Harvey, David. *A Brief History of Neoliberalism.* Oxford: Oxford University Press, 2007.

———. *A Companion to Marx's Capital.* London: Verso, 2010.

———. *The Condition of Postmodernity.* London: Basil Blackwell, 1989.

Harvie, Jen. *Fair Play: Art, Performance and Neoliberalism.* Houndmills, UK: Palgrave Macmillan, 2013.

Hayek, Friedrich von. *The Road to Serfdom.* Chicago: University of Chicago Press, 1944.

Hearn, Alison. "Brand Me 'Activist.'" In *Commodity Activism: Cultural Resistance in Neoliberal Times*, edited by Roopali Mukherjee and Sarah Banet-Weiser, 23–38. New York: New York University Press, 2012.

Heise, Heather. "Opera for Everyone." *Ampersand*, October 24, 2015. http://www.ampersandla.com/opera-for-everyone-yuval-sharon-invisible-cities/.

Hess, Amanda. "The Trump Resistance Will Be Commercialized." *New York Times*, March 17, 2017. https://www.nytimes.com/2017/03/17/arts/the-trump-resistance-will-be-commercialized.html?_r=0.

Heussner, Ki Mae. "YouTube Orchestra: Online Auditions Open Today." *ABC News*, October 12, 2010. https://abcnews.go.com/Technology/youtube-symphony-orchestra-online-auditions-open-today/story?id=11862738.

Hickel, Jason. "The Microfinance Delusion: Who Really Wins?" *Guardian* US edition, June 10, 2015. https://www.theguardian.com/global-development-professionals -network/2015/jun/10/the-microfinance-delusion-who-really-wins.

Hickman, Steve. "You Can Innovate while You Meditate." *Mindful*, November 9, 2016. https://www.mindful.org/innovate-while-you-meditate/.

Hochschild, Arlie Russell. *The Commercialization of Intimate Life: Notes from Home and Work*. Berkeley: University of California Press, 2003.

Hoffmann, E. T. A. "Beethoven's Instrumental Music." In *Source Readings in Music History: The Romantic Era*, edited by Oliver Strunk, 35–41. New York: W. W. Norton, 1965.

Howe, Brian. Review of Nico Muhly, *I Drink the Air before Me*. Pitchfork, December 8, 2010. https://pitchfork.com/reviews/albums/14914-i-drink-the-air-before-me-a-good -understanding/.

Huang, Erica. "NovaTrio Brings Live Visual Technology to Classical Music." *Creators*, November 1, 2012. https://creators.vice.com/en_us/article/kbgd9w/inovatrioi-brings -live-visual-technology-to-classical-music.

Humphreys, Ashlee, and Craig J. Thompson. "Branding Disaster: Reestablishing Trust through the Ideological Containment of Systemic Risk Anxieties." *Journal of Consumer Research* 41, no. 4 (December 2014): 877–910.

Huyssen, Andreas. *After the Great Divide: Modernism, Mass Culture, Postmodernism*. Bloomington: Indiana University Press, 1986.

Intel. "The Human Radio." Video, 1:53, published February 1, 2016. https://www .youtube.com/watch?v=wP5NKn68S50.

———. "Intel's Efforts to Achieve a 'Conflict-Free' Supply Chain." White paper, May 2018. https://www.intel.com/content/dam/www/public/us/en/documents/white-papers/ conflict-minerals-white-paper.pdf.

IntelCanada. "Symphony of One." Video, 1:43, published February 11, 2016. https:// www.youtube.com/watch?v=Zvp-Tg0F5Bc.

IntelDeutschland. "Inside the Tech." Video, 1:06, published March 7, 2017. https://www .youtube.com/watch?v=0b1RgCjYt0U.

Jameson, Fredric. *Postmodernism: Or, the Cultural Logic of Late Capitalism*. Durham, NC: Duke University Press, 1991.

Janeway, William H. *Doing Capitalism in the Innovation Economy*. Cambridge: Cambridge University Press, 2012.

Johnson, Daniel. "Judd Greenstein: Pulsating Complexity with Indie-Classical Populism." WXQR, February 3, 2012. https://www.wqxr.org/story/172816-portal-judd -greenstein/.

Johnson, Julian. *Who Needs Classical Music? Cultural Choice and Musical Value*. Oxford: Oxford University Press, 2002.

Jones, Jonathan. "Artwashing: The New Watchword for Anti-gentrification Protesters." *Guardian* US edition, July 18, 2016. https://www.theguardian.com/artanddesign/ jonathanjonesblog/2016/jul/18/artwashing-new-watchword-for-anti-gentrification -protesters.

Kapur, Akash. "Couldn't Be Better: The Return of the Utopians." *New Yorker*, October 3, 2016, 66–71.

Keay, Douglas. "Aids, Education, and the Year 2000!" *Woman's Own*, September 23, 1987, 8–10.

Keefe, Josh, and David Sirota. "Trump Administration Conflicts of Interest: How Gary Cohn Could Sell U.S. Infrastructure to Goldman Sachs." *International Business Times*, May 26,

2017. http://www.ibtimes.com/political-capital/trump-administration-conflicts-interest
-how-gary-cohn-could-sell-us-infrastructure.

Keller, Douglas. "Adorno and the Dialectics of Mass Culture." In *Adorno: A Critical Reader*,
edited by Nigel Gibson and Andrew Rubin, 86–109. Oxford: Blackwell, 2002.

Kim, Sojin. "All Roads Lead to Boyle Heights: Exploring a Los Angeles Neighborhood."
In *Common Ground: The Japanese American National Museum and the Culture of Collabo-
rations*, edited by Akemi Kikumura-Yano, Lane Ryo Hirabayashi, and James A. Hirabayashi, 149–66. Boulder: University of Colorado Press, 2005.

Kramer, Lawrence. *Why Classical Music Still Matters*. Berkeley: University of California
Press, 2009.

LaBarre, Polly. "Who's the Best at Innovating Innovation?" *Harvard Business Review*, February 25, 2013. https://hbr.org/2013/02/whos-the-best-at-innovating-in/.

Lal, Deepak. *Reviving the Invisible Hand: The Case for Liberalism in the Twenty-First Century*.
Princeton, NJ: Princeton University Press, 2006.

Landau, Deb Miller. "Kawehi Harnesses Tech, Creates One-Woman Orchestra." *iQ by Intel*, February 2, 2016. https://iq.intel.com/kawehi-harnesses-tech-creates-one-woman
-orchestra/.

Lanz, Michelle. "'Invisible Cities' Opera Moves from Union Station to Your Listening Device." *The Frame*, SCPR.org, November 5, 2014. https://www.scpr.org/programs/the
-frame/2014/11/05/40158/the-industrys-invisible-cities-opera-union-station/.

Latour, Bruno. "Why Has Critique Run out of Steam? From Matters of Fact to Matters of
Concern." *Critical Inquiry* 30 (Winter 2004): 225–48.

Leavitt, Jacqueline. "Art and the Politics of Public Housing." *Progressive Planning Magazine*,
October 24, 2005. http://www.plannersnetwork.org/2005/10/art-and-the-politics-of
-public-housing/.

Lebrecht, Norman. *Who Killed Classical Music? Maestros, Managers, and Corporate Politics*.
New York: Birch Lane Press, 1997.

Lees, Loretta, Tom Slater, and Elvin Wyly. *Gentrification*. New York: Routledge, 2008.

Leppert, Richard. "The Musician of the Imagination." In *The Musician as Entrepreneur,
1700–1914*, edited by William Weber, 25–58. Bloomington: Indiana University Press,
2004.

Levine, Lawrence. *Highbrow/Lowbrow: The Emergence of Cultural Hierarchy in America*.
Cambridge, MA: Harvard University Press, 1988.

Levy, Ariel. "Lesbian Nation." *New Yorker*, March 2, 2009. https://www.newyorker.com/
magazine/2009/03/02/lesbian-nation.

Li Qiang. "Apple Should Not Profit at the Expense of Low-Wage Workers." China Labor
Watch, April 1, 2015. http://www.chinalaborwatch.org/newscast/435.

Llopis, Glenn. "Diversity Management Is the Key to Growth: Make It Authentic." *Forbes*,
June 13, 2011. https://www.forbes.com/sites/glennllopis/2011/06/13/diversity-manage
ment-is-the-key-to-growth-make-it-authentic/#28a2743a66f3.

Lobel, Orly. *Talent Wants to Be Free: Why We Should Learn to Love Leaks, Raids, and Free Riding*. New Haven, CT: Yale University Press, 2013.

Long, Michael. *Beautiful Monsters: Imagining the Classic in Musical Media*. Berkeley: University of California Press, 2008.

Lovett, Ian. "Los Angeles Bridge's Demolition Is a Sign of Changes Sweeping the City."
New York Times, December 2, 2015. http://www.nytimes.com/2015/12/03/us/los
-angeles-gentrification.html.

Macek, Steve. *Urban Nightmares: The Media, the Right, and the Moral Panic over the City*.
Minneapolis: University of Minnesota Press, 2006.

Mandel, Ernest. *Late Capitalism*. Translated by Joris De Bres. London: Verso, 1978.

Manent, Pierre. *An Intellectual History of Liberalism*. Translated by Rebecca Balinsky. Princeton, NJ: Princeton University Press, 1994.

Mann, Geoff. *Disassembly Required: A Field Guide to Actually Existing Capitalism*. Edinburgh: AK Press, 2013.

Marlow, Jeffrey. "Is This the Opera of the Future?" *Wired*, October 22, 2013. http://www .wired.com/2013/10/is-this-the-opera-of-the-future/.

Martin, Will. "Nobel Prize–Winning Economist Stiglitz Tells Us Why 'Neoliberalism Is Dead.'" *Business Insider*, August 19, 2016. www.businessinsider.com/joseph-stiglitz -says-neoliberalism-is-dead-2016-8.

Marx, Karl. *Capital: A Critique of Political Economy*. Translated by Ben Fowkes. Vol. 1. London: Pelican Books, 1976.

———. *Grundrisse: Foundations of the Critique of Political Economy (Rough Draft)*. Translated by Martin Nicolaus. London: Penguin Books, 1993.

Marx, Karl, and Frederick Engels. *The Communist Manifesto: A Modern Edition*. London: Verso, 1998.

Matthews, Steve. "The Do-It-Yourself Economy Just Hired 1 Million American Entrepreneurs." *Bloomberg*, June 5, 2015. http://www.bloomberg.com/news/articles/2015-06 -05/the-do-it-yourself-economy-just-hired-1-million-american-entrepreneurs.

Mauro, Evan. "The Death and Life of the Avant-Garde: Or, Modernism and Biopolitics." *Mediations* 26: 1–2 (Fall/Spring 2012–13): 119–42.

McGuigan, Jim. *Neoliberal Culture*. Houndmills: Palgrave Macmillan, 2016.

McMaster, H. R., and Gary D. Cohn. "America First Doesn't Mean America Alone." *Wall Street Journal*, May 30, 2017. http://www.wsj.com/articles/america-first-doesnt-mean -america-alone-1496187426.

McRobbie, Angela. *Be Creative: Making a Living in the New Culture Industries*. Cambridge: Polity Press, 2016.

Meiksins Wood, Ellen. *Democracy against Capitalism: Renewing Historical Materialism*. Cambridge: Cambridge University Press, 1995.

Melamed, Jodi. *Represent and Destroy: Rationalizing Violence in the New Racial Capitalism*. Minneapolis: University of Minnesota Press, 2011.

———. "The Spirit of Neoliberalism: From Racial Liberalism to Neoliberal Multiculturalism." *Social Text* 89 (Winter 2006): 1–25.

Metzer, David. *Musical Modernism at the Turn of the Twenty First Century*. Cambridge: Cambridge University Press, 2009.

———. "Sharing a Stage: The Growing Proximity between Modernism and Popular Music." In *Transformations of Musical Modernism*, edited by Erling E. Guldbrandsen and Julian Johnson, 97–116. Cambridge: Cambridge University Press, 2015.

Midgette, Anne. "A Composer Offers the Field Just What It Needs." *Washington Post*, April 2, 2016. https://www.washingtonpost.com/entertainment/music/a-composer -offers-the-field-just-what-it-needs/2016/03/31/9bd82884-d428-11e5-be55-2cc3c1 e4b76b_html.

Miles, Malcolm. *Limits to Culture: Urban Regeneration vs. Dissident Art*. New York: Pluto Press, 2015.

Miles, Raymond E., Charles C. Snow, and Grant Miles. "The Ideology of Innovation." *Strategic Organization* 5, no. 4 (November 2007): 423–35.

Mirowski, Philip. "Postface: Defining Neoliberalism." In *The Road from Mont Pèlerin*, edited by Philip Mirowski and Dieter Plehwe, 417–56. Cambridge, MA: Harvard University Press, 2009.

Mirowski, Philip, and Dieter Plehwe, eds. *The Road from Mont Pèlerin*. Cambridge, MA: Harvard University Press, 2009.

Mohl, Raymond A. *The Interstates and Cities: Highways, Housing, and the Freeway Revolt*. Research Report to the Poverty and Race Research Action Council, 2002.

Monllos, Kristina. "This Creative Agency Is Trying to Brand the Anti-Trump Movement." *AdWeek*, April 4, 2017. http://www.adweek.com/agencies/this-creative-agency-is-trying-to-brand-the-anti-trump-movement/.

Moore, Andrea. "Neoliberalism and the Musical Entrepreneur." *Journal of the Society for American Music* 10, no. 1 (2016): 33–53.

Morse, Jennifer Roback. "The Appeal of the Empire of Lies." *Independent Review* 5, no. 2 (Fall 2000): 283–93.

Moulitsas, Markos. "Be Happy for Coal Miners Losing Their Health Insurance. They're Getting Exactly What They Voted For." *Daily Kos*, December 12, 2016. www.dailykos.com/story/2016/12/12/1610198/-Be-happy-for-coal-miners-losing-their-health-insurance-They-re-getting-exactly-what-they-voted-for.

Muhly, Nico. "Hindi Classical." *Nico Muhly* (blog), June 21, 2012. http://nicomuhly.com/news/2012/hindi-classical/.

———. "Lots of Things." *Nico Muhly* (blog), April 15, 2012. http://nicomuhly.com/news/2012/3366/.

———. "Think Fast." *Nico Muhly* (blog), July 1, 2014. http://nicomuhly.com/news/2014/think-fast/.

Mukherjee, Roopali, and Sarah Banet-Weiser, eds. *Commodity Activism: Cultural Resistance in Neoliberal Times*. New York: New York University Press, 2012.

Murray, Bill. "Hollenbeck Station Celebration: Grand Opening." Los Angeles Community Policing, September 20, 2009. http://www.lacp.org/2009-Articles-Main/091909-HollenbeckOpens.htm.

Mylonas, Yiannis. "Amateur Creation and Entrepreneurialism: A Critical Study of Artistic Production in Post-Fordist Structures." *tripleC: Communication, Capitalism, and Critique* 10, no. 1 (January 2012): 1–11.

Nadhan, E. G. "Drones Align the Business of Music with the Technology of Information." *Intel Peer Network* (blog), January 25, 2016. https://itpeernetwork.intel.com/drones-align-the-business-of-music-with-the-technology-of-information/.

National Post. "Why the Boston Orchestra Is Giving Its Patrons iPads," January 20, 2016. https://nationalpost.com/entertainment/music/why-the-boston-orchestra-is-giving-its-patrons-ipads.

Niebur, Louis. *Special Sound: The Creation and Legacy of the BBC Radiophonic Workshop*. Oxford: Oxford University Press, 2010.

NPR staff. "Missy Mazzoli: A New Opera and New Attitude for Classical Music." *Deceptive Cadence* (blog), November 20, 2012. NPR Classical, http://www.npr.org/blogs/deceptivecadence/2012/11/23/165585232/missy-mazzoli-a-new-opera-and-new-attitude-for-classical-music.

Nye, David. *American Technological Sublime*. Cambridge, MA: MIT Press, 1994.

Paddison, Max. "Authenticity and Failure in Adorno's Aesthetics of Music." In *The Cambridge Companion to Adorno*, edited by Tom Huhn, 198–221. Cambridge: Cambridge University Press, 2004.

Parkhurst, Bryan J., and Stephan Hammel. "On Theorizing a 'Properly Marxist' Musical Aesthetics." *International Review of the Aesthetics and Sociology of Music* 48, no. 1 (June 2017): 33–55.

Peck, Jamie. *Constructions of Neoliberal Reason*. Oxford: Oxford University Press, 2010.

Pederson, Sanna. "Defining the Term 'Absolute Music' Historically." *Music and Letters* 90, no. 2 (May 2009): 240–62.

Peterson, Richard A., and Roger M. Kern. "Highbrow Taste: From Snob to Omnivore." *American Sociological Review* 61, no. 5 (October 1996): 900–907.

Pippen, John Robison. "Toward a Postmodern Avant-Garde: Labour, Virtuosity, and Aesthetics in an American New Music Ensemble." PhD diss., University of Western Ontario. 2014.

Politico. "'Indie Classical' Goes Uptown: Judd Greenstein on New Music." January 17, 2011. https://www.politico.com/states/new-york/city-hall/story/2011/01/indie-classical-goes -uptown-judd-greenstein-on-new-music-000000.

Pomerleau, Mark. "How Technology Has Changed Intelligence Collection." Defense Systems.com, April 22, 2015. https://defensesystems.com/articles/2015/04/22/tech nology-has-changed-intelligence-gathering.aspx.

Press, Joy, and Simon Reynolds. *The Sex Revolts.* Cambridge, MA: Harvard University Press, 1995.

Priest, eldritch. *Boring Formless Nonsense: Experimental Music and the Aesthetics of Failure.* London: Bloomsbury Academic, 2013.

Reixeira, Ruy. "What Right-Wing Populism? Polls Reveal That It's Liberalism That's Surging." *Vox*, May 22, 2017. https://www.vox.com/platform/amp/the-big-idea/2017/5/ 22/15672530/opinion-polls-liberal-immigration-trade-role-government-aca.

Rich, Frank. "No Sympathy for the Hillbilly." *New York Magazine*, March 19, 2017. www .nymag.com/daily/intelligencer/2017/03/frank-rich-no-sympathy-for-the-hillbilly.html.

Richards, Patricia. *Race and the Chilean Miracle: Neoliberalism, Democracy, and Indigenous Rights.* Pittsburgh: University of Pittsburgh Press, 2013.

Ricker, Ramon. "YouTube Symphony—Year Two Coming." Blog post, Polyphonic Archive, Institute for Music Leadership, Eastman School of Music, October 18, 2010. https://iml.esm.rochester.edu/polyphonic-archive/youtube-symphony-year-two -coming/.

Ritchey, Marianna. "Amazing Together: Mason Bates, Classical Music, and Neoliberal Values." *Music and Politics* 11, no. 2 (Summer 2017). https://quod.lib.umich.edu/m/mp/ 9460447.0011.202?view=text;rgn=main.

———. "New Music in a Borderless World." In *The Routledge Companion to Expanding Approaches for Popular Music Analysis*, edited by Ciro Scotto, John Brackett, and Kenneth Smith. New York: Routledge, forthcoming.

———. "The (R)evolution of Steve Jobs." *Musicology Now*, August 11, 2017. http:// musicologynow.ams-net.org/2017/08/the-revolution-of-steve-jobs-html.

Robin, William. "Classical Music Isn't Dead." *New Yorker*, January 29, 2014. https://www .newyorker.com/culture/culture-desk/the-fat-lady-is-still-singing.

———. "'Hopscotch' Takes Opera into the Streets." *New York Times*, October 30, 2015. http://www.nytimes.com/2015/10/31/arts/music/hopscotch-takes-opera-into-the -streets.html.

———. "The Rise and Fall of 'Indie Classical': Tracing a Controversial Term in Twenty-First Century New Music." *Journal of the Society for American Music* 12, no. 1 (February 2018): 55–88.

———. "A Scene without a Name: Indie Classical and American New Music in the Twenty-First Century." PhD diss., University of North Carolina at Chapel Hill, 2016.

Robinson, Sarah May. "Chamber Music in Alternative Venues in the 21st-Century U.S.: Investigating the Effects of New Venues on Concert Culture, Programming and the Business of Classical Music." DMA thesis, University of South Carolina, 2013.

Rockwell, John. *All American Music: Composition in the Late Twentieth Century.* New York: Da Capo, 1997.

Ross, Alex. "Opera on Location." *New Yorker,* November 16, 2015. https://www.newyorker.com/magazine/2015/11/16/opera-on-location.

Rutherford-Johnson, Tim. *Music after the Fall: Modern Composition and Culture since 1989.* Berkeley: University of California Press, 2017.

Sanchez, George. "'What's Good for Boyle Heights Is Good for the Jews': Creating Multiracialism on the Eastside during the 1950s." *American Quarterly* 56, no. 3 (September 2004): 633–61.

Sandow, Greg. "YouTube (Sigh) Symphony." *Arts Journal,* April 16, 2009. http://www.artsjournal.com/sandow/2009/04/youtube_sigh_symphony.html.

Scherzinger, Martin. "Music, Corporate Power, and Unending War." *Cultural Critique* 60 (Spring 2005): 23–67.

Schumpeter, Joseph. *Capitalism, Socialism, and Democracy.* New York: Harper and Brothers, 1942.

Schwartz, Gary A. "Urban Freeways and the Interstate System." *Southern California Law Review* 49 (March 1976): 406–513.

Serve the People LA. "Against Art (Galleries, Their Investors, Apologists, and Media Lapdogs)." Tumblr, July 18, 2016. http://servethepeoplela.tumblr.com/post/147621681245/against-art-galleries-their-investors.

———. "Against Gentrification, Against Bourgeois Art." *Serve the People LA* (blog), October 4, 2015. https://servethepeoplela.wordpress.com/2015/10/04/against-gentrification-against-bourgeois-art/.

———. "The Youth Will Lead the Revolutionary Struggle." *Serve the People LA* (blog), November 22, 2015. https://servethepeoplela.wordpress.com/page/3/.

Sharon, Yuval. "Invisible Cities: The Dematerialization of Opera." *Artbound,* October 10, 2013. https://www.kcet.org/shows/artbound/invisible-cities-the-dematerialization-of-the-opera.

Sheridan, Molly. "Judd Greenstein—a World of Difference." *New Music Box,* January 17, 2011. http://www.newmusicbox.org/articles/judd-greenstein-a-world-of-difference/.

Sirota, Nadia. "New Music Fight Club." *Meet the Composer* podcast, episode 15, May 15, 2017.

Slater, Tom. "The 'Eviction' of Critical Perspectives from Gentrification Research." *International Journal of Urban and Regional Research* 30, no. 4 (December 2006): 737–57.

Slefo, George. "Intel Mixes Beethoven with Its Iconic Mnemonic in Spot about 'Amazing Experiences.'" *Creativity Online,* January 19, 2016. http://creativity-online.com/work/intel-experience-amazing/45143.

Smith, Adam. *The Theory of Moral Sentiments.* Edited by Knud Haakonssen. Cambridge: Cambridge University Press, 2002.

Smith, Jean. "Surviving the Underground: On Making Art and Getting By." Blog post, NPR Music, November 18, 2009. https://www.npr.org/sections/monitormix/2009/11/surviving_the_underground_on_m.html.

Smith, Neil. "New Globalism, New Urbanism: Gentrification as Global Urban Strategy." *Antipode* 34, no. 3 (2002): 427–50.

———. "Toward a Theory of Gentrification: A Back to the City Movement by Capital, Not People." *Journal of the American Planning Association* 45, no. 4 (1979): 538–48.

Smith, Noah. "Centrism Takes on the Extremes." *Bloomberg,* May 23, 2017. https://www.bloomberg.com/view/articles/2017-05-23/centrism-takes-on-the-extremes.

Standing, Guy. *The Precariat: The New Dangerous Class.* London: Bloomsbury, 2011.

Steigerwald, Megan. "Bringing Down the House: Situating and Mediating Opera in the Twenty First Century." PhD diss., Eastman School of Music, 2017.

Subotnik, Rose Rosengard. *Developing Variations: Style and Ideology in Western Music*. Minneapolis: University of Minnesota Press, 1991.

Taruskin, Richard. "The Musical Mystique." In *The Danger of Music: And Other Antiutopian Essays*, 330–53. Berkeley: University of California Press, 2009.

———. *The Oxford History of Western Music*. Oxford: Oxford University Press, 2005.

Taylor, Dorceta. *Toxic Communities: Environmental Racism, Industrial Pollution, and Residential Mobility*. New York: New York University Press, 2014.

Taylor, Timothy D. *Music and Capitalism: A History of the Present*. Chicago: University of Chicago Press, 2016.

———. *The Sounds of Capitalism: Advertising, Music, and the Conquest of Culture*. Chicago: University of Chicago Press, 2012.

Tiee, Charlise. "Bay Area Composer Mason Bates to Create New Steve Jobs Opera." *KQED Arts*, August 7, 2015. https://ww2kqed.org/arts/2015/08/07/bay-area-composer -mason-bates-to-create-new-steve-jobs-opera/.

Toffler, Alvin. *The Third Wave*. New York: Bantam Books, 1980.

Tommasini, Anthony. "Claire Chase Invites Young Musicians to Create New Paths." *New York Times*, December 26, 2013.

———. "YouTube Orchestra Melds Music Live and Online." *New York Times*, April 16, 2009.

Townley, Barbara, and Nic Beech, eds. *Managing Creativity: Exploring the Paradox*. Cambridge: Cambridge University Press, 2010.

Tsing, Anna Lowenhaupt. *The Mushroom at the End of the World: On the Possibility of Life in Capitalist Ruins*. Princeton, NJ: Princeton University Press, 2015.

van Dijk, Hans, Marloes van Engen, and Jaap Paauwe. "Reframing the Business Case for Diversity: A Values and Virtues Perspective." *Journal of Business Ethics* 111, no. 1 (November 2012): 73–84.

Vanhoenacker, Mark. "Requiem: Classical Music in America is Dead." *Slate*, January 2, 2014. http://www.slate.com/articles/arts/culturebox/2014/01/classical_music_sales _decline_is_classical_on_death_s_door.html.

von Rhein, John. "What Can Be Done to Make Classical Music More Relevant to Today's Culture? Ask Young Musicians." *Chicago Tribune*, April 29, 2010.

Wacquant, Loïc. *Punishing the Poor: The Neoliberal Government of Social Insecurity*. Durham, NC: Duke University Press, 2009.

Wade, Bonnie. *Music in Japan: Experiencing Music, Expressing Culture*. New York: Oxford University Press, 2005.

Wagner, Alex. "The Pontiff versus the Mogul." *Atlantic*, May 23, 2017. https://www .theatlantic.com/politics/archive/2017/05/the-pontiff-versus-the-mogul/527856/.

Wagner, Tony. *Creating Innovators: The Making of Young People Who Will Change the World*. New York: Scribner, 2012.

Wakin, Daniel J. "Getting to Carnegie via YouTube." *New York Times*, December 1, 2008.

Waleson, Heidi. "'Hopscotch,' a Mobile Opera in 24 Cars." *Wall Street Journal*, November 11, 2015.

Walker, Peter. "Donald Trump's Muslim Ban: Steve Jobs Was Son of Syrian Migrant." *Independent* UK edition, January 25, 2017. https://www.independent.co.uk/news/ world/americas/donald-trump-muslim-ban-steve-jobs-apple-son-of-syrian-migrant -refugee-mexico-border-wall-a7544636.html.

Watkins, Glenn. *Proof through the Night: Music and the Great War.* Berkeley: University of California Press, 2003.

Weber, Max. *The Protestant Ethic and the Spirit of Capitalism.* Translated by Stephen Kalberg. Los Angeles: Roxbury, 2002.

Weber, William. *Music and the Middle Class: The Social Structure of Concert Life in London, Paris and Vienna between 1830 and 1848.* 2nd ed. Burlington, VT: Ashgate, 2004.

———. *The Musician as Entrepreneur, 1700–1914.* Bloomington: Indiana University Press, 2004.

Weininger, David. "Flute Genius Claire Chase Brings Entrepreneurial Spirit to Boston." *Boston Globe*, November 19, 2014. https://www.bostonglobe.com/arts/music/2014/11/19/flute-genius-claire-chase-brings-entrepreneurial-spirit-boston/Ccqg4cKnv4R42kE47LeaLN/story.html.

Weston, Hillary. "Going between the Notes with Nico Muhly." *BlackBook*, May 16, 2013. http://bbook.com/music/going-between-the-notes-with-nico-muhly/.

Wilkie, Rob. *The Digital Condition: Class and Culture in the Information Network.* New York: Fordham University Press, 2011.

Williams, Raymond. "Base and Superstructure in Marxist Cultural Theory." *New Left Review* 82 (1973): 3–16.

Xia, Rosanna, and Christopher Goffard. "6th Street Bridge, Spanning Much of LA's Past, Finally Starts to Fall to Demolition Crews." *Los Angeles Times*, February 6, 2016. http://www.latimes.com/local/california/la-me-0207-bridge-demolition-20160207-story.html.

Zaslaw, Neal. "Mozart as Working Stiff." In *On Mozart*, edited by James Morris, 102–12. Cambridge: Cambridge University Press, 1994.

Zukin, Sharon. *Loft Living: Culture and Capital in Urban Change.* New Brunswick, NJ: Rutgers University Press, 1982.

INDEX

Adorno, Theodor W.: on atomized listening, 127–28; on autonomy, 9–10, 140, 145; on Beethoven's Fifth Symphony, 126–28; and critique, 16–17, 159; on music's potential to change society, 152–53; on new music, 80; and the New Musicology, 9–10; on repetition, 127; on subjective freedom, 147–48; on tradition, 123
Afrofuturism, 44
"Aging of the New Music, The" (Adorno), 80
alienation: of audiences by modernism, 3, 8, 65–66, 69, 77, 153; autonomous music and, 10, 127, 152; contemporary composers' attempts to resolve, 53; of labor, 56, 187n20; as a social problem, 56, 83, 148–49, 187n20
Alsop, Marin, 25
Amadeus (film), 12
Apple (corporation), 38, 42, 47, 115, 136, 138, 141. *See also* Jobs, Steve
Applebaum, Richard, 34
appropriation, cultural, 70–71, 81
artistic critique of capitalism. *See under* Boltanski and Chiapello
Attali, Jacques, 152; and neoliberalism, 11–12; and the New Musicology, 10
audience (in classical music): hatred of, 8, 66; pleasing or reaching of, 3, 4, 19, 65–66, 69, 77–78, 80, 94, 97, 144, 147, 153, 176n52; widening of, 19, 25, 30, 65, 92, 118–19, 128, 140. *See also* participatory art

automation, 23, 51
autonomy, 6, 7; the academy and, 24, 66; Adorno and, 140, 145; collective vs. individual, 61, 75, 83, 144–46; as musical ideal, 9, 144, 160–61; musicology and, 7–10; as resistance against market logic, 8–9, 24, 55, 66, 144–46, 160–61
avant-garde, 47, 58, 70, 77–78, 95, 111, 147, 176n52
Avila, Eric, 108

Babbitt, Milton, 8–9, 65–66
Babes in Toyland (band), 84
Bach, J. S., 20, 26
Bang on a Can, 60, 78
Barton, William, 42
Baskin, Ozgur, 41, 42
Bates, Mason: education and awards, 21, 24; and tech entrepreneurship, 47–48, 55; and techno, 25, 30–32; "Mothership," 26, 30–33, 35, 44–45; *The (R)evolution of Steve Jobs*, 47–48; "The Rise of Exotic Computing," 21, 48–52
BBC Radiophonic Workshops, 23
Beethoven, Ludwig van, 6, 25, 51–52. *See also* Beethoven's Fifth Symphony
Beethoven's Fifth Symphony, 1, 7, 114; Adorno on, 126–38; and the canon, 123; and marketing, 118, 128, 132; military associations of, 135, 185n63; organicism in, 125, 127, 131; and the spirit world of the infinite, 123, 124–26, 138; "There is no Fifth Symphony," 151

Ross, Alex, 92, 98
Rutherford-Johnson, Tim, 150

Sanders, Bernie, 19
Sanders, Ed, 30, 34
Sandow, Greg, 30, 46
Scherzinger, Martin, 167n5
Schoenberg, Arnold, 152
Schubert, Franz, 26
Schumann, Robert, 26
Schumpeter, Joseph, 28–29
self-management: contemporary classical
    music and, 4, 59, 148–49; as freedom,
    63–64, 86; gentrification and, 109; the
    gig economy and, 75–76; as index of
    worth, 3, 64, 138; neoliberalism and,
    63, 109; precarity and, 75–76, 83, 87;
    See also entrepreneurship; individual-
    ism; self-reliance
self-reliance: 109, 117, 129–30, 148. See
    also entrepreneurship; individualism
Sennheiser (corporation), 92–93, 96
Serve The People LA, 103, 105, 107, 112
Sharon, Yuval, 90, 91, 94, 95, 96, 97, 98,
    107, 108, 111, 112. See also Industry, The
Shrigley, David, 93
Sirota, Nadia, 72, 73; Meet the Composer,
    78–80
Slater, Tom, 110
slavery. See capitalism: slavery and; racism
Smith, Adam, 4, 61, 100, 119
Smith, Jean, 146–47, 151, 155
Smith, Neil, 113
social critique of capitalism. See under
    Boltanski and Chiapello
socialism, 12, 18, 19, 28, 29, 41, 119, 123,
    140
spirit of capitalism. See under Weber, Max
Stanford University, 23, 155
Stanyek, Jason, 179n7
Stravinsky, Igor, 26
subjective freedom. See under Adorno,
    Theodor W.
surveillance state, 20; and connectivity, 22,
    52–55; and incarceration, 136; technol-
    ogy corporations' role in, 20, 52–54,
    133–38; as utopia, 53–54
Sydney Opera House, 26, 32, 40, 43
symphony (genre), 124–27

Taruskin, Richard, 12–13
Taylor, Timothy, 5, 9–10, 17, 129–30
Thatcher, Margaret, 63, 87
"THIS IS WHY PEOPLE O.D. ON PILLS / AND JUMP
    FROM THE GOLDEN GATE BRIDGE" (Walshe),
    150–51. See also Walshe, Jennifer
Tilson Thomas, Michael, 25, 26–27, 35,
    42, 55
Tommasini, Anthony, 46, 83
Toy Factory Lofts (Los Angeles), 105, 110
Trump, Donald, 19, 140–43
Tsing, Anna, 43, 148–49
Twitter, 96

Union de Vecinos, 103
utopia, 11, 17, 76, 144, 155–58; capitalism
    as, 37, 53, 100, 156–57

Vampire Weekend (band) 78
"Vers une musique informelle" (Adorno),
    147–48

Wagner, Richard, 126
Walshe, Jennifer, 149–50, 151
war. See endless war; military-industrial
    complex
Weber, Max, 16, 77; on "the calling," 77,
    170n40, 176n49; on profit-seeking, 121,
    184n20; on the rationalization of work,
    167n3; on "the spirit of capitalism,"
    121–22, 149
Webern, Anton, 152
Werzowa, Walter, 116, 127–28
"Why Is the New Art So Hard to Under-
    stand?" (Adorno), 145
Wilkie, Rob, 43
Williams, Raymond, 151
Wood, Ellen Meiksins, 15
work/life boundary, 34, 77, 137. See also
    creativity
Wuorinen, Charles, 79

Yale University, 59
YouTube Symphony Orchestra, 1, 22,
    25–27, 30, 45–46; critical reception of,
    45–46; and labor, 34; and multicultur-
    alism, 35–43

Zaslaw, Neal, 12–13